# EXAMINING THE LANDSCAPE OF TRANSFER SUPPORT

## RESULTS FROM THE 2021 NATIONAL STUDY OF TRANSFER STUDENT INITIATIVES

Catherine Hartman and Jeffrey Mayo

Research Report No.

# 12

Cite as:

Hartman, C., & Mayo, J. (2024). *Examining the landscape of transfer support: Results from the 2021 National Study of Transfer Student Initiatives.* University of South Carolina, National Resource Center for The First-Year Experience & Students in Transition.



ISBN: 978-1-942072-74-4 (paperback)
ISBN: 978-1-942072-75-1 (epub)
ISBN: 978-1-942072-76-8 (ebrary)

Library of Congress Control Number: 2024953141
Published by:
National Resource Center for The First-Year Experience® and Students in Transition
University of South Carolina
701 Assembly Street, Suite 1000, Columbia, SC 29201
www.sc.edu/fye



Production Staff for the National Resource Center:

| | |
|---|---|
| Project Managers: | Catherine Hartman, North Carolina State University |
| | Jennifer Keup, Association of Public and Land-grant Universities, APLU |
| Design and Production: | Jenna A. Seabold, Production Manager |
| | Stephanie L. McFerrin, Graphic Artist |
| | Makayla Rippy, Graphic Artist |
| Reviewers: | Jamil D. Johnson, National Resource Center for the First-Year Experience & Students in Transition, University of South Carolina |
| | Kathleen J. Lehman, National Resource Center for the First-Year Experience & Students in Transition, University of South Carolina |
| | Janet Marling, National Institute for the Study of Transfer Students, NISTS |
| | Scott Peska, Waubonsee Community College |
| | Cielo Ruiz, National Resource Center for the First-Year Experience & Students in Transition, University of South Carolina |
| | Riley Shoemaker, National Resource Center for the First-Year Experience & Students in Transition, University of South Carolina |
| | Kevin Wenger, National Resource Center for the First-Year Experience & Students in Transition, University of South Carolina |

# About the Publisher

The National Resource Center for The First-Year Experience and Students in Transition was born out of the success of the University of South Carolina's much-honored University 101 course and a series of annual conferences focused on the freshman year experience. The momentum created by the educators attending these early conferences paved the way for the development of the National Resource Center, which was established at the University of South Carolina in 1986. As the National Resource Center broadened its focus to include other significant student transitions in higher education, it underwent several name changes, adopting the National Resource Center for The First-Year Experience and Students in Transition in 1998.

Today, the Center collaborates with its institutional partner, University 101 Programs, in pursuit of its mission to advance and support efforts to improve student learning and transitions into and through higher education. We achieve this mission by providing opportunities for the exchange of practical and scholarly information as well as the discussion of trends and issues in our field through convening conferences and other professional development events such as institutes, workshops, and online learning opportunities; publishing scholarly practice books, research reports, a peer-reviewed journal, electronic newsletters, and guides; generating, supporting, and disseminating research and scholarship; hosting visiting scholars; and maintaining several online channels for resource sharing and communication, including a dynamic website, listservs, and social media outlets.

The National Resource Center serves as the trusted expert, internationally recognized leader, and clearinghouse for scholarship, policy, and best practice for all postsecondary student transitions.

## Institutional Home

The National Resource Center is located at the University of South Carolina's (USC) flagship campus in Columbia. Chartered in 1801, USC Columbia's mission is twofold: to establish and maintain excellence in its student population, faculty, academic programs, living and learning environment, technological infrastructure, library resources, research and scholarship, public and private support and endowment; and to enhance the industrial, economic, and cultural potential of the state. The Columbia campus offers 324 degree programs through its 15 degree-granting colleges and schools. In fiscal year 2024, faculty generated $309 million in funding for research, outreach, and training programs. USC is among the top tier of universities receiving Research and Community Engagement designations from the Carnegie Foundation.

# Contents

# Tables and Figures

## Tables



## Figures

# Acknowledgements

The authors would like to thank the other members of the research team who were instrumental in facilitating the research design, data collection, and analysis phases of this project: Elizabeth Bartles (George Mason University), Jessica Hopp (The Chronicle of Higher Education), and Isaac Portillo (University of Georgia). We also thank our colleagues at the National Institute for the Study of Transfer Students, including Janet Marling, Judith Brauer, and Emily Kittrell, as well as Heather Maietta (Regis College) for their helpful feedback and support on the survey portion of this project.

# Introduction

Transfer students are an important yet often understudied and underserved population within postsecondary education. Cohort data from the National Student Clearinghouse indicate that across two- and four-year schools in the United States, 38% of students transfer from one institution to another within 6 years of starting postsecondary education (Shapiro et al., 2018). In particular, transfer plays a pivotal role within two-year schools, as one mission of these open-access institutions is to support vertical transfer, which involves movement from two- to four-year schools (Cohen et al., 2013). Millions of students rely on the transfer function of two-year schools to earn bachelor's degrees, including many low-income and racially and ethnically minoritized students (Community College Research Center, 2023). The transfer function will remain significant as data indicate that despite a decline in transfer rates that aligned with a fall in overall higher education enrollment at the beginning of the COVID-19 pandemic, transfer-out rates for students from two-year institutions have since returned to and surpassed pre-pandemic rates (National Student Clearinghouse Research Center, 2024).

However, few students who aspire to transfer do so successfully. Nationally representative data have indicated that approximately 80% of incoming community college students report that they intend to transfer to four-year schools. However, only 32% of community college students transfer within 6 years of enrollment, and of those students who do transfer, only 49% complete a bachelor's degree within 6 years of starting college (National Student Clearinghouse Research Center, 2022; Shapiro et al., 2018). In addition to this vertical transfer gap, research has indicated a racial transfer gap, in which Black and Latino/a/x students transfer at lower rates than White students (Crisp & Núñez, 2014). Low student transfer and bachelor's degree completion rates indicate a leaky transfer pipeline that is often the effect of several bureaucratic hurdles and a lack of dedicated institutional support for transfer and transfer-intending students. These barriers may manifest in the form of institutional policies, practices, and procedures that implicitly or explicitly exclude or present challenges for transfer students (Tobolowsky & Cox, 2012). For example, transfer students may have difficulty accessing and navigating information about transfer and degree requirements provided within institutional resources, including college or university websites and/or relevant policy documents such as articulation agreements and transfer credit and articulation procedures (Schudde et al., 2020). Also, advising structures at two-year colleges may not sufficiently support transfer-intending students; limited support can be seen in complicated information provided to students by academic advisors, unclear program or transfer maps, and confusing policies associated with degree completion (Schudde et al., 2021).

Additional bureaucratic hurdles can be seen as students transition into their new, or receiving, institutions (Flaga, 2006; Santiago & Stettner, 2013; Townsend & Wilson, 2006). Transfer students may lose academic credit and/or may not be able to apply their previously earned credit toward major or degree requirements at their receiving institutions (Laanan, 2007), resulting in students repeating courses and prolonging progress toward completion of their bachelor's degrees. Institutions also often lack dedicated resources designed specifically for transfer or transfer-intending students that could promote students' retention by helping them develop a sense of belonging and connection to campus (Roberts et al., 2019), including asset-based mentoring experiences (Crisp et al., 2020) and social support opportunities (Hernández et al., 2017). Unintentional support may be combined with negative experiences students have with institutional agents (including faculty, staff, and peers) and their environments, which may result in students believing that their institutions are unreceptive to their needs, that they do not matter to faculty and staff and their institutions overall (Núñez & Yoshimi, 2016), and that they are different from and less worthy than their non-transfer peers (Castro & Cortez, 2016).

In sum, the transfer process is complex and often riddled with multiple barriers created and maintained by institutions. Insufficient institutional support for transfer students may have dire consequences for their success (Tobolowsky & Cox, 2012), which is often dependent on intentional services and supports. If students do not have resources that aid their academic and social transitions, their persistence toward their educational goals may falter (Melguizo et al., 2011). To facilitate impactful services, institutional agents such as faculty, staff, and leaders must engage in activities that allow them to understand students' experiences during their transitions. It is crucial that institutions accept responsibility for their role in supporting students' educational journeys, and this commitment is even more crucial now, in the wake of the COVID-19 pandemic, which resulted in declines in enrollment and student transfer (National Student Clearinghouse Research Center, 2022). The pandemic unearthed and exacerbated disparities in educational access and student well-being, including food and housing insecurity, financial uncertainty, lack of access to technology and internet resources, and increased familial caretaking responsibilities (Fishman & Nguyen, 2021). As such, not only do institutional agents need to understand issues that transfer and transfer-intending students face, but they need to build asset-based approaches to support, building on students and the wealth that they bring with them to campus (Jain et al., 2011).

Given the growing interest and increase in transfer and transfer-intending students across the postsecondary landscape and the longstanding challenges to completing their educational goals these students often face, institutional leaders and staff must understand how they can best support these learners and bolster their persistence. For this reason, the National Resource Center for The First-Year Experience and Students in Transition created the inaugural National Study of Transfer Student Initiatives (NSTSI). This report details the results from 2021 NSTSI and is intended to provide leaders, researchers, and policymakers with a national overview of transfer-related policies, practices, and procedures as well as institutional and bureaucratic barriers to their development, coordination, and implementation. In addition, it prompts discussions for leaders and staff as they consider how transfer-related efforts may be improved to better meet the needs of students.

This report is divided into two sections. An overview of the 2021 NSTSI is provided first, followed by a discussion of the results and key takeaways for practice and future research. The Appendices include a partial list of participating institutions[1], the survey questionnaire, and the frequency distributions of responses to the NSTSI, disaggregated by institutional characteristics (i.e., type, control, and size of undergraduate enrollment). The information and tables in this report provide points of conversation for leaders and educators looking for ways to create, innovate, and sustain successful programs related to the transfer experience.

---

[1] Institutions could opt out of identification as a survey respondent.

# Examining the Landscape of Transfer Support: Results From the 2021 National Study of Transfer Student Initiatives

In 2021, a research team organized by the National Resource Center for The First-Year Experience and Students in Transition began the National Study of Transfer Student Initiatives (NSTSI). The purpose of this study was to explore how transfer personnel at community colleges and four-year schools support transfer and transfer-intending students, including pre- and post-transfer. Specifically, we, as members of the research team, aimed to

- identify the academic and social support services that institutions offer to transfer and transfer-intending students,

- understand the most prevalent and salient transfer-specific issues that institutional agents report students face,

- explore the role that transfer programs play in students' transitions, and

- understand the ways in which institutions do or do not promote a transfer-receptive culture.

In the following section, we describe the transfer-receptive culture framework (Jain et al., 2011), which guided the development of and analyses associated with NSTSI. In addition, we describe the method and the respondents as well as the analyses and subsequent results. We conclude this report with a discussion about future directions that transfer professionals, researchers, and policy-oriented staff may take to best support transfer and transfer-intending student progress and success.

## Guiding Framework

Insufficient support for transfer students can be consequential for their success. As such, we sought to understand how institutions work toward establishing a commitment to transfer, using the framework of *transfer-receptive culture* to guide our inquiry (Jain et al., 2011). By its definition, a transfer-receptive culture requires a commitment from transfer-sending institutions (i.e., whose mission is to prepare students for transfer to another school) and transfer-receiving institutions (i.e., whose mission is to recruit, enroll, and retain transfer students) to supporting transfer student success. As Jain et al. (2011) noted,

A transfer culture, or transfer sending culture, at the community college level can be seen as an institutional effort to normalize the transfer function so that all students who seek to transfer are able to do so. Extending the definition of a transfer culture to a four-year campus, we define a transfer-receptive culture as an institutional commitment by a four-year college or university to provide the support needed for students to transfer successfully—that is, to navigate the community college, take the appropriate coursework, apply, enroll, and successfully earn a baccalaureate degree in a timely manner. (p. 257)

The transfer-receptive framework shifts the responsibility for successful transfer from the student to both the transfer-sending and the transfer-receiving institutions. Through this approach, institutions must develop a shared commitment to students and accept their role and responsibility in promoting transfer student success. Institutions that are not considered to be transfer receptive have weak or nonexistent structures and few commitments designed to recognize and validate transfer students and their educational choices. Foundationally, transfer-receptive culture requires institutional staff to use an asset-based approach to transfer, meaning that they must foreground students' assets, strengths, and knowledge (Del Real Viramontes, 2020). Ultimately, a transfer-receptive culture can help institutional leaders and staff identify how institutional services and spaces may or may not center transfer students' needs, aspirations, and identities. The framework also offers an opportunity for educators to consider how to address such gaps in services and to strengthen institutional commitments to transfer student success. Further, the transfer-receptive culture framework may be useful with mitigating the effects of both the vertical and the racial transfer gaps, discussed in the introduction of this report.

## Method

NSTSI is a mixed-methods project that focuses on the availability and structure of transfer student services, programs, and initiatives at two- and four-year schools across the United States and its associated territories. NSTSI fills a significant gap in the field of higher education, as no other national-level survey solely dedicated to examining transfer student initiatives and programs on campuses currently exists. The data collection included two phases: (a) the distribution of an online survey to faculty, staff, and administrators whose roles support transfer students (completed in Fall 2021) and (b) individual interviews with survey participants to further understand transfer services on their specific campuses (completed in Summer 2022).

In September 2021, we began the first phase of the study, the distribution of the NSTSI survey, which was created in Qualtrics. To identify a sample, we used data from the Integrated Postsecondary Education Data System (IPEDS) to inventory all degree-granting institutions that offered Title IV financial aid to undergraduate students (3,788 institutions). We then used data from HigherEd Direct (n.d.) to identify an individual in a role related to transfer success at each institution (e.g., transfer-year experience coordinator or director, director of transfer admissions and articulation, director of a transfer center, provost, or vice provost of academics). If we were unable to find anyone at an institution who served in such a role by using information from HigherEd Direct, the research team then reviewed the website of the institution to identify an individual and their email contact information. We found contact information for 2,722 institutions, resulting in 2,574 valid invites (the discrepancy in these values was primarily due to invalid invites, determined when email bounced back to us). The survey invitation email also contained language that asked participants to forward the survey to individuals at their institution who may be more knowledgeable about transfer and transfer-intending student initiatives if they believed that they were not the best contact to complete the survey. Reminder emails were sent via Qualtrics approximately every 3 weeks to participants who had not completed the survey.

From the 2,574 institutions from which individuals were invited, 169 participants responded to the survey during the time it was active, September to December 2021 (response rate of 6.6%). Ultimately, survey participants mostly included directors and assistant directors of first-year experience programs, academic advising staff, faculty members, institutional research staff, assistant vice presidents, and campus provosts.

Of the 169 survey participants, 58 (34.3% of the sample) were employed at public or private two-year schools, and 111 worked at public or private four-year schools (65.7% of the sample). Seven individuals from for-profit institutions participated (4% of the sample), representing six four-year schools and one technical college. Minority-serving institutions (MSIs) in the sample were underrepresented; one participant worked at a four-year, private historically Black university. Table 1 shows characteristics of the institutions represented in the 2021 NSTSI compared to a national profile of degree-granting institutions in the United States. Our survey sample included an overrepresentation of public institutions and an underrepresentation of private, for-profit schools. In addition, the sample included a disproportionately large number of respondents from institutions with more than 10,000 undergraduate students enrolled.

Table 1

*Characteristics of Institutions Represented in the 2021 NSTSI Compared to a National Profile of Institutions in the United States*

| Institutional characteristic | Frequency and percentages of sample responding to 2021 NSTSI Survey (*N* = 169) | Frequency and percentage, national profile (*N* = 4,250) |
|---|---|---|
| Type[a] | | |
| Two-year | 58 (34.3%) | 1,272 (29.9%) |
| Four-year | 111 (65.7%) | 2,680 (63.1%) |
| Control | | |
| Public | 89 (52.7%) | 1,720 (40.5%) |
| Private, not-for-profit | 73 (43.2%) | 1,766 (41.6%) |
| Private, for-profit | 7 (4.1%) | 764 (18.0%) |
| Undergraduate enrollment[b] | | |
| Under 1,000 students | 20 (11.8%) | 1,619 (38.1%) |
| 1,001–4,999 students | 74 (43.8%) | 1,482 (34.9%) |
| 5,000–9,999 students | 28 (16.6%) | 472 (11.1%) |
| 10,000–19,999 students | 23 (13.6%) | 311 (7.3%) |
| More than 20,000 students | 24 (14.2%) | 211 (5.0%) |

*Note.* Figures for the national percentages are from the Integrated Postsecondary Education Data System (IPEDS) by the National Center for Education Statistics (2021).

[a]Size and setting data for 298 schools were reported in IPEDS as "Not applicable, not in Carnegie universe (not accredited or nondegree-granting)."

[b]Undergraduate enrollment data for 155 schools were reported in IPEDS as "Not available" or "Not applicable."

After closing the survey, the research team engaged in the second phase of data collection. We invited all survey participants to take part in individual interviews to further elaborate on their survey responses and to discuss transfer support services on their campuses. To identify these institutions and individuals, we used the contact information gathered from the survey and emailed the individuals, asking them to talk with a member of the research team to share more about their transfer-related work at their institution. Additionally, to diversify our sample and to hear more from individuals at MSIs, we invited select nonsurvey participants to engage in interviews; to determine these potential interviewees, we used IPEDS to identify all historically Black colleges and universities (HBCUs) and Tribal Colleges and Universities (TCUs) in the United States and reviewed information from HigherEd Direct and institutional websites (i.e., a similar strategy as that used for the survey) to find names and contact information. In total, we interviewed 30 individuals from 30 different institutions, including 8 two-year schools and 22 four-year schools (11 private and 11 public institutions). The sample included two HBCUs, two for-profit institutions, and five Hispanic-serving institutions. The roles of the participants varied and included dean of instruction, dean of the college, director (e.g., of transfer and articulation, first-year experience offices, transfer centers), provost and associate provost/vice president of academic affairs, registrar, and vice president of student engagement.

The interviews lasted approximately 60 minutes, were semistructured, and were conducted over Zoom. During the interviews, participants provided details about transfer services available, the structure of services within institutions, and plans for transfer services in the future. They also answered questions focused on student- and institutional-level challenges associated with integration and sense of belonging and specific questions about advising structures, challenges, and plans related to transfer and about developmental education policies and practices and the role they play in supporting transfer and transfer-intending students. Finally, participants responded to questions about how they perceived equality as considered and operationalized in transfer services and how the COVID-19 pandemic affected the delivery, coordination of, and future planning for transfer services.

## Data Analysis

We began data analysis by conducting descriptive analyses of the survey data to gather an understanding of the initiatives and associated objectives that institutions offered for transfer and transfer-intending students. Comprehensive frequency distributions and sample percentages for each reported item were tabulated in the aggregate (total) across institution type, control, and size. Members of the research team then reviewed these descriptive statistics for patterns and to better determine the initiatives that the institutions reported offering, any differences across institution types, and any challenges related to delivery and coordination of services. We used this information to inform the development of the interview protocol we used with transfer professionals. After interviews were completed, we used Dedoose, a qualitative software system, to code interview transcripts to further address how transfer-related efforts on campuses are designed, coordinated, and evaluated for their effectiveness. We used a hybrid coding method, first creating deductive codes using the transfer-receptive culture framework. We then created subcodes inductively (primarily using in vivo codes) and created a data matrix in Excel to generate themes. Throughout the process of analyzing the data, the research team developed analytic memos to capture connections, thoughts, and questions and met consistently to discuss emerging findings.

## Results

In the following sections, we share results from our analyses of the survey and interview data, starting with a discussion about institutions' attention to transfer. Specifically, we focus on several main areas, including institutions' role in the transfer landscape, initiatives and objectives associated with transfer, length of time institutions devoted to transfer, academic advising and transfer, equity and transfer, campuswide coordination and assessment of transfer services, and high-impact transfer-related practices, among others. Considering the importance of the commitment between two- and four-year schools in fostering and sustaining a transfer-receptive culture, in this report we focus primarily on differences across institutional type (i.e., differences among two- and four-year schools). Additional information about results by institutional control and size can be found in the data table in Appendix C.

### *Institutions' Role in the Transfer Landscape*

To understand how institutional agents (including faculty, staff, and administrators) perceived their school's role in the transfer landscape, we highlight findings from a survey question that asked participants to describe their institutions. Participants could indicate that their institution was primarily one of the following: transfer sending (i.e., the institution's mission and/or purpose included supporting student transfer to another institution), transfer receiving (i.e., the institution's mission and/or purpose included supporting the enrollment of transfer students), or a hybrid of both (i.e., they were transfer sending and receiving).

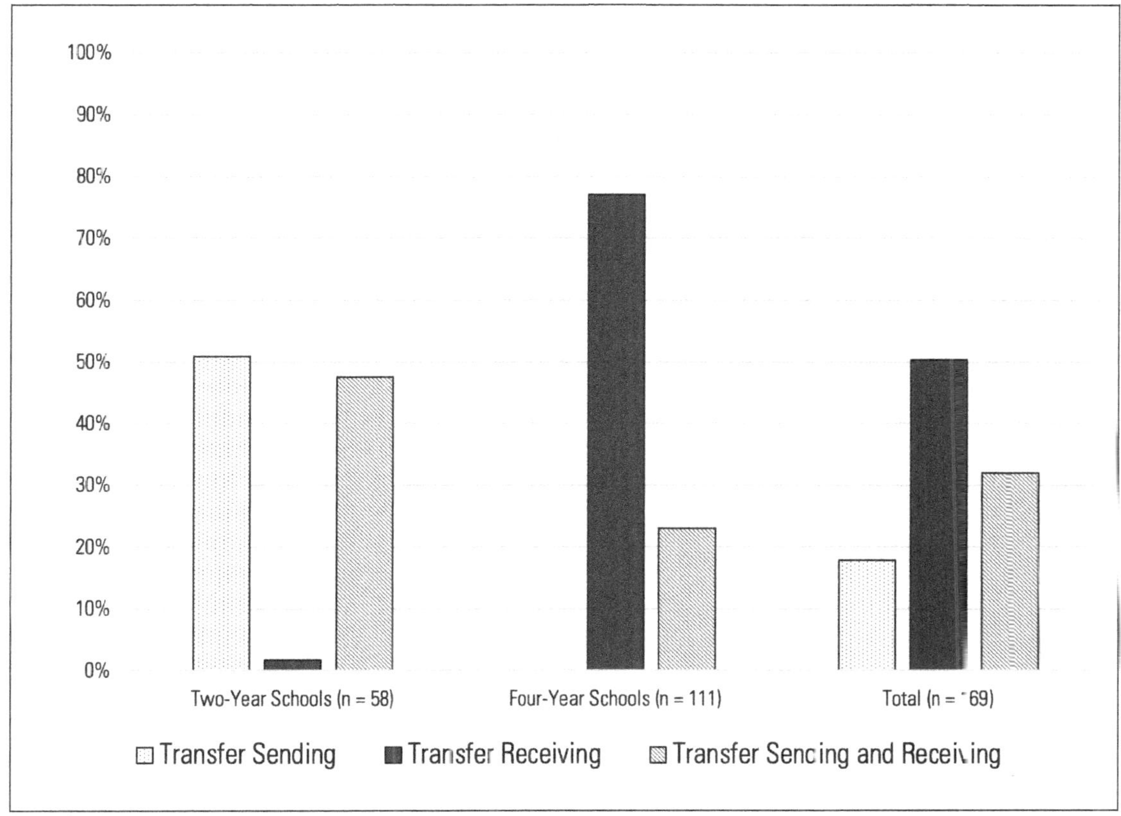


*Figure 1.* Percentage of survey participants reporting their institution's role in the transfer landscape (*n* = 169).

Figure 1 shows that no representatives of four-year schools in the sample described their institutions as exclusively transfer sending. However, 22.9% of respondents described their four-year schools as both transfer sending and transfer receiving. In contrast, most respondents from two-year schools indicated that their institutions were transfer sending; however, the difference between the subset that described their institutions as transfer sending and the subset that described them as both transfer sending and transfer receiving is narrow (50.9% vs 47.5%, respectively).

These findings recall the historic mission of two-year schools, highlighting the existence of the transfer function that facilitates movement to four-year schools (Cohen et al., 2013). These findings also underscore a contemporary function in that two-year schools support multiple categories of students with different mobility and goals, including swirling students, visiting students, students seeking to transfer to four-year schools, and more (Taylor & Jain, 2017). Among four-year schools, some respondents' identification of their institution as serving hybrid functions may be a result of recent enrollment trends, particularly resulting from the COVID-19 pandemic. For instance, an interview participant described how enrollment has declined at their public four-year school since 2020, and this decline was problematic for the vitality of their school, which relies heavily on partnerships with local community colleges to sustain enrollment. This participant shared,

> Most of our students who were admitted and supposed to come chose not to come. When we look at the [National Student] Clearinghouse data, they didn't just not choose us and go somewhere else; they just stopped out. That terrifies me that we will have several years of students who have missed out on this opportunity if we're thinking about just social mobility.

Other participants highlighted an increased focus away from supporting transfer toward focusing on increasing enrollment, as an interviewee from a two-year college described:

I don't think we have prioritized transfer as much as we possibly could. Part of it is just because of the external and internal factors. We're down in enrollment right now, and can we dedicate resources to transfer? We need to dedicate more resources into getting folks to come into our institution to stabilize our financials. Those are some of the things that we are doing.

The importance of transfer can also be seen in institutional strategic planning efforts. Most respondents reported that issues related to transfer and transfer-intending students were included in the institutional strategic planning at their institutions (74.7% of the overall sample; see Figure 2), with more participants from two-year schools than from four-year schools agreeing (87.0% vs. 66.7%, respectively). While these findings seem to illuminate institutional attention to transfer, they may instead be indicative of bias of those who self-selected to participate in this research study, and, as such, may not be indicative of all postsecondary institutions.

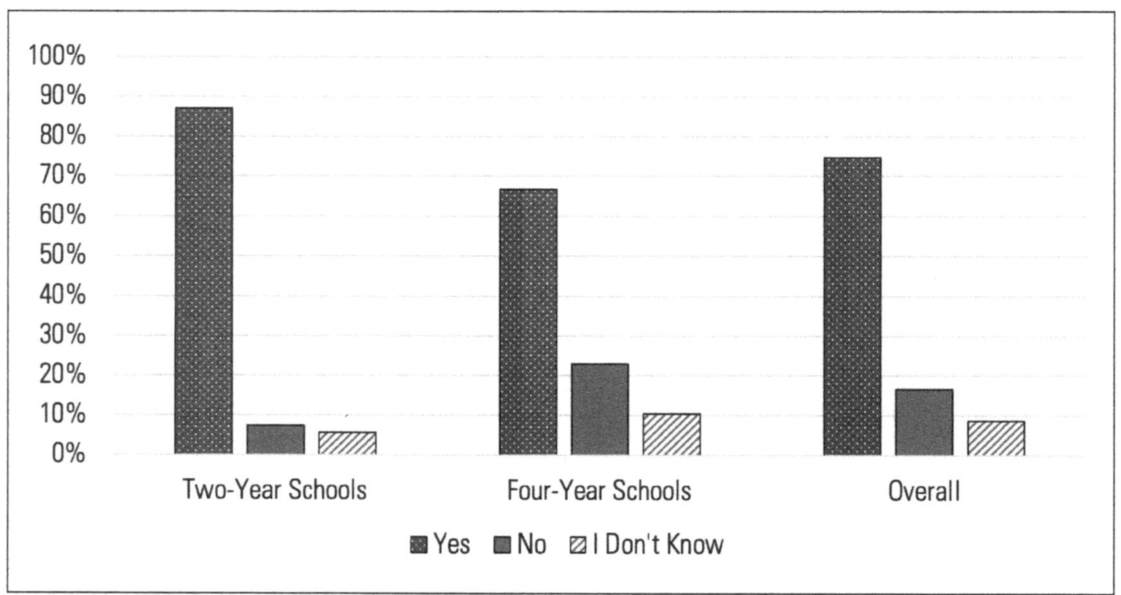


*Figure 2.* Percentage of participants reporting that transfer is included in institutional strategic planning (*n* = 150). *Note.* Responses included 54 from two-year schools and 96 from four-year schools.

Most participants also indicated that their institution was moderately to highly committed to prioritizing transfer and transfer-intending student success when considering current practices, institutional resources, and students' encountered challenges. Specifically, 30.0% of respondents (including 25.9% from two-year schools and 33.3% from four-year schools) reported that they believed their institution was moderately committed, 28.7% of respondents (including 31.5% from two-year schools and 27.1% from four-year schools) reported that their schools were between moderately and highly committed, and 33.3% of respondents (38.9% from two-year schools and 29.2% from four-year schools) reported that their schools were highly committed to transfer student success.

### *Equity and Transfer*

Centering equity within transfer planning and initiatives is another crucial component of building a transfer-receptive culture. As such, we asked survey and interview participants how they made sense of equity and applied this understanding to their work. We defined equity as "ensur[ing] that transfer resources are used not just to provide access but also to promote equal transfer outcomes," particularly for racially and ethnically minoritized groups (Chase et al., 2012, p. 671).

To explore these relationships, we asked survey participants if their institutions had any specific goals associated with equity and transfer. We discovered that 77.8% of respondents from two-year schools indicated their institutions did. In contrast, 52.1% of participants from four-year schools noted that their institutions had specific goals associated with equity and transfer (see Figure 3), leading us to question why this number was not higher and what barriers might be prohibiting the creation and sustainability of these goals.

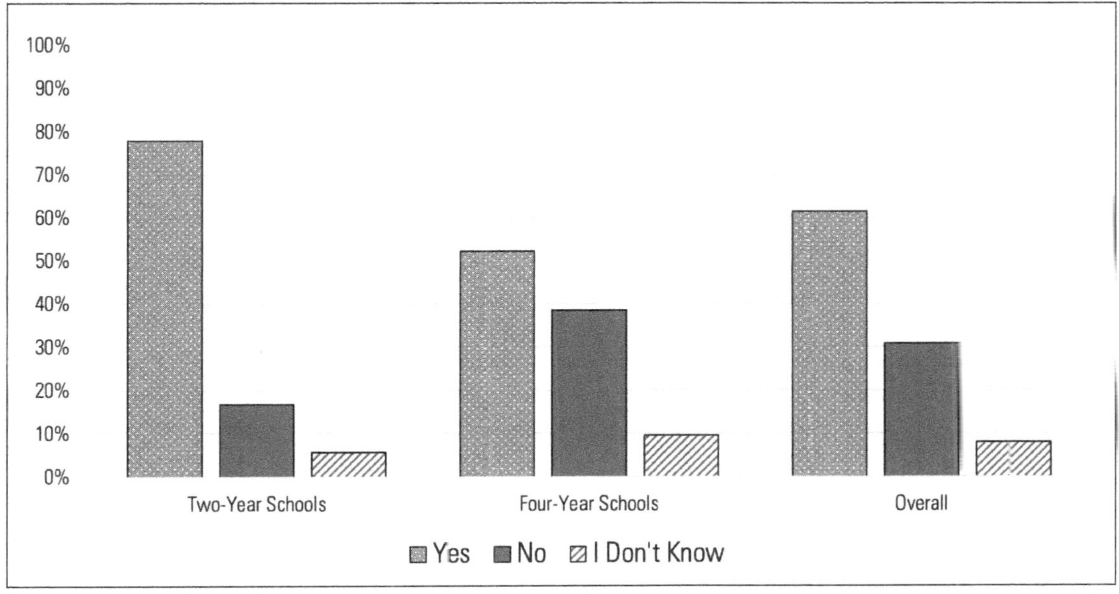


*Figure 3.* Percentage of survey participants indicating that their institution has goals associated with equity and transfer (*n* = 150).

*Note.* Responses included 54 from two-year schools and 96 from four-year schools.

In the interviews, transfer personnel described how they made sense of equity and applied this understanding to their work. Mostly, faculty and staff indicated that equity for transfer and transfer-intending students required having an awareness and understanding of these learners and the challenges they face across their educational experiences. For example, participants indicated that transfer students are a unique population that requires an understanding of their diversity. As a participant from a private four-year university noted, "Transfer students are not a homogeneous population … when you disaggregate the data, you find there are different subgroups, so one must consider tailoring resource support to different student needs … it is not one size fits all." This quote highlights the wide-ranging diversity of transfer and transfer-intending student populations, which is especially important for practitioners to consider as recent data has revealed increased rates of transfer among Black and Latino/a/x students and lower-income students (National Student Clearinghouse Research Center, 2024).

Participants expressed concerns about whether equity-oriented goals were actionable or performative. As a participant from a community college shared, "There is more stated commitment than actual commitment." Staff also understood that transfer students were motivated by different goals than non-transfer students were and that the knowledge and navigational capital that transfer students bring with them to the receiving institution were assets. As another participant from a public four-year school indicated,

> We tend to find our transfer students because they've now lived the college experience, they've had that transitional time and understand time management … They tend to be really focused on graduating. We know that they're going to finish off their degree program, which you can't always say about a first-year student.

While having an awareness of transfer was a key step in promoting equity, multiple cross-functional and cross-institutional barriers prevented and/or hindered commitments to doing so, which we discuss in the subsequent section of this report.

### *Challenges to and Opportunities for Supporting Transfer Success*

Multiple opportunities exist to support transfer student success and to develop and sustain a transfer-receptive culture. The primarily cited examples among interviewee participants included resource constraints and creating buy-in among stakeholders.

**Resource Constraints.** One of the most frequent resource-related challenges discussed by participants was related to personnel, including faculty constraints on time and faculty attitudes toward transfer. Specifically, one participant from a public four-year school noted, "We face challenges recruiting faculty to work on cross-institutional and state-level work related to course development and curricular pathways due to constraints on faculty's time and efforts." Even when an institution had faculty who were potentially available to support transfer-related efforts, participants described difficulties with breaking through faculty (mis)perceptions and convincing faculty that transfer students were an important population worthy of time and dedicated resources. As an individual from a different public four-year school discussed, "Faculty mindset around supporting transfer students and creating transfer-friendly policies is lacking. Senior leadership would love to grow transfer support, and student-facing staff would love to see transfer support increase, but the faculty barrier is very real."

Interviewees also noted that creating robust transfer supports often required a cultural shift toward caring about transfer across the institution. Some participants mentioned using their social capital and familiarity with an institution (established sometimes through long tenures of employment) to create partnerships. A participant from a public four-year school shared how such closeness was beneficial to their work and to supporting transfer students' success:

> I have to admit, this is where longevity plays a part. I've had many, many years on this campus. You begin to develop a relationship with these spaces, with people. That helps to create an opportunity there for increased engagement.

This participant continued to describe the impact of the university's transfer center and its recognition on campus:

> I think that, the transfer center having the longevity on the campus … having that presence, that longevity is established. It's not new. It's not something we're launching; it's something that's been in place and in play for decades. It's facilitated building new partnerships and maintaining existing ones … That helps a lot, I think. It's also about being a good partner. We're here to serve students. We know the experience, we can lend our expertise right to the work that you are doing in your program or your area, that may help facilitate your work … That exchange of ideas and the exchange of the willingness to exchange in resources and information I think has gone a long way.

Similarly, a participant from a different public four-year school highlighted how relationships with campus partners generated excitement about the work of the institution's transfer center:

> I joke [about] how we built our space was by building FOMO [fear of missing out], where we worked with the people who wanted to work with us first and then showed the results widely on why these partnerships were successful.

Other methods for generating change and bolstering transfer-related supports included using grassroots efforts to connect with other institutions, such as through the creation of a transfer organization between schools within the same university system, and identifying ways to connect with coworkers across the institution through informal transfer working groups.

**Building Buy-In.** Participants spoke about the importance of identifying innovative and fun ways to build buy-in for transfer. For example, one participant described the creation of a transfer champion belt, fashioned in the style of a wrestling belt. The respondent from a community college who designed the belt shared,

> [The belt is for] those faculty members that are going above and beyond. We're going to end up awarding them, and they will be able to have the belt for that year. The cool thing is we're going to be able to put their names on the particular shields as well … I'm hoping that this helps to change transfer and the culture of transfer.

Determining the challenges that may exist between institutional partnerships (i.e., cross-institutionally) is another necessary component of sustaining a transfer-receptive culture. Notably, participants discussed that they perceived several transfer-related issues to be associated with prestige and power. In particular, some participants at two-year schools described neighboring four-year schools as exclusionary and elitist in their attitudes and practices related to two-year partnerships and students. As one participant from a community college noted, "I think the biggest challenge is the varying degree of cooperation we receive from area four-year colleges and universities."

Perceived insufficient or inefficient collaboration often manifested in challenges associated with academic transfer credit and applicability policies, as a participant from a public technical college shared: "We struggle to get four-year universities to automatically accept our classes that are exactly the same as ones offered at nearby comprehensives." In addition, participants observed that staff at some four-year schools questioned the rigor of coursework completed at two-year schools, or the "underlying bias still held by many faculty around the value of community college programs," according to a participant at a private, not-for-profit four-year school. Ultimately, four-year schools often shape and hold power within transfer partnerships (Cohen et al., 2013), and such dynamics and (mis)conceptions about the value of two-year curricula can be deleterious for transfer and transfer-intending students' progress toward transfer and degree completion.

### *Initiatives Associated with Transfer and Transfer-Intending Student Success*

To better understand how institutions reached transfer and transfer-intending students, we asked NSTSI participants to identify initiatives (i.e., transfer-related policies, practices, and programs) that their institutions were using to support student mobility, transitions, and success. As shown in Figure 4, the majority of respondents (73.8%, with 87.0% of respondents from two-year schools and 65.3% from four-year schools) indicated that they had at least one initiative specifically or intentionally geared toward transfer.

Table 2 shows the initiatives that were offered, disaggregated by institutional type. Academic advising was the most frequent initiative overall, reported by 91.0% of participants. At two-year schools, the most common transfer initiatives were academic advising (91.3%) and articulation and/or admissions agreements (91.3%). Other common services or strategies at two-year schools included honor societies (e.g., Tau Sigma or Phi Theta Kappa; 82.6%), Guided Pathways (80.4%), informational sessions about navigating transfer (78.3%), and academic program maps (73.9%), the last of which may be related to the growth in institutions that have implemented Guided Pathways (Bailey et al., 2015). At four-year schools, academic advising was also most frequently reported (89.2% of participants); other frequently reported initiatives included articulation and/or admissions agreements (84.6%), institution-wide orientation (76.9%), standardized policies for awarding transfer credit (73.8%), and financial aid (67.7%).

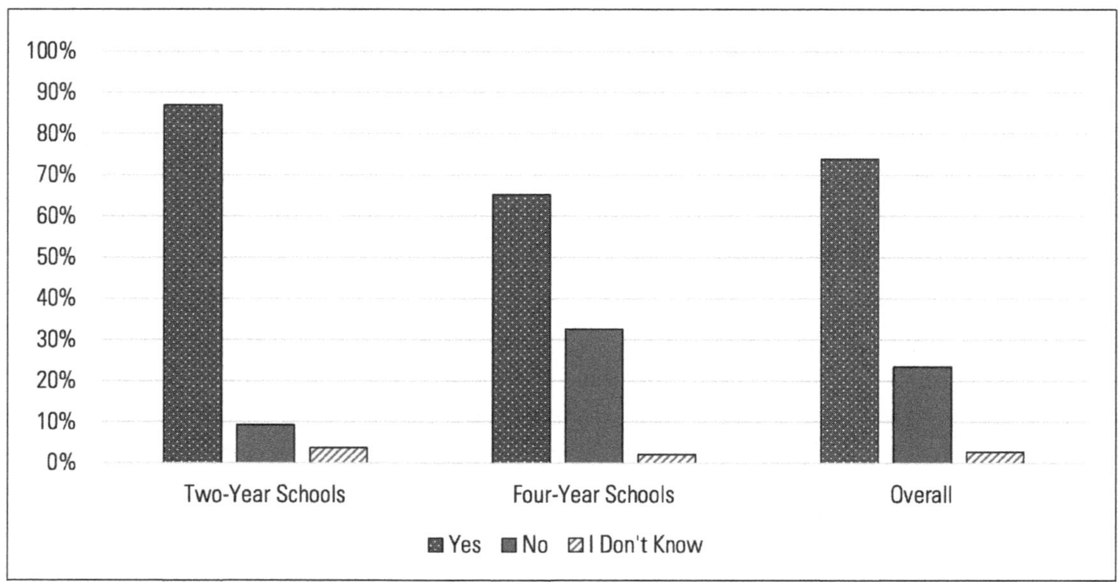


*Figure 4.* Percentage of participants indicating that transfer initiatives are offered by their institutions (*n* = 149). *Note.* Responses included 54 from two-year schools and 95 from four-year schools.

Table 2

*Percentage of Survey Participants Reporting Transfer Student Success Programs, Policies, and Practices Offered Specifically for Transfer/Transfer-Intending Students*

| | Institutional type | | | |
| --- | --- | --- | --- | --- |
| | Two-year | | Four-year | |
| Institutional initiative | Freq. | % | Freq. | % |
| Academic advising | 42 | 91.3 | 58 | 89.2 |
| Academic coaching or mentoring | 24 | 52.2 | 38 | 58.5 |
| Academic program maps | 34 | 73.9 | 40 | 61.5 |
| Articulation and/or admissions agreements | 42 | 91.3 | 55 | 84.6 |
| Awarding of experiential learning credits (e.g., prior-learning assessments, credit "badges," and/or CLEP) | 25 | 54.3 | 28 | 43.1 |
| Bridge programs | 12 | 26.1 | 11 | 16.9 |
| Campus-based event (e.g., common reading experiences, dinners, fairs) | 21 | 45.7 | 25 | 38.5 |
| Career exploration | 34 | 73.9 | 33 | 50.8 |
| Career planning | 29 | 63.0 | 35 | 53.8 |
| Communication or publications (e.g., social media, newsletters, emails, brochures) | 24 | 52.2 | 33 | 50.8 |
| Course-specific support for classes with high dropout, fail, or withdraw rates (e.g., supplemental instruction) | 21 | 45.7 | 12 | 18.5 |
| Credit-bearing course (e.g., transfer seminar) | 3 | 6.5 | 10 | 15.4 |
| Cultural enrichment activities (e.g., plays, musical events, multicultural fairs) | 23 | 50.0 | 16 | 24.6 |
| Early alert systems | 34 | 73.9 | 31 | 47.7 |
| Equal Opportunity Program (EOP) | 12 | 26.1 | 10 | 15.4 |
| Faculty or staff mentors | 13 | 28.3 | 26 | 40.0 |

*Table continues on page 23*

*Table continued from page 22*

*Percentage of Survey Participants Reporting Transfer Student Success Programs, Policies, and Practices Offered Specifically for Transfer/Transfer-Intending Students*

| | Institutional type | | | |
| --- | --- | --- | --- | --- |
| | Two-year | | Four-year | |
| **Institutional initiative** | **Freq.** | **%** | **Freq.** | **%** |
| Financial aid (e.g., transfer scholarships, loans) | 28 | 60.9 | 44 | 67.7 |
| Financial planning, coaching, and information | 15 | 32.6 | 15 | 23.1 |
| Guided pathways | 37 | 80.4 | 31 | 47.7 |
| Honor societies (e.g., Tau Sigma, Phi Theta Kappa, etc.) | 38 | 82.6 | 25 | 38.5 |
| Informational sessions about navigating transfer (including admission, policies, and more) | 36 | 78.3 | 42 | 64.6 |
| Internships or co-ops | 24 | 52.2 | 23 | 35.4 |
| Leadership development | 19 | 41.3 | 8 | 27.7 |
| Learning communities (i.e., students take two or more linked courses as a group) | 9 | 19.6 | 9 | 13.8 |
| Major exploration and selection | 21 | 45.7 | 21 | 32.3 |
| Mentoring from others outside of the institution (e.g., peers at other institutions, alumni, and more) | 6 | 13.0 | 8 | 12.3 |
| Next-steps enrollment checklist (i.e., details about to-do items students must complete before enrollment) | 21 | 45.7 | 40 | 61.5 |
| Off-campus event (e.g., retreat, outdoor adventure) | 10 | 21.7 | 8 | 12.3 |
| Opportunities to co-teach or assist in teaching a class | 1 | 2.2 | 6 | 9.2 |
| Orientation (institution-wide) | 24 | 40.0 | 50 | 76.9 |
| Peer mentoring across institutions (e.g., transfer students at four-year institutions mentoring students at partner community colleges) | 4 | 8.7 | 6 | 9.2 |
| Peer mentoring by transfer/transfer-intending students (i.e., transfer/transfer-intending students mentoring other students at the same institution) | 4 | 8.7 | 8 | 12.3 |
| Peer mentoring by undergraduate students (i.e., undergraduate students mentoring transfer/transfer-intending students at the same institution) | 4 | 8.7 | 15 | 23.1 |
| Practica or other supervised practice experiences | 4 | 8.7 | 12 | 18.5 |
| Regional institutional partnerships that include joint transfer programs and/or staff positions | 17 | 37.0 | 14 | 21.5 |
| Residence life—transfer live-on-campus requirement | 2 | 4.3 | 11 | 16.9 |
| Residence life—transfer-specific residential curriculum | 0 | 0.0 | 3 | 4.6 |
| Residence life—transfer-specific living–learning community | 1 | 2.2 | 10 | 15.4 |
| Service learning or community service | 14 | 30.4 | 22 | 33.8 |
| Signature course (i.e., introductory academic credit-bearing course on various interdisciplinary topics) | 12 | 26.1 | 18 | 27.7 |
| Standardized policies for awarding transfer credit | 27 | 58.7 | 48 | 73.8 |
| Statewide articulation agreements | 33 | 71.7 | 30 | 46.2 |
| Student government (e.g., designated transfer student representative or council) | 11 | 23.9 | 18 | 27.7 |
| Study abroad | 15 | 32.6 | 23 | 35.4 |
| Targeted admissions recruitment of transfer students | 14 | 30.4 | 49 | 75.4 |

*Table continues on page 24*

*Table continued from page 23*

*Percentage of Survey Participants Reporting Transfer Student Success Programs, Policies, and Practices Offered Specifically for Transfer/Transfer-Intending Students*

| | Institutional type | | | |
| | Two-year | | Four-year | |
| **Institutional initiative** | **Freq.** | **%** | **Freq.** | **%** |
|---|---|---|---|---|
| Transfer fairs (e.g., admissions fairs) | 37 | 80.4 | 34 | 52.3 |
| Transfer planning guide (i.e., how-to, things to consider) | 20 | 43.5 | 18 | 27.7 |
| Transfer student center | 15 | 32.6 | 9 | 13.8 |
| Transfer student organization(s) | 3 | 6.5 | 14 | 21.5 |
| Transfer/college student success skills course | 19 | 41.3 | 21 | 32.3 |
| Undergraduate research | 14 | 30.4 | 20 | 30.8 |
| Other | 1 | 2.2 | 5 | 7.7 |
| Total | 46 | 100.0 | 65 | 100.0 |

*Note.* Of the 169 total survey participants, 46 from two-year schools and 65 from four-year schools answered this question. Survey participants were asked to select any programs, practices, and policies they perceived to be offered specifically for transfer/transfer-intending students.

As shown in Figure 4, 23.5% of respondents across two- and four-year schools indicated having no initiatives targeted to transfer. These participants ($n$ = 38) gave a variety of reasons for this lack of initiatives. The most frequent responses indicated that institutions lacked funding for transfer support (36.8%) and that institutions did not have a large enough population of transfer or transfer-intending students at their institution to warrant such attention (36.8%). Other reported reasons associated with a lack of services included transfer not being an institutional priority (34.2%), limited availability of staff time to devote to initiatives (34.2%), and a lack of staff or faculty buy-in (29.0%). The least reported reason for not offering transfer initiatives was a lack of staff expertise about transfer (18.4%).

A lack of institutional support for transfer or unavailability of transfer initiatives may also be the result of competing demands for focus. A participant from a public four-year school shared that their office had attempted to build transfer programs but the efforts had been stalled by shifts in leaders' and institutional priorities: "We would like to offer these programs but have stopped and started several times. In some cases, it has been due to limited resources, and in others it has stopped due to a shift in priorities."

### Institutional Objectives Associated with Transfer Initiatives

The survey component of NSTSI also included questions regarding the objectives associated with the programs, policies, and practices available at each school. Table 3 shows that the objective most often reported across both two- and four-year schools was academic planning (reported by 89.1% of participants from two-year schools and 83.1% from four-year schools). Among respondents from two-year schools, other common objectives included career exploration and/or preparation (65.2%), gateway course completion (56.5%), oral communication (58.7%), and writing skills (58.7%). Respondents from four-year schools frequently reported that knowledge of institutional resources and services (70.8%), academic success strategies (66.2%), introduction to institutional-specific academic expectations (55.4%), and career exploration and/or preparation (55.4%) were objectives associated with transfer initiatives.

Table 3

*Percentage of Survey Participants Reporting Specific Objectives Associated With Transfer Student Success Programs, Policies, and Practices*

| Institutional objective | Institutional type | | | |
| --- | --- | --- | --- | --- |
| | Two-year | | Four-year | |
| | Freq. | % | Freq. | % |
| Academic planning | 41 | 89.1 | 54 | 83.1 |
| Academic success strategies | 27 | 45.0 | 43 | 66.2 |
| Analytical, critical-thinking, or problem-solving skills | 21 | 45.7 | 22 | 33.8 |
| Career exploration and/or preparation | 30 | 65.2 | 36 | 55.4 |
| Civic engagement | 10 | 21.7 | 12 | 18.5 |
| Common transfer-year experience | 8 | 17.4 | 17 | 26.2 |
| Connection with the institution or campus | 16 | 34.8 | 34 | 52.3 |
| Developmental education, remediation, and/or review | 17 | 37.0 | 6 | 9.2 |
| Digital literacy | 19 | 41.3 | 14 | 21.5 |
| Discipline-specific knowledge | 20 | 43.5 | 19 | 29.2 |
| Financial literacy | 20 | 43.5 | 17 | 26.2 |
| Gateway course completion | 26 | 56.5 | 13 | 20.0 |
| Global education | 8 | 17.4 | 16 | 24.6 |
| Graduate or professional school preparation (e.g., pre-med, pre-law) | 4 | 8.7 | 16 | 24.6 |
| Health and wellness | 19 | 41.3 | 24 | 36.9 |
| Information literacy | 18 | 39.1 | 19 | 29.2 |
| Integration of learning and reflection | 8 | 17.4 | 24 | 36.9 |
| Integrative and applied learning | 12 | 26.1 | 16 | 24.6 |
| Intercultural competence, diversity skills, or engaging with different perspectives | 20 | 43.5 | 25 | 38.5 |
| Introduction to a major, discipline, or career path | 14 | 30.4 | 24 | 36.9 |
| Introduction to institutional-specific academic expectations | 22 | 47.8 | 36 | 55.4 |
| Introduction to the liberal arts | 10 | 21.7 | 19 | 29.2 |
| Knowledge of institution or campus resources and services | 22 | 47.8 | 46 | 70.8 |
| Leadership skill development | 13 | 28.3 | 24 | 36.9 |
| Library science education | 5 | 10.9 | 11 | 16.9 |
| Major exploration | 22 | 47.8 | 24 | 36.9 |
| On-time graduation rates (i.e., 4-year or 6-year graduation rate for transfers) | 14 | 30.4 | 34 | 52.3 |
| Oral communication skills | 27 | 58.7 | 17 | 26.2 |
| Persistence of transfer/transfer-intending students | 24 | 52.2 | 25 | 38.5 |
| Personal exploration or development | 16 | 34.8 | 19 | 29.2 |
| Project planning, teamwork, or management skills | 8 | 17.4 | 12 | 18.5 |
| Research skill building | 10 | 21.7 | 17 | 26.2 |
| Retention of transfer/transfer-intending students | 22 | 47.8 | 31 | 47.7 |
| Social support networks (e.g., peer connections and friendships) | 9 | 19.6 | 30 | 46.2 |
| Student–faculty interaction | 20 | 43.5 | 34 | 52.3 |
| Writing skills | 27 | 58.7 | 28 | 43.1 |
| Other | 0 | 0.0 | 4 | 6.2 |

*Table continues on page 26*

*Table continued from page 25*

*Percentage of Survey Participants Reporting Specific Objectives Associated With Transfer Student Success Programs, Policies, and Practices*

| | Institutional type | | | |
| | Two-year | | Four-year | |
| Institutional objective | Freq. | % | Freq. | % |
| --- | --- | --- | --- | --- |
| My institution has not identified objectives for initiatives available to transfer/transfer-intending students | 1 | 2.2 | 4 | 6.2 |
| Total | 46 | 100.0 | 65 | 100.0 |

*Note.* Of the 169 total survey participants, 46 from two-year schools and 65 from four-year schools answered this question. Survey participants were asked to select any objectives they perceived to be associated with their institution's transfer practices.

The adoption and implementation of targeted programs, policies, and practices for transfer and transfer-intending students were relatively recent efforts among NSTSI-participating institutions (i.e., they started within the last 10 years). This finding was true for 42.3% of respondents who reported that their institution offered transfer programs (including 41.3% of respondents from two-year schools and 41.6% from four-year schools). NSTSI participants were also asked to report, based on their knowledge, how long institution-wide efforts included a concerted focus on transfer and transfer-intending students; some examples included accreditation efforts (e.g., quality enhancement plans), curricular or gateway course redesign, institutional assessment, participation in a national survey (e.g., Community College Survey of Student Engagement, National Survey of Student Engagement), retention studies, and transfer advisory councils. Most respondents whose institutions offered transfer initiatives (33.1%) reported that efforts had been focused on transfer for 2 to 5 years (see Figure 5). Among two-year schools, 25.0% of respondents revealed that they did not know how long institution-wide efforts had been focused on transfer, 22.9% reported that efforts had been in place for 2 to 5 years, and 20.8% indicated a duration of 6 to 10 years. Respondents from four-year schools also indicated that institution-wide efforts for transfer were relatively new, as 38.1% reported their institution participated in these actions within the last 2 to 5 years and 15.5% noted such steps had been taken within the last 6 to 10 years.

In addition, more than half of the participants (57.0% of all respondents, including 59.6% from two-year schools and 54.5% from four-year schools) reported considering or currently developing future initiatives specifically or intentionally geared toward transfer/transfer-intending students. However, despite this focus, 19.1% of respondents from two-year schools and 23.8% from four-year schools were unsure of whether any transfer-related efforts were under development, possibly indicating challenges with cross-functional and cross-institutional communication, coordination, and planning. Frequently reported objectives that respondents indicated would be measured in the upcoming initiatives included academic planning (63.6% of all respondents, including 60.7% of participants from two-year schools and 66.7% from four-year schools), retention of transfer/transfer-intending students (61.0% of all respondents; 57.1% from two-year schools and 64.6% from four-year schools), and persistence of transfer and transfer-intending students (53.2% of all respondents; 53.6% from two-year schools and 54.2% from four-year schools).

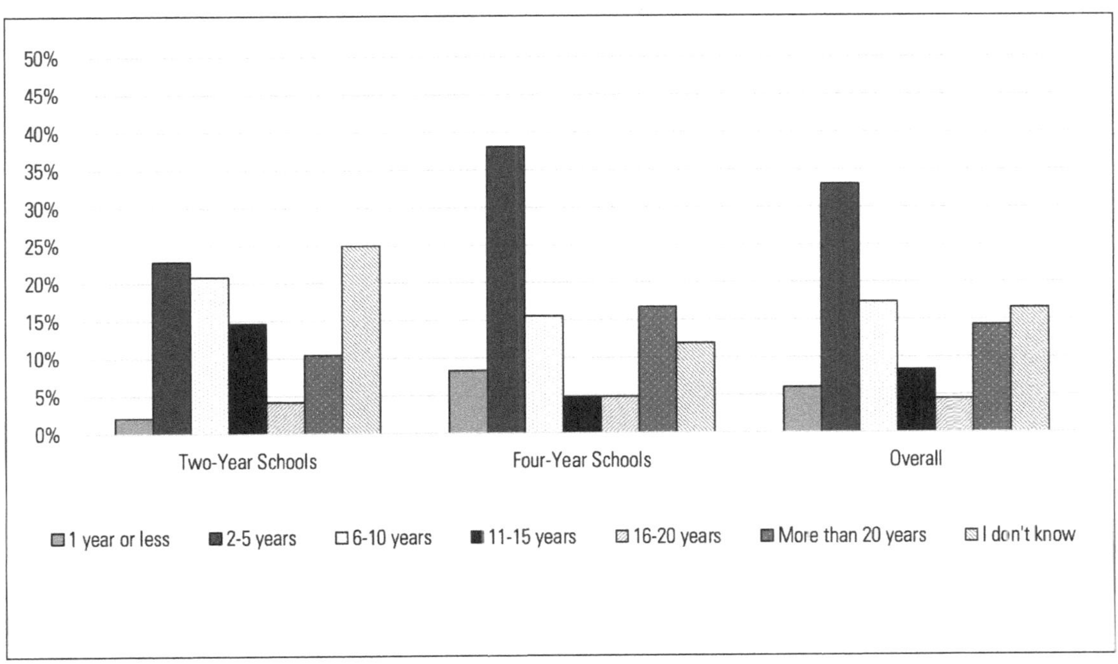



*Figure 5.* Length of time institution-wide efforts have included a concerted focus on transfer and transfer-intending students (*n* = 133).

*Note.* Responses included 48 from two-year schools and 84 from four-year schools.

### *Coordination of Transfer Initiatives*

Data from the survey revealed differences in terms of how transfer-related efforts were coordinated across institutions, including which organizational units were involved in these efforts and which institution-wide efforts included a transfer focus. Regarding the extent to which transfer initiatives were coordinated across campus, 39.2% of respondents (including 38.0% from two-year schools and 39.8% from four-year schools) indicated services were somewhere between decentralized and centralized, revealing that not all efforts were collectively organized. The second most frequent response in terms of extent of coordination indicated that efforts were almost all centralized and coordinated (28.7% of all respondents, including 32.0% from two-year schools and 25.8% from four-year schools). A more detailed breakdown of responses by institution type is shown in Figure 6.

During the interviews, participants spoke about barriers associated with streamlining coordination across campus. For example, a staff member at a community college noted that "communication and collaboration among departments and faculty needs to improve" to achieve such a goal. In addition, a respondent from a public four-year school shared that decentralized services inherently "means that different units have different transfer services, but these units aren't always working in alignment with each other." Institutional attention and focus on nontransfer student populations, especially first-time-in-college and nontransfer or transfer-intending students, also affected coordination and delivery of services, as a participant at a private not-for-profit four-year school described:

> [Transfer students] are an overlooked population. We have some events for them, but they are not coordinated in a meaningful way. Because we are so first-year focused, and because transfer students make up only 3% of our undergraduate population, they don't always get the support that they need.

A lack of focus on transfer students can result in nonexistent or weak structures available to guide them through the transfer process and support their progress toward obtaining bachelor's degrees. Furthermore, uncoordinated efforts among offices and institutional partners can exacerbate this lack of support and leave students to navigate a complex transfer process.

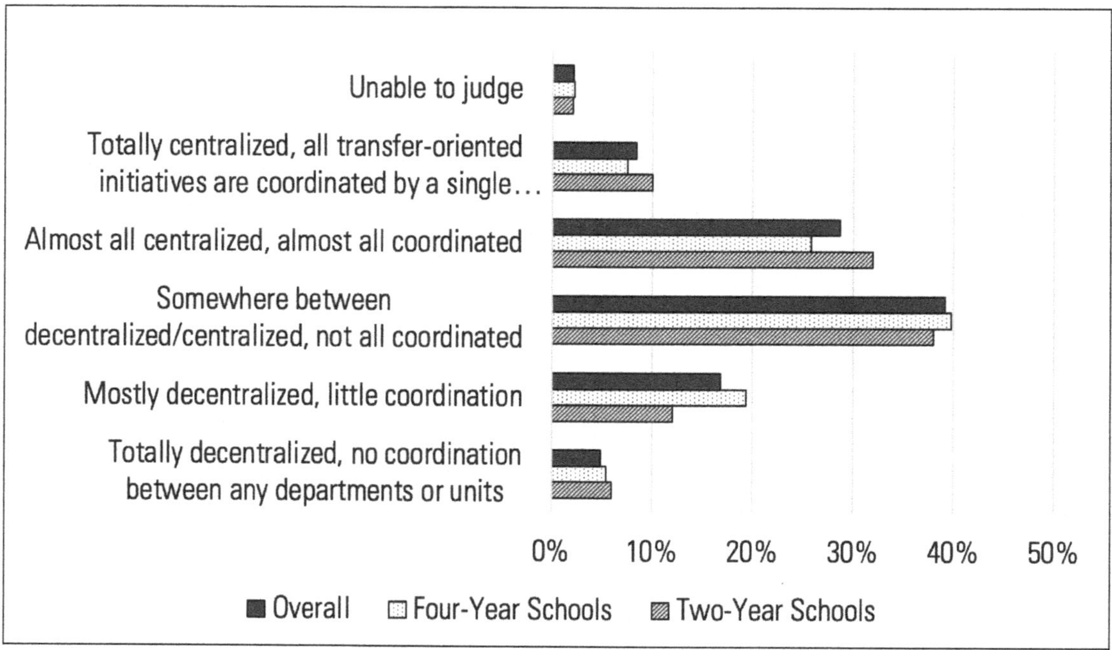


*Figure 6.* Degree of centralization of transfer initiatives reported by respondents (*n* = 143).
*Note.* Responses included 50 from two-year schools and 93 from four-year schools.

Reviewing the data on how campus units participate in the coordination of transfer-related services, we discovered that academic advising was the most frequently reported unit, indicated by 84.6% of respondents. Other frequently reported offices and positions included the admissions office (70.6% of all respondents), the academic affairs office (59.4%), the registrar or transfer evaluation coordinator (55.2%), and the orientation office (46.2%). A detailed breakdown of units that work to develop and deliver transfer-related services is shown in Table 4.

When asked which organizational structures their institution uses to facilitate the coordination of the transfer experience, 37.8% of respondents (including 36.0% from two-year schools and 39.8% from four-year schools) indicated that their schools did not have any organizational structures to do so. Among two-year respondents whose institutions did have teams, offices, and services that supported coordination, 32.0% had a transfer center or designated space on campus, and 20.0% reported the existence of a transfer program office (e.g., a transfer-year experience program). At four-year schools with such initiatives, 23.7% of respondents reported a transfer program committee, task force, or advisory board helping to coordinate the transfer experience. A cross-institutional transfer team (i.e., a team inclusive of representatives across multiple institutions) was reported by 18.0% of respondents from two-year schools and 17.2% of respondents from four-year schools. Most often, academic affairs central offices were reported as the institutional division that housed transfer-specific services, indicated by 52.4% of respondents from four-year schools and 28.6% from two-year schools. In addition, some respondents reported that their institution had a transfer programs office to aid with supporting transfer (30.1% of respondents, including 44.0% from two-year schools and 22.6% from four-year schools). A majority of participants from institutions with a transfer programs office noted that the individual overseeing this office held a position not solely focused on transfer, indicating that the job required that they oversee and support additional initiatives related to other student populations (57.1% all participants indicating such, including 57.1% from two-year schools and 57.1% from four-year schools).

The survey data also revealed differences in institution-wide efforts designed to enhance student learning across two- and four-year schools. Among respondents from two-year schools, 69.4% noted that pathways programs (such as Guided Pathways) included a specific focus on transfer. In addition, 51.0% of respondents from two-year schools indicated that curricular or gateway course redesign efforts included a consideration of transfer, and 46.9% reported the same about student services programming. Among respondents from four-year schools, frequent responses specified that enrollment management efforts (e.g., admissions, financial aid, and/or registrar offices; 72.8%) and institutional assessment (i.e., analysis of data collected with a specific focus on transfers, including enrollment data; 48.9%) included an emphasis on transfer.

Table 4

*Percentage of Survey Participants Endorsing Each Campus Unit Participating in Coordination of Transfer Initiatives*

| | Institutional type | | | |
| | Two-year | | Four-year | |
| **Participating unit** | **Freq.** | **%** | **Freq.** | **%** |
|---|---|---|---|---|
| Academic advising | 46 | 92.0 | 75 | 80.6 |
| Academic affairs office | 29 | 58.0 | 56 | 60.2 |
| Academic department(s), please specify | 19 | 38.0 | 25 | 26.9 |
| Admissions office | 20 | 40.0 | 81 | 87.1 |
| Career services | 20 | 40.0 | 23 | 24.7 |
| Center for teaching excellence | 3 | 6.0 | 9 | 9.7 |
| Enrollment management | 12 | 24.0 | 51 | 54.8 |
| Financial aid office | 17 | 34.0 | 46 | 49.5 |
| First-year experience/transfer-year experience office | 11 | 22.0 | 17 | 18.3 |
| Institutional research office | 13 | 26.0 | 18 | 19.4 |
| Library services | 5 | 10.0 | 12 | 12.9 |
| Orientation | 10 | 20.0 | 55 | 59.1 |
| Registrar or transfer evaluation coordinator | 14 | 28.0 | 64 | 68.8 |
| Residence life or housing | 1 | 2.0 | 23 | 24.7 |
| Student activities and leadership | 7 | 14.0 | 13 | 14.0 |
| Student affairs office | 14 | 28.0 | 30 | 32.3 |
| Student success center | 13 | 26.0 | 32 | 34.4 |
| Transfer center | 15 | 30.0 | 8 | 8.6 |
| Other, please specify | 4 | 8.0 | 7 | 7.5 |
| I don't know | 0 | 0.0 | 0 | 0.0 |
| Total | 50 | 100.0 | 93 | 100.0 |

### *High-Impact and Promising Practices Related to Transfer and Transfer-Intending Student Success*

When exploring efforts associated with supporting transfer student learning and success, it is important to understand the role and impact of high-impact practices (HIPs). HIPs have long been touted for their relationship to student engagement and success. As originally outlined by the American Association of Colleges and Universities (AAC&U; Kuh, 2008), HIPs include 10 initiatives that may help contribute to student retention (Provencher & Kassel, 2019), student learning, and student integration on campus. The list of AAC&U-designated HIPs includes capstone courses and projects, collaborative assignments and projects, common intellectual experiences, diversity/global learning, ePortfolios, first-year seminars and experiences, internships, learning communities, service learning and community-based learning, undergraduate research, and writing-intensive courses (AAC&U, 2023). For transfer and transfer-intending students in particular, HIPs may be crucial ways that institutions help students prepare for transfer, develop academic aspirations and goals, and form connections with peers, faculty, and staff at their receiving institutions. Additionally, when considering the HIPs identified by AAC&U and their applicability across institutional types, it is important to understand that these impactful practices may not be offered by two-year schools and/or may not be most useful to two-year student success. Instead, two-year schools may provide different educational practices, tailored to the student and to institutional needs and goals.

To help bridge this understanding and examine the educational practices in the two-year sector that were most significant to transfer student engagement and learning, the Center for Community College Student Engagement (2013) identified 13 promising educational practices in the two-year sector that they described as high impact, based on the gains that participating students experience as a result of them. These HIPs include academic goal setting and planning, orientation, accelerated or fast-track developmental education, first-year experience, student success courses, learning communities, experiential learning beyond the classroom, tutoring, supplemental instruction, assessment and placement, registration before classes begin, class attendance, and alert and intervention.

To understand HIPs across the transfer experience, which spans multiple institutional sectors, we included expanded modules in the survey to examine three HIPs likely to be offered at two- and four-year schools and that have been identified in the literature as significant to supporting transfer and transfer-intending student success. These practices include orientation, transfer or college success skills courses, and academic advising.

**Orientation.** Orientation has been identified as an important initiative to connect incoming transfer and transfer-intending students to institutional resources, services, and staff (Hoover, 2010; Peska, 2011; Wyner et al., 2016). During orientation, students may be provided with opportunities to connect with academic advisors, who can help them to decide on an academic major or area of study and can provide additional focus for students already aware of what they would like to study. At two-year schools, orientation efforts may include opportunities to prepare academically for transfer and to learn about the curricular requirements needed to complete a transfer-oriented associated degree. Orientation may also offer opportunities for staff to develop programming so that students become aware of institutional traditions, activities, and events. These events can be supportive in helping to reinforce that students belong at their institution (Wyner et al., 2016). As transfer students may have previous experience within higher education, research has shown that tailored orientation experiences for transfer students that validate their previous knowledge and experiences while connecting them to useful and relevant information about processes at their new institution can be beneficial for their success (Hoover, 2010; Peska, 2011). As such, it is important for transfer personnel to understand the orientation activities they offer, including whether they are available to and specifically geared for transfer students rather than only for first-year (nontransfer) students.

Among respondents who answered a question about whether their institution offered orientation programming for incoming transfer or transfer-intending students, 69.6% indicated such. Differences in frequencies across institutional type were apparent, as more respondents from four-year schools (80.0%) than from two-year schools (50.0%) noted that their college or university offered orientation.

Additionally, the type and focus of orientation programming differed greatly across the sample. When asked to indicate the best description of their institution's orientation programming for incoming transfer or transfer-intending students, a majority of respondents from two-year schools (62.5%) noted that their institution offered an orientation and that transfer/transfer-intending students attended the same sessions as first-year (nontransfer or transfer-intending) students, while 20.8% indicated that their institution offered an orientation for all incoming students, with specific programs and sessions for transfers/transfer-intending students. Among four-year schools, 52.1% of respondents reported that their institution offered an orientation specifically for transfer/transfer-intending students, 23.9% indicated that their institution offered an orientation for all students but with specific programs and sessions for transfer/transfer-intending students, and 22.5% noted that transfer/transfer-intending students attended the same sessions as first-year (nontransfer) students during orientation.

The availability of and requirements for participation in orientation also differed across the sample. Most respondents indicated that their institution offered orientation programming for incoming students who transfer outside of the Fall semester or quarter (86.3% of respondents, including 79.2% of respondents from two-year schools and 88.7% from four-year schools). Offering midyear transfer orientation can be an impactful way to support students and to customize orientation programming to meet the needs of those transitioning at different points (Peska, 2011). We also discovered that 68.4% of respondents overall (including 66.7% of respondents from two-year schools and 69.0% from four-year schools) noted that their institution required incoming transfer or transfer-intending students to participate in orientation programming.

Colleges and universities in the sample offered a variety of orientation activities to transfer and transfer-intending students. Participants from two-year schools frequently reported online orientation (83.3% of respondents), pre-term advising or registration (66.7%), welcome week activities (50.0%), and on-campus preterm activities (50.0%). Among four-year schools, preterm advising or registration (81.7%), online orientation (56.3%), and welcome week activities (54.9%) were most often reported. Less common orientation activities included bridge programs (5.3% of respondents indicating such) and outdoor adventure/wilderness experiences (8.4%).

When reporting content covered and engagement activities offered through orientation, nearly all respondents indicated that programming shared an introduction to campus resources and services (92.6% of all respondents, including 83.3% from two-year schools and 95.8% from four-year schools). Respondents also indicated that academic advising (83.3% of participants from two-year schools, 84.5% from four-year schools) and college- or university-specific policies (87.5% from two-year schools, 88.7% from four-year schools) were commonly discussed during orientation. Structured interactions with faculty were reported as an orientation-related activity by 25.0% of respondents from two-year schools and 33.8% from four-year schools. Critically, 25.0% of the respondents from two-year schools and 26.8% from the four-year schools indicated that employment opportunities were discussed during orientation, which may indicate a significant gap in programming as students seek jobs and monetary support to provide for themselves and their families as well as to finance their education (Center for Community College Student Engagement, 2020). The least frequently reported activity was common reading (i.e., a book or article students read before and discuss during orientation); only 8.3% of respondents from two-year schools and 18.3% from four-year schools indicated that common reading was available at their institution.

When asked about the campus units that directly administer orientation programming for incoming transfer or transfer-intending students, 91.3% of respondents from two-year schools reported that a student affairs/student services office was tasked with these efforts, compared to 59.4% from four-year schools. Respondents from four-year schools also reported that academic affairs offices (21.7%) as well as academic departments (13.0%) played a role in the administration of orientation.

Overall, a substantial proportion of respondents (50.0% of respondents from two-year schools and 29.6% of four-year schools) noted that their orientation programming had not been formally assessed or evaluated within the last four years at the time the survey was administered. Furthermore, 16.7% of respondents from two-year schools and 36.6% from four-year schools shared that they were unaware of whether any assessment had taken place.

Among respondents who indicated that formal assessment of orientation had taken place (33.3% of respondents from two-year schools and 33.8% from four-year schools), the types of assessment measures varied. The most frequently reported efforts included analysis of institutional data (e.g., GPA, retention rates, and/or graduation) and the use of a survey instrument, with 68.8% of respondents indicating that their institution used both efforts. A survey was the most commonly reported assessment method at two-year schools (87.5% of respondents, compared to 66.7% of the respondents at four-year schools), whereas analysis of institutional data was the most frequently reported effort among respondents from four-year schools (75.0%, compared to 37.5% of the respondents from two-year schools). Finally, when asked about the benefit of orientation programming for supporting transfer student success when considering staff time, resources, and other costs, most respondents (84.0% from two-year schools and 83.1% from four-year schools) indicated that orientation had medium- to high-benefit for students.

**Transfer or College Student Success Skills Courses.** Another HIP that may be available at two- and four-year schools is the use of success skills courses designed for transfer or college students. These courses are often introductory and guide students regarding college or university academic requirements, degree programs, and major and/or transfer pathways as well as provide information about campus activities, support services, and learning and study strategies (Fematt et al., 2021). Transfer and college student success skills courses can also promote student engagement as they facilitate student–faculty interactions, peer relationships, and active learning opportunities and bolster interactions with support services. These courses can be especially helpful for transfer-intending students to learn more about how to identify and interpret information related to transfer, including credit and articulation policies, transfer maps, and degree timelines. For incoming transfer students, these courses can provide valuable support, especially as students navigate their new institution and its associated spaces and cultures (Cooper et al., 2020).

Among survey respondents, 30.9% noted their institution offered a transfer or college student success skills course that included a focus on transfer for students. More two-year schools than four-year schools provided this initiative (31.7% vs. 25.3%). The majority of respondents reported that their institution had offered these courses for 10 or fewer years (68.4% from two-year schools and 65.2% from four-year schools). Whether students were required to participate in such courses differed across institution type, with 57.9% of respondents from two-year schools and 27.3% from four-year schools reporting that transfer or transfer-intending students were required to take a transfer or college success skills course.

Respondents most frequently reported that college or transfer success skills courses lasted either half a term (57.9% of respondents from two-year schools, 4.3% from four-year schools) or one semester (47.4% from two-year schools, 73.9% from four-year schools). A majority of respondents reported that students earned one academic credit (63.2% from two-year schools, 52.2% from four-year schools), and some indicated that these courses carried three credits (31.6% from two-year schools, 17.4% from four-year schools). Regarding applicability of credit earned from the course, 42.1% of respondents from two-year schools and 47.8% from four-year schools noted that the course counted as an elective, whereas 47.4% from two-year schools and 43.5% of four-year schools indicated the course counted toward general education requirements. Nearly all participants indicated that students could apply financial aid toward the tuition and fees associated with the transfer or college success skills course (100.0% from two-year schools, 90.9% from four-year schools).

Content covered and learning facilitated within transfer and college success skills courses varied across institutions. Among respondents from two-year schools, the five most important course objectives included learning academic success strategies (84.2%), academic planning (68.4%), career exploration and/or preparation (68.4%), knowledge of institution or course resources and services (57.9%), and introduction to a major, discipline, or career path (36.8%). Among four-year respondents, developing academic success strategies was the most frequently reported important course objective (65.2% of respondents), followed by knowledge of institution or campus resources and services (52.2%), academic planning (43.5%), retention of students (39.1%), and connection with the institution or campus (34.8%).

When asked about crucial topics that comprised the content of transfer or college success skills courses and related directly to course objectives, respondents from two-year schools most frequently reported academic planning or advising (78.9%), academic success strategies such as study skills and time management (73.7%), academic resources (52.6%), career exploration or preparation (42.1%), and financial information, including financial aid and scholarships (42.1%). Respondents from four-year schools indicated academic success strategies (69.6%), academic planning or advising (65.2%), academic resources (52.2%), campus activities and involvement (39.1%), and campus resources (34.8%). At two-year schools, full-time, non-tenure-track faculty (reported by 78.9% of respondents) and adjunct faculty (57.9%) most frequently taught the transfer or college success skills courses, whereas academic advisors (reported by 56.5% of respondents) and student affairs professionals (39.1%) most often taught the transfer or college success skills courses at four-year schools.

Regarding whether their institution's transfer or college success skills courses had been formally assessed or evaluated, 55.8% of the respondents noted that such initiatives had been undertaken within four years of the dissemination of the survey, including 68.4% from two-year schools and 43.5% from four-year schools. Common types of assessment indicated by participants from two-year schools were analysis of institutional data, including GPA, retention rates, and graduation (76.9% of respondents); direct assessment of student learning outcomes (69.2%); program review (69.2%); and student course evaluation (69.2%). Respondents from four-year schools noted that common approaches to assessment included direct assessment of student learning outcomes (66.7%) and analysis of institutional data (55.6%). However, student course evaluation also emerged as a frequent form of assessment at four-year schools (66.7%). Additionally, 89.5% of participants from two-year schools and 86.4% from four-year schools reported that they perceived their institution's transfer or college student success skills course to be of medium to high benefit to supporting transfer students.

**Academic Advising.** As previously noted, academic advising is a frequently used and important means through which institutions support transfer and transfer-intending student success. Multiple studies underscore the impact of advising on students' planning for transfer, their adjustment and engagement, and their satisfaction with transfer, among other outcomes (Center for Community College Student Engagement, 2018; Hunter & White, 2004; Zhang, 2016). Recent scholarship suggests that academic advising may be characterized as a HIP because of its inherent requirement for students and staff to invest time and effort into the practice and because it facilitates engagement among students and faculty (Keup & Young, 2022). However, despite the benefits of academic advising, transfer and transfer-intending students often face multiple challenges associated with it. For example, they may receive unclear or conflicting information about navigating the transfer process from institutional representatives and advisors, and they may have to make sense of transfer policies, such as articulation and admissions agreements (Fay et al., 2022; Schudde et al., 2021).

Given evidence of a racial transfer gap in which White students transfer from community colleges more frequently than Black and Hispanic or Latina/o/x students do (Crisp & Núñez, 2014), it is crucial to understand the impact advising may have on the transfer and transfer-intending student experience. Advising is an institutional service that can have powerful or detrimental implications, particularly for racially and ethnically minoritized students (Del Real Viramontes, 2020; Zhang, 2016). Students rely on guidance from institutional agents, particularly advisors, to navigate the transfer process and gather information about admissions requirements, financial aid, and transfer credit policies (Fink et al., 2023). If students do not receive useful information or if their learning goals are not validated by staff, they may not transfer successfully. As such, it is important that institutional leaders and staff understand characteristics associated with advising and how advising may be organized or improved to increase students' engagement and the benefits gained from interactions with these services.

Most participants who responded to the survey question about whether their institution offers academic advising to transfer or transfer-intending students indicated that their institutional advising did (97.9% of participants from two-year schools and 94.4% from four-year schools). However, 52.1% of respondents from two-year schools and 45.2% from four-year schools reported that advising services had been offered for 10 years or less, whereas 27.4% of respondents from four-year schools shared that their institutions have had dedicated resources and have provided targeted advising services and initiatives for transfer students for 16 to 20 years.

Of the participants whose institutions offered advising to transfer and transfer-intending students, 70.0% (63.0% of participants from two-year schools and 73.8% from four-year schools) reported that incoming transfer or transfer-intending students were required to participate in academic advising. Ninety percent of respondents (84.8% from two-year schools and 92.9% from four-year schools) noted their school assigned incoming students to academic advisors, although the requirements varied in terms of frequency of meeting with the advisor (faculty or staff member) during a student's first academic year. Of the participants from two-year schools, 20.5% reported that students were required to meet with an advisor only once during the first term, 30.8% reported that students met with an advisor once during each term of their first year, and 10.3% indicated that students were required to meet with an advisor two or more times each term of their first year. Of respondents from four-year schools, 34.6% noted that their schools required students to meet with an advisor once during each term of their first year, whereas 10.3% reported students were required to meet with an advisor only once during the first term and 15.4% reported students were required to meet with an advisor two or more times each term of their first year.

Over a third (36.8%) of respondents, and 43.6% from four-year schools, reported that students were required to meet with their assigned advisor once each term after their first academic year. However, 38.5% of respondents from two-year schools indicated that transfer or transfer-intending students were not required to meet with their assigned advisor after their first year. Such policies or guidelines may have a negative impact on student progress, particularly as students move toward completing their academic programs and prepare to transfer to four-year schools. Continued conversations with advising staff could provide valuable opportunities for students to monitor and understand their progress toward achieving their academic goals.

The availability of advising services differed across institution type. Many survey respondents noted their institutions first offered academic advising services to students after they confirmed their acceptance at the institution (37.7% of respondents from two-year schools and 47.6% from four-year schools). Respondents from 28.8% of two-year schools and 32.1% of four-year schools reported their institutions offered advising prior to confirmation of acceptance (i.e., before students are admitted to the institution).

The forms of advising offered also varied across institution type. All respondents from two-year schools (100.0%) reported that one-on-one advising (i.e., individual meetings between students and advisors) was available, and 69.6% reported that online or distance advising was available. Participants from four-year schools also reported their institutions offered one-on-one advising (96.4%) as well as online or distance advising (61.9%).

Respondents identified a variety of campus units involved in directly administering transfer-related advising. Respondents from two-year schools noted that student affairs (58.7%) and academic departments (30.4%) participated in these efforts. Among four-year schools, 22.6% of respondents indicated that individuals working in academic departments most frequently administered advising, and 32.1% identified academic affairs staff as having this role. Professionally trained advisors were reported as the most common type of advisors (80.4% of respondents from two-year schools and 70.2% from four-year schools), followed by faculty (52.2% of respondents from two-year schools and 67.9% from four-year schools).

Regarding preparation and professional development, 69.6% of respondents from two-year schools reported that their institution's advisors received training about student transfer, compared to 45.2% of respondents from four-year schools. This finding may indicate that institutional staff could benefit from professional development opportunities to learn more about barriers associated with transfer student mobility and success, transfer student demographics, and strengths that transfer students possess.

Respondents also identified varying methods to monitor transfer and transfer-intending student academic progress. Advising services for students often included early warning/academic alert systems (87.0% of respondents from two-year schools and 76.2% from four-year schools); 42.5% of survey participants from two-year schools that used early alerts also indicated that they used a hybrid approach combining technology- and human-based approaches, compared with 53.1% of respondents from four-year schools. Most respondents indicated that faculty or instructors participated in some aspect of the early alert/academic warning systems for transfer or transfer-intending students (92.5% of respondents from two-year schools and 89.1% from four-year schools), with 80.0% of respondents from two-year schools and 93.8% from four-year schools also noting that academic advisors participated in these programs. Additionally, 82.8% of respondents from four-year schools indicated that academic support personnel were involved in these alert systems. Respondents most frequently noted that students are contacted by phone, letter, or electronic means (e.g., email and/or text "nudges"; 92.5% of participants from two-year schools and 96.9% from four-year schools) and/or that students are informed about opportunities to seek academic assistance (70.0% from two-year schools and 70.3% from four-year schools).

Respondents also provided insight into activities and processes related to advising that their institutions were engaged in at the time the NSTSI was disseminated. They reported that their schools provided ongoing professional development and training for advisors (80.4% of respondents at two-year schools and 62.2% from four-year schools) as well as evaluation and continuous improvement of advising (71.7% from two-year schools and 63.4% from four-year schools). While this finding is promising, it may point to a concerted effort of continuous improvement of advising in general and not specifically to transfer-related advising.

Asked whether their institutions had conducted some form of assessment and evaluation of academic advising within the last four years, 47.8% of respondents from two-year schools agreed, compared to 24.4% of respondents from four-year schools (24.4%). Respondents who indicated that their institution had completed a formal assessment most often reported analysis of institutional data (63.6% from two-year schools and 80.0% from four-year schools) and the use of survey instrument(s) (54.5% from two-year schools and 60.0% from four-year schools). Again, these data may reveal a focus on overall improvement of advising and not necessarily efforts targeted toward understanding and supporting transfer-related advising.

We also asked respondents to identify the outcome(s) measured by the assessment methods they used. Respondents most often identified academic planning as an objective (68.2% from two-year schools and 70.0% from four-year schools). Respondents from four-year schools also identified on-time (i.e., four-year or six-year) graduation rates (60.0% of respondents). When considering time, costs, and resources associated with academic advising, 41.3% of respondents from two-year schools and 34.1% from four-year schools noted that they believed advising is highly beneficial to support transfer student success. In addition, 56.5% of respondents from two-year schools and 56.1% from four-year schools reported that advising has a medium or medium to high benefit.

# Future Directions and Considerations

When colleges and universities establish a shared commitment to transfer and continuously act on delivering and supporting that vision, a transfer-receptive culture can be sustained. The results from this 2021 NSTSI point to multiple promising practices and opportunities for maintaining such partnerships. We identified challenges associated with sustaining a transfer-receptive culture, prompting multiple questions and implications for supporting transfer and transfer-intending students. We thus offer some discussion points for transfer-oriented researchers and practitioners to consider as they continue their important roles in prompting student and institutional success.

## Understanding and Committing to Supporting Transfer

NSTSI participants from a variety of two- and four-year schools described their roles as crucial in supporting student transfer and mobility. As institutions continue to grapple with enrollment challenges and serve incoming and outgoing transfer students, staff may consider questions related to their college or university's role in transfer landscape, such as what it means to be a transfer-sending institution, what it means to be a transfer-receiving institution, what it means to be both transfer sending and transfer receiving, and what responsibilities are associated with these roles. Through reflections on the institutional transfer function, staff may begin to observe potential instances of misalignment between the institution's mission and its function, including the actions the institution takes toward transfer and what the institution espouses it values or prioritizes.

Future research can continue to explore the changing landscape of transfer. Inquiries may include not only how institutions interpret their roles (i.e., are they transfer sending, transfer receiving, or both?) but also how institutions respond to students' needs through initiatives and objectives. Understanding institutional responses and commitment to transfer may be especially significant in light of the COVID-19 pandemic, during which transfer rates declined, particularly at two-year institutions (Causey et al., 2022). Student mobility has and will continue to take multiple and complex forms (e.g., swirling) as student goals and responsibilities shift. Institutional staff will be tasked with responding to these changes and ameliorating challenges that students face related to their enrollment and retention.

Transfer personnel cited a lack of institutional support and resources as impediments to providing transfer-related support. As such, it would be worthwhile to explore how support and resource allocation for transfer or transfer-intending initiatives were affected during the COVID-19 pandemic (e.g., in the face of budget cuts, shifting modalities of instruction). In addition, given the faculty-related issues participants described, future work may examine the impact of faculty commitment to transfer with an aim to create resources that staff and faculty can use as they build buy-in and seek to transform institutional cultures around transfer.

## Identifying and Improving Key Initiatives and Practices

Institutions must provide early and consistent supports for students across the transfer pipeline. In particular, sustained initiatives can be important ways to provide students with clear, accurate, and relevant information about transfer. Given that NSTSI participants endorsed advising as an important means for transfer-related success, advising may be a key initiative to address. The success of advising and other transfer initiatives is dependent on cultivating and maintaining cross-functional coordination (i.e., within institution) as well as cross-institutional coordination (i.e., the strength of relationships between two- and four-year schools). Partnerships are especially critical to consider, given that admissions and articulation agreements were cited by NSTSI participants as frequent and important initiatives. To ensure that these services work as intended and benefit students, relationships must promote collaboration, share information and resources, and connect students to important information, support services, and people to aid their progress on their academic pathways.

Because transfer is a key pathway of mobility for multiple marginalized student populations, equity must be centered within the creation, implementation, and assessment of partnerships. Partners must identify shared goals for equity, use asset-based approaches to the shared work, and understand the role of structural forces in transfer student success outcomes (Crisp et al., 2022). Ultimately, robust transfer partnerships can help to validate students' learning through acceptance of transfer credit and clear discussions about how that credit will apply. Strong forms of coordination can help to sustain students' experiences across institutions, particularly when considering how students' experiences at two-year schools may connect to and support those they encounter after enrollment at a four-year school.

The identification and celebration of transfer champions, or individuals committed to transfer and transfer-intending students, can be crucial in ensuring the sustainability of partnerships. Transfer champions may be allies with prior experience as transfer students themselves or individuals committed to equity and student success; they can serve as points of contact and proud supporters of transfer efforts and can foster relationships with both students and partners, across the institution and externally. Students benefit because useful and supportive interactions with these individuals or offices contribute to engagement, help them feel connected with the institution, and offer opportunities to receive meaningful and tailored support and information related to transfer and degree completion. Individuals with knowledge of and commitment to transfer students and the transfer process can enhance student–staff/faculty relationships. Staff and faculty may be well poised to advocate for transfer students and initiatives to support these students using approaches informed by empathy and care.

A potential concern associated with singular points of contact may be sustainability, especially when considering what happens when staff turnover occurs or when institutions do not have enough money or are not committed to growing services. The data reported here suggest that the responsibility to educate the rest of the institution on transfer issues often falls on transfer champions and their offices. As such, it is necessary to understand how transfer champions and partners can work together to inform and strengthen each other. In tandem, these efforts can prompt conversations about how commitment to transfer can be successfully diffused within and across institutions to support buy-in and allocation of time and resources for transfer.

## Strengthening Equity-Minded Approaches Toward Transfer Research and Practice

Finally, results from NSTSI point toward equity-related implications as well as questions associated with transfer. Nearly 80% of the respondents from two-year schools indicated that their institutions had specific goals related to equity and transfer, compared to about half of the participants from four-year schools. This difference aligns with the gap in the numbers of two-year and four-year schools that included transfer in their institutional strategic plans. While these results may not be surprising given differences in outcomes associated with transfer across institution type, the disconnect between transfer and equity, especially at four-year schools, provides opportunities for new directions in research and practice in the future. As such, we encourage institutions to collect, analyze, and share transfer student data as consistently as they share data regarding first-time-in-college students. A better understanding of the demographic, recruitment, enrollment, and outcome data would raise awareness of the transfer students on their campuses and could lead to development of institutional goals tailored to the transfer experience. Student voices should also be included in such datasets to help explore nuances in the quantitative data and differences between transfer students and their first-year-in-college peers. Readied with data, administrators can address key questions about transfer student access to student support programs on campus. For instance, are transfer students eligible for programs that serve first-generation college students or programs that serve students from historically marginalized communities? Relatedly, do transfer-serving programs recognize intersectional identities held by transfer students, including race/ethnicity, age, and status as a veteran or parent?

Commitments to transfer equity are resource-intensive, and, as such, institutions should consider barriers to staff, faculty, and administrative involvement in processes that promote and facilitate transfer. For instance, in the promotion and tenure process, recognition of faculty efforts using data from course evaluations as well as participation in cross-functional and cross-institutional partnerships with common sending/receiving institutions may provide an incentive for faculty to invest time in transfer practices. Rewarding these efforts contributes to building a transfer-receptive culture on campus and focuses on the ways that institutions can work to eliminate barriers to transfer success.

Within an equity-driven approach, faculty, staff, and leaders must work to identify the strengths and assets of their transfer and transfer-intending populations consciously and explicitly. For instance, one participant from a four-year school shared in their interview that transfer students at their institution excelled in time management and were motivated to graduate. Practitioners should determine how to collect such information (e.g., through assessment and evaluation efforts) to recognize students' assets and leverage them in the design of transfer support programs.

Ultimately, success for transfer and transfer-intending students cannot occur without discussing equity, as clear evidence of a racial transfer gap highlights a significant failure in support for Black and Latino/a/x students' academic pathways (Crisp & Núñez, 2014). Adapting asset-based approaches to understanding transfer student success can help staff and faculty uncover the multiple discriminatory and exclusionary systems students have to navigate (including societal and institutional systems) and the role that these systems play in students' educational outcomes. It may also help them to understand the role they play in perpetuating such systems and to consider ways to reconceptualize definitions and outcomes related to student success and associated assessment efforts.

# Appendix A:
# Survey Instrument: 2021 National Survey of Transfer Student Initiatives

Q1 National Survey of Transfer Student Initiatives

The National Resource Center for The First-Year Experience and Students in Transition at the University of South Carolina invites you to take the National Survey of Transfer Student Initiatives (NSTSI). NSTSI seeks to understand how transfer personnel at community colleges and four-year institutions support transfer and transfer-intending students, specifically examining academic and social support services associated with transfer.

This survey will take approximately 30 minutes to complete. It should be completed in one sitting, as your responses may not be saved.

NSTSI asks questions about:

- Transfer student enrollment at your institution
- Institutional objectives and initiatives associated with transfer
- Assessment of institutional initiatives associated with transfer
- Academic advising for transfer/transfer-intending students
- Orientation programming for transfer/transfer-intending students
- Transfer or college success skills courses at your institution
- Future transfer initiatives your institution plans to implement

We ask that you consult with relevant colleagues across your institution who can assist you with answering questions related to the above bullets. Thank you for sharing your knowledge and perspectives.

Q2. Full name of institution:

_________________________________________________________________

Q3. Institution city:

_________________________________________________________________

Q4. Institution state:

_________________________________________________________________

Q5. Your first name:

_______________________________________________

Q6. Your last name:

_______________________________________________

Q7. Your job title:

_______________________________________________

Q8. Your email address:

_______________________________________________

End of Block: Introduction

Start of Block: Transfer Students on Your Campus

Q9: Transfer Students at your Institution
In this section, you will be asked questions about trends and issues associated with transfer at your institution.

Q126. Which of the following best describes your institution? (Select only one.)

- ❏ Transfer sending (i.e., my institution aims to support student transfer from the institution) (1)
- ❏ Transfer receiving (i.e., my institution aims to support student transfer to the institution) (2)
- ❏ Transfer sending and receiving (i.e., my institution aims to support student transfer to and from the institution) (4)

*Skip To: Q12 If Q126 = 1*
*Skip To: Q106 If Q126 = 2*
*Skip To: Q134 If Q126 = 4*

Q106. During the 2019–2020 academic year, what percentage of your institution's overall undergraduate student body was comprised of students who had transferred **to your** institution?

- ❏ 10% or less (1)
- ❏ 11–20% (2)
- ❏ 21–30% (3)
- ❏ 31–40% (4)
- ❏ 41–50% (5)
- ❏ 51–60% (6)
- ❏ 61–70% (7)
- ❏ 71–80% (8)
- ❏ 81–90% (9)
- ❏ 91–100% (10)
- ❏ I don't know (11)

*Skip To: Q13 If Q106 = 1*
*Skip To: Q13 If Q106 = 2*

*Skip To: Q13 If Q106 = 3*
*Skip To: Q13 If Q106 = 4*
*Skip To: Q13 If Q106 = 5*
*Skip To: Q13 If Q106 = 6*
*Skip To: Q13 If Q106 = 7*
*Skip To: Q13 If Q106 = 8*
*Skip To: Q13 If Q106 = 9*
*Skip To: Q13 If Q106 = 10*
*Skip To: Q13 If Q106 = 11*

Q12. During the 2019–2020 academic year, what percentage of your institution's overall undergraduate student body transferred **from your** institution?

- ☐ 10% or less (1)
- ☐ 11–20% (2)
- ☐ 21–30% (3)
- ☐ 31–40% (4)
- ☐ 41–50% (5)
- ☐ 51–60% (6)
- ☐ 61–70% (7)
- ☐ 71–80% (8)
- ☐ 81–90% (9)
- ☐ 91–100% (10)
- ☐ I don't know (11)

*Display This Question:*
*If Q126 = 4*

Q134. During the 2019–2020 academic year, what percentage of your institution's overall undergraduate student body transferred:

| | To the institution (1) | From the Institution (2) |
| --- | --- | --- |
| 10% or less (1) | ☐ | ☐ |
| 11–20% (2) | ☐ | ☐ |
| 21–30% (10) | ☐ | ☐ |
| 31–40% (11) | ☐ | ☐ |
| 41–50% (12) | ☐ | ☐ |
| 51–60% (13) | ☐ | ☐ |
| 61–70% (14) | ☐ | ☐ |
| 71–80% (15) | ☐ | ☐ |
| 81–90% (16) | ☐ | ☐ |
| I don't know (17) | ☐ | ☐ |

Q13. Transfer-Related Issues among Faculty, Staff, and Administrators
In your opinion, what are the most common issues associated with transfer that staff, faculty, and administrators at your institution face? Please drag the arrows to indicate the prominence of the issue (0 = not at all a concern, 100 = a major concern at your institution).

| | 0 10 20 30 40 50 60 70 80 90 100 |
|---|---|
| Budget constraints that impact transfer-related programs and services () | |
| Availability of resources and institutional services tailored for transfer/transfer-intending students () | |
| Inadequate staffing for transfer-related programs and services () | |
| Lack of institutional commitment to transfer () | |
| Lack of training/professional development about transfer/transfer-intending students () | |
| Lack of information about transfer/transfer-intending students, including students' needs and characteristics () | |
| Intra-institutional coordination (e.g., communication and coordination within the institution) () | |
| Cultivating and maintaining cross-institutional partnerships (e.g., articulation agreements) () | |

Q135. Are there any additional concerning issues associated with transfer that staff, faculty, and administrators at your institution face? If so, please briefly describe these below:

_______________________________________________________________

_______________________________________________________________

_______________________________________________________________

_______________________________________________________________

Q118. Transfer-Related Issues among Students
In your opinion, what are the most concerning issues associated with transfer that students at your institution face? Please drag the arrows to indicate the prominence of the issue (0 = not at all a concern, 100 = a major concern at your institution).

| | 0 10 20 30 40 50 60 70 80 90 100 |
|---|---|
| Academic advising, including lack of support from advisors and/or lack of accurate and helpful information () | |
| Basic needs insecurity (food and/or housing insecurity and/or homelessness) () | |
| Financial aid and/or scholarship availability or access to financial resources () | |

| | |
|---|---|
| Gateway course completion () | |
| Progress toward graduation and/or transfer () | |
| Accessing and navigating institutional services () | |
| Social connections and sense of belonging (e.g., with peers, campus, and community) () | |
| Transfer credit processes (including credit articulation timelines, credit appeals, and loss of and/or inapplicability of transfer credit) () | |
| Academic adjustment, including developing skills and strategies necessary to succeed () | |

Q136. Are there any additional concerning issues associated with transfer that students at your institution face? If so, please briefly describe these below:

______________________________________________________________________

______________________________________________________________________

______________________________________________________________________

______________________________________________________________________

Q14. Which campus units participate in the coordination of their sophomore-year initiatives? (Select all that apply.)

- ❑   Yes (1)
- ❑   No (2)
- ❑   I don't know (3)

Q101. Does your institution have specific goals associated with equity and transfer/transfer-intending students?

- ❑   Yes (1)
- ❑   No (2)
- ❑   I don't know (3)

Q15. In your opinion, how committed is your institution currently to prioritizing transfer student success?

- ❑   1 – Not committed at all (1)
- ❑   2 (2)
- ❑   3 – Moderately committed (3)
- ❑   4 (4)
- ❑   5 – Highly committed (5)
- ❑   Unable to judge (6)

End of Block: Transfer Students on Your Campus
Start of Block: Institutional Objectives and Initiatives for Transfer Students

Q16. Institutional Objectives and Initiatives for Transfer Students This section will ask about initiatives for supporting transfer/transfer-intending students and the objectives associated with these programs.

Q18. Does your institution offer success programs, policies, or practices specifically or intentionally geared toward transfer/transfer-intending students?

- ❐ Yes (1)
- ❐ No (2)
- ❐ I don't know (3)

*Skip To: Q19 If Q18 = 1*

Q25. If your institution does not offer any transfer initiatives, indicate the reason(s) why: (Select all that apply.)

- ❐ Lack of expertise (41)
- ❐ Lack of funding (42)
- ❐ Lack of staff or faculty buy-in (43)
- ❐ Limited time (44)
- ❐ Not an institutional priority (45)
- ❐ Not a large enough population of transfer/transfer-intending students (47)
- ❐ Other, please specify: _________________________________________________

*Skip To: End of Block If Q25 = 41*
*Skip To: End of Block If Q25 = 42*
*Skip To: End of Block If Q25 = 43*
*Skip To: End of Block If Q25 = 44*
*Skip To: End of Block If Q25 = 45*
*Skip To: End of Block If Q25 = 46*

Q19. Which of the following transfer student success programs, policies, and practices does your institution offer specifically or intentionally for transfer/transfer-intending students? (Select all that apply.)

- ❐ Academic advising (1)
- ❐ Academic program maps (2)
- ❐ Academic coaching or mentoring (3)
- ❐ Articulation and/or admissions agreements (54)
- ❐ Awarding of experiential learning credits (e.g., prior-learning assessments, credit "badges," and/or CLEP) (4)
- ❐ Bridge programs (6)
- ❐ Campus-based event (e.g., common reading experiences, dinners, fairs) (7)
- ❐ Career exploration (8)
- ❐ Career planning (9)
- ❐ Communication or publications (e.g., social media, newsletters, emails, brochures) (10)
- ❐ Course-specific support for classes with high dropout, fail, or withdraw rates (e.g., supplemental instruction) (11)
- ❐ Credit-bearing course (e.g., transfer seminar) (12)

- ❐ Cultural enrichment activities (e.g., plays, musical events, multicultural fairs) (13)
- ❐ Early alert systems (14)
- ❐ Equal Opportunity Program (EOP) (15)
- ❐ Faculty or staff mentors (16)
- ❐ Financial aid (e.g., transfer scholarships, loans) (17)
- ❐ Financial planning, coaching, and information (18)
- ❐ Guided pathways (19)
- ❐ Honors societies (e.g., Tau Sigma, Phi Theta Kappa, etc.) (20)
- ❐ Informational sessions about navigating transfer (including admission, policies, and more) (21)
- ❐ Internships or co-ops (22)
- ❐ Leadership development (23)
- ❐ Learning communities (i.e., students take two or more linked courses as a group) (24)
- ❐ Major exploration and selection (25)
- ❐ Mentoring from others outside of the institution (e.g., peers at other institutions, alumni, and more) (26)
- ❐ Next-steps enrollment checklist (i.e., details about to-do items students must complete before enrollment) (52)
- ❐ Off-campus event (e.g., retreat, outdoor adventure) (28)
- ❐ Opportunities to co-teach or assist in teaching a class (29)
- ❐ Orientation (institution-wide) (30)
- ❐ Peer mentoring across institutions (e.g., transfer students at four-year institutions mentoring students at partner community colleges) (53)
- ❐ Peer mentoring by transfers/transfer-intending students (i.e., transfer/transfer-intending students mentoring other students at the same institution) (31)
- ❐ Peer mentoring by undergraduate students (i.e., undergraduate students mentoring transfers/transfer-intending students at the same institution) (32)
- ❐ Practica or other supervised practice experiences (33)
- ❐ Regional institutional partnerships that include joint transfer programs and/or staff positions (34)
- ❐ Residence life—transfer live-on-campus requirement (35)
- ❐ Residence life—transfer-specific living–learning community (36)
- ❐ Residence life—transfer-specific residential curriculum (37)
- ❐ Service learning or community service (38)
- ❐ Signature course (i.e., introductory academic credit-bearing course on various interdisciplinary topics) (39)
- ❐ Standardized policies for awarding of transfer credit (40)
- ❐ Statewide articulation agreements (41)
- ❐ Student government (e.g., designated transfer student representative or council) (42)
- ❐ Study abroad (43)

❑ Targeted admissions recruitment of transfer students (44)

❑ Transfer fairs (e.g., admissions fairs) (45)

❑ Transfer/college student success skills course (46)

❑ Transfer planning guide (i.e., how-to, things to consider) (51)

❑ Transfer student center (47)

❑ Transfer student organization(s) (48)

❑ Undergraduate research (49)

❑ Other, please specify: _______________________________________________

Q17. Which of the following objectives are associated with the transfer-specific programs, policies, and practices available to transfer/transfer-intending students on your campus? (Select all that apply.)

❑ Academic planning (1)

❑ Academic success strategies (2)

❑ Analytical, critical-thinking, or problem-solving skills (3)

❑ Career exploration and/or preparation (4)

❑ Civic engagement (5)

❑ Common transfer-year experience (6)

❑ Connection with the institution or campus (7)

❑ Developmental education, remediation, and/or review (8)

❑ Digital literacy (9)

❑ Discipline-specific knowledge (10)

❑ Financial literacy (11)

❑ Gateway course completion (12)

❑ Global education (36)

❑ Graduate or professional school preparation (e.g., pre-med, pre-law) (13)

❑ Health and wellness (14)

❑ Information literacy (15)

❑ Integrative and applied learning (16)

❑ Intercultural competence, diversity skills, or engaging with different perspectives (17)

❑ Introduction to a major, discipline, or career path (18)

❑ Introduction to institutional-specific academic expectations (19)

❑ Introduction to the liberal arts (20)

❑ Integration of learning and reflection (39)

❑ Knowledge of institution or campus resources and services (21)

❑ Leadership skill development (38)

❑ Library science education (37)

❑ Major exploration (22)

- ❒ On-time graduation rates (i.e., 4-year or 6-year graduation rate for transfers) (23)
- ❒ Oral communication skills (24)
- ❒ Persistence of transfer/transfer-intending students (25)
- ❒ Personal exploration or development (26)
- ❒ Project planning, teamwork, or management skills (27)
- ❒ Research skill building (35)
- ❒ Retention of transfer/transfer-intending students (28)
- ❒ Social support networks (e.g., peer connections and friendships) (29)
- ❒ Student–faculty interaction (30)
- ❒ Writing skills (31)
- ❒ Other, please specify: _______________________________________________
- ❒ My institution has not identified objectives for initiatives available to transfer/transfer-intending students (33)

*Carry Forward Selected Choices from "Q19"*

Q23. You indicated that the following transfer-specific programs, policies, and practices are available at your institution. In your opinion, which of these are most important to transfer/transfer-intending student success? (Select all that apply.)

- ❒ Academic advising (1)
- ❒ Academic program maps (2)
- ❒ Academic coaching or mentoring (3)
- ❒ Articulation and/or admissions agreements (4)
- ❒ Awarding of experiential learning credits (e.g., prior-learning assessments, credit "badges," and/or CLEP) (5)
- ❒ Bridge programs (6)
- ❒ Campus-based event (e.g., common reading experiences, dinners, fairs) (7)
- ❒ Career exploration (8)
- ❒ Career planning (9)
- ❒ Communication or publications (e.g., social media, newsletters, emails, brochures) (10)
- ❒ Course-specific support for classes with high dropout, fail, or withdraw rates (e.g., supplemental instruction) (11)
- ❒ Credit-bearing course (e.g., transfer seminar) (12)
- ❒ Cultural enrichment activities (e.g., plays, musical events, multicultural fairs) (13)
- ❒ Early alert systems (14)
- ❒ Equal Opportunity Program (EOP) (15)
- ❒ Faculty or staff mentors (16)
- ❒ Financial aid (e.g., transfer scholarships, loans) (17)
- ❒ Financial planning, coaching, and information (18)

- ❏ Guided pathways (19)
- ❏ Honors societies (e.g., Tau Sigma, Phi Theta Kappa, etc.) (20)
- ❏ Informational sessions about navigating transfer (including admission, policies, and more) (21)
- ❏ Internships or co-ops (22)
- ❏ Leadership development (23)
- ❏ Learning communities (i.e., students take two or more linked courses as a group) (24)
- ❏ Major exploration and selection (25)
- ❏ Mentoring from others outside of the institution (e.g., peers at other institutions, alumni, and more) (26)
- ❏ Next-steps enrollment checklist (i.e., details about to-do items students must complete before enrollment) (27)
- ❏ Off-campus event (e.g., retreat, outdoor adventure) (28)
- ❏ Opportunities to co-teach or assist in teaching a class (29)
- ❏ Orientation (institution-wide) (30)
- ❏ Peer mentoring across institutions (e.g., transfer students at four-year institutions mentoring students at partner community colleges) (31)
- ❏ Peer mentoring by transfers/transfer-intending students (i.e., transfer/transfer-intending students mentoring other students at the same institution) (32)
- ❏ Peer mentoring by undergraduate students (i.e., undergraduate students mentoring transfers/transfer-intending students at the same institution) (33)
- ❏ Practica or other supervised practice experiences (34)
- ❏ Regional institutional partnerships that include joint transfer programs and/or staff positions (35)
- ❏ Residence life—transfer live-on-campus requirement (36)
- ❏ Residence life—transfer-specific living–learning community (37)
- ❏ Residence life—transfer-specific residential curriculum (38)
- ❏ Service learning or community service (39)
- ❏ Signature course (i.e., introductory academic credit-bearing course on various interdisciplinary topics) (40)
- ❏ Standardized policies for awarding of transfer credit (41)
- ❏ Statewide articulation agreements (42)
- ❏ Student government (e.g., designated transfer student representative or council) (43)
- ❏ Study abroad (44)
- ❏ Targeted admissions recruitment of transfer students (45)
- ❏ Transfer fairs (e.g., admissions fairs) (46)
- ❏ Transfer/college student success skills course (47)
- ❏ Transfer planning guide (i.e., how-to, things to consider) (48)
- ❏ Transfer student center (49)
- ❏ Transfer student organization(s) (50)

❒ Undergraduate research (51)

❒ Other, please specify: _______________________________________________

Q24. How long has your institution provided targeted programs, policies, and practices for transfer/transfer-intending students?

❒ 1 year or less (71)

❒ 2–5 years (72)

❒ 6–10 years (73)

❒ 11–15 years (74)

❒ 16–20 years (75)

❒ More than 20 years (76)

❒ I don't know (77)

End of Block: Institutional Objectives and Initiatives for Transfer Students
Start of Block: Future Transfer Initiatives

Q91. Future Transfer Initiatives We are interested in learning about future initiatives associated with transfer that your institution is considering or planning to implement.

Q92. Is your institution considering or developing any future initiatives specifically or intentionally geared toward transfer students?

❒ Yes (28)

❒ No (29)

❒ I don't know (30)

*Skip To: End of Block If Q92 = 29*
*Skip To: End of Block If Q92 = 30*

Q93. Please describe the future transfer initiative(s) your institution is considering or developing:

_______________________________________________________________________

_______________________________________________________________________

_______________________________________________________________________

_______________________________________________________________________

Q94. Select the objectives(s) that will be measured in the upcoming initiative(s) you described:

❒ Academic planning (1224)

❒ Academic success strategies (1225)

❒ Analytical, critical-thinking, or problem-solving skills (1226)

❒ Career exploration and/or preparation (1227)

❒ Civic engagement (1228)

❒ Common transfer-year experience (1229)

❒ Connection with the institution or campus (1230)

❒ Developmental education, remediation, and/or review (1231)

❑ Digital literacy (1232)

❑ Discipline-specific knowledge (1233)

❑ Financial literacy (1234)

❑ Gateway course completion (1235)

❑ Graduate or professional school preparation (e.g., premed, prelaw) (1236)

❑ Health and wellness (1237)

❑ Information literacy (1238)

❑ Integrative and applied learning (1239)

❑ Intercultural competence, diversity skills, or engaging with different perspectives (1240)

❑ Introduction to a major, discipline, or career path (1241)

❑ Introduction to institutional-specific academic expectations (1242)

❑ Introduction to the liberal arts (1243)

❑ Knowledge of institution or campus resources and services (1244)

❑ Major exploration (1245)

❑ On-time graduation rates (i.e., 4-year or 6-year graduation rate for transfers) (1246)

❑ Oral communication skills (1247)

❑ Persistence of transfer students (1248)

❑ Personal exploration or development (1249)

❑ Project planning, teamwork, or management skills (1250)

❑ Retention of transfer students (1251)

❑ Social support networks (e.g., peer connections and friendships) (1252)

❑ Student–faculty interaction (1253)

❑ Writing skills (1254)

❑ Other, please specify: _______________________________________________

❑ My institution has not identified which objectives will be measured. (1256)

Q117. How has COVID-19 affected the planning, development, and implementation of future transfer-related initiatives at your institution?

_______________________________________________________________________

_______________________________________________________________________

_______________________________________________________________________

_______________________________________________________________________

End of Block: Future Transfer Initiatives
Start of Block: Coordination and Assessment of Transfer Services

Q27. Coordination and Assessment of Transfer Services

This section will ask questions about the coordination and assessment of transfer student programs and services on your campus.

Q28. On your campus, how coordinated are transfer initiatives? (Select the most appropriate answer.)

- ❑  1– Totally decentralized, no coordination between any departments or units associated with transfer initiatives (82)
- ❑  2 (83)
- ❑  3 (84)
- ❑  4 (85)
- ❑  5– Totally centralized, all transfer-oriented initiatives are coordinated by a single director or office (86)
- ❑  Unable to judge (87)

Q29. Which units on your campus participate in the coordination of transfer-related initiatives? (Select all that apply.)

- ❑  Academic advising (172)
- ❑  Academic affairs office (173)
- ❑  Academic department(s), please specify: (174) _______________________________________
- ❑  Admissions office (189)
- ❑  Career services (175)
- ❑  Center for teaching excellence (176)
- ❑  Enrollment management (177)
- ❑  Financial aid office (188)
- ❑  First-year experience/transfer-year experience office (185)
- ❑  Institutional research office (186)
- ❑  Library services (178)
- ❑  Orientation (187)
- ❑  Registrar or transfer evaluation coordinator (190)
- ❑  Residence life or housing (179)
- ❑  Student activities and leadership (180)
- ❑  Student affairs office (181)
- ❑  Student success center (182)
- ❑  Transfer center (191)
- ❑  Other, please specify: (183) _______________________________________
- ❑  I don't know (184)

Q30. Which of the following organizational structures does your institution offer to coordinate the transfer experience? (Select all that apply).

- ❑  Cross-institutional transfer team (e.g., team inclusive of various institutions) (77)
- ❑  Transfer center/designated space on campus (78)
- ❑  Transfer curriculum committee (79)
- ❑  Transfer program committee, task force, or advisory board (80)

❏ Transfer program office (e.g., transfer-year experience program) (81)

❏ Other campuswide transfer coordination, please describe: (82) _______________________

❏ My institution does not have any organizational structures to coordinate transfer experiences. (83)

Q121. Does your institution have a transfer programs office?

❏ Yes (1)

❏ No (2)

❏ I don't know (3)

*Skip To: Q37 If Q121 = 2*
*Skip To: Q37 If Q121 = 3*

Q31. Which of the following describe the institutional division(s) where transfer-specific services are housed at your institution? (Select all that apply.)

❏ Academic affairs central office (74)

❏ Academic department(s), please specify: (75) _______________________________

❏ College or school (e.g., College of Liberal Arts) (76)

❏ Enrollment management central office (77)

❏ Student affairs central office (78)

❏ Other, please specify: (79) _______________________________________

Q33. What is the job title of the individual who is responsible for transfer programs office at your institution (e.g., director, coordinator, dean of transfer student programs)?

_______________________________________________________________________

Q122. Is this position solely dedicated to transfer programs and initiatives on a full-time basis (approximately 40 hours per week), or does it include other duties and responsibilities?

❏ Yes, the position is solely focused on transfer (1)

❏ No, the position oversees other populations/initiatives, as well (2)

❏ I don't know (3)

Q123. Does the person responsible for transfer programs and initiatives have another position on campus?

❏ Yes (1)

❏ No (2)

❏ I don't know (3)

*Skip To: Q37 If Q123 = 2*
*Skip To: Q37 If Q123 = 3*

Q125. The other role of the person responsible for transfer programs and initiatives is: (Select all that apply.)

❏ Academic affairs administrator (1)

❏ Adjunct or part-time faculty member (2)

❏ Full-time or tenure-track faculty member (3)

❒   Student affairs staff member (4)

❒   Other, please specify: (5) _______________________________________________

Q37. Which of the following institution-wide efforts include a specific focus on transfer/transfer-intending students? (Select all that apply.)

❒   Accreditation (e.g., Action Project or Quality Enhancement Plan focused on transfer/transfer-intending students) (378)

❒   Curricular or gateway course redesign (380)

❒   Employment or job-placement study (381)

❒   Enrollment management (e.g., Admissions, Financial Aid, and/or Registrar) (396)

❒   Graduation study (382)

❒   Grant-funded project (383)

❒   Institutional assessment (i.e., analysis of data collected with a specific focus on transfers, including enrollment data) (384)

❒   Participation in a national survey (e.g., CCSSE, NSSE, SERU) (386)

❒   Pathways programs (387)

❒   Program self-study (i.e., using a set of professional standards, such as CAS standards, to engage in a self-study of transfer-oriented programs) (388)

❒   Retention study (389)

❒   Strategic planning (390)

❒   Student services programming (391)

❒   Transfer advisory council (392)

❒   Other, please specify: (393) _______________________________________________

❒   My institution is not engaged in any efforts with a specific focus on transfers/transfer-intending students (394)

*Skip To: End of Block If Q37 = 394*

Q38. Based on your knowledge, how long have your institution-wide efforts included a concerted focus on transfer/transfer-intending students?

❒   1 year or less (40)

❒   2–5 years (41)

❒   6–10 years (42)

❒   11–15 years (43)

❒   16–20 years (44)

❒   More than 20 years (45)

❒   I don't know (46)

End of Block: Coordination and Assessment of Transfer Services
Start of Block: Specific Transfer Initiatives: Transfer/College Success Skills Course

Q39. Specific Transfer Initiatives: Transfer or College Success Skills Course In this section, we will ask specific questions about your institution's transfer or college success skills course (that includes a focus on transfer).

Q40. Does your institution offer a transfer success or college success skills course (that includes a focus on transfer)?

- ❏ Yes (25)
- ❏ No (26)
- ❏ I don't know (27)

*Skip To: End of Block If Q40 = 26*
*Skip To: End of Block If Q40 = 27*


Q99. Please provide the course title(s), department(s), and number(s) of your institution's transfer or college success skills course (e.g., SDV 100: College Success Skills).

_______________________________________________________________________
_______________________________________________________________________
_______________________________________________________________________
_______________________________________________________________________


Q42. Approximately how many years has your institution offered a transfer or college success skills course?

- ❏ 2 years or less (53)
- ❏ 3–5 years (54)
- ❏ 6–10 years (55)
- ❏ 11–15 years (56)
- ❏ 16–20 years (57)
- ❏ More than 20 years (58)
- ❏ I don't know (59)

Q128. Are transfer/transfer-intending students required to take a transfer or college success skills course at your institution?

- ❏ Yes, transfer/transfer-intending students are required to take a course at my institution (1)
- ❏ No, transfer/transfer-intending students are not required to take a course at my institution (2)
- ❏ Other, please specify: (4) _______________________________________________
- ❏ I don't know (5)

Q141. Which transfer/transfer-intending students, by category, are not required to take a transfer or college success skills course at your institution? (Select all that apply.)

- ❏ All transfer/transfer-intending students are required to participate (627)
- ❏ Anyone not interested in participating (626)
- ❏ Adult learners (602)
- ❏ Formerly or currently incarcerated students (604)
- ❏ Full-time students (605)
- ❏ Honors students (606)

❏ Institutionally deemed academically underprepared students (e.g., students enrolled in developmental or remedial courses) (607)

❏ International students (608)

❏ Learning community participants (609)

❏ Non-degree students (629)

❏ Online students (610)

❏ Part-time students (611)

❏ Preprofessional students (e.g., pre-law, pre-med) (612)

❏ Reentry students (613)

❏ Student athletes (614)

❏ Students caring for dependents (615)

❏ Students on probationary status (617)

❏ Students residing within a particular residence hall (618)

❏ Students within specific majors, please list: (620) _______________________________

❏ TRIO participants (621)

❏ Undeclared students (622)

❏ Veterans (623)

❏ Visiting students (630)

❏ Other, please specify: (624) _______________________________

❏ I don't know (625)

Q43. What is the approximate percentage of transfer/transfer-intending students who take a transfer or college success skills course at your institution?

❏ Less than 10% (136)

❏ 10–19% (137)

❏ 20–29% (138)

❏ 30–39% (139)

❏ 40–49% (140)

❏ 50–59% (141)

❏ 60–69% (142)

❏ 70–79% (143)

❏ 80–89% (144)

❏ 90–99% (145)

❏ 100% (146)

❏ I don't know (147)

Q44. What is the duration of the transfer or college success skills course? (Select all that apply.)

❒ Half a term (29)

❒ One quarter (30)

❒ One semester (31)

❒ One year (32)

❒ Other, please specify: (33) ________________________________________________

❒ I don't know (34)

Q45. How many credits does the transfer or college success skills course carry?

❒ None (67)

❒ 1 credit (68)

❒ 2 credits (69)

❒ 3 credits (70)

❒ 4 credits (71)

❒ 5 credits (72)

❒ 6 or more credits (73)

❒ I don't know (74)

Q46. How is the transfer or college success skills course credit applied? (Select all that apply.)

❒ As an elective (20)

❒ Toward general education requirements (21)

❒ Toward major requirements (22)

❒ Other, please specify: (23) ________________________________________________

❒ I don't know (24)

Q129. Can students apply financial aid toward the tuition and fees associated with the transfer or college success skills course?

❒ Yes (1)

❒ No (2)

❒ I don't know (3)

Q47. Select the five most important course objectives for the transfer or college success skills course:

❒ Academic planning (1378)

❒ Academic success strategies (1379)

❒ Analytical, critical-thinking, or problem-solving skills (1380)

❒ Career exploration and/or preparation (1381)

❒ Civic engagement (1382)

❒ Common transfer-year experience (1383)

❒ Connection with the institution or campus (1384)

❏ Developmental education, remediation, and/or review (1385)

❏ Digital literacy (1386)

❏ Discipline-specific knowledge (1387)

❏ Financial literacy (1388)

❏ Gateway course completion (1389)

❏ Graduate or professional school preparation (e.g., premed, prelaw) (1390)

❏ Health and wellness (1391)

❏ Information literacy (1392)

❏ Integrative and applied learning (1393)

❏ Intercultural competence, diversity skills, or engaging with different perspectives (1394)

❏ Introduction to a major, discipline, or career path (1395)

❏ Introduction to institutional-specific academic expectations (1396)

❏ Introduction to the liberal arts (1397)

❏ Knowledge of institution or campus resources and services (1398)

❏ Major exploration (1399)

❏ On-time graduation rates (i.e., 4-year or 6-year graduation rate for transfers) (1400)

❏ Oral communication skills (1401)

❏ Persistence of transfer students (1402)

❏ Personal exploration or development (1403)

❏ Project planning, teamwork, or management skills (1404)

❏ Retention of transfer students (1405)

❏ Social support networks (e.g., peer connections and friendships) (1406)

❏ Student–faculty interaction (1407)

❏ Writing skills (1408)

❏ Other, please specify: (1409) _______________________________________________

Q48. Select the five most important topics that comprise the content of the transfer or college success skills course:

❏ Academic integrity (1225)

❏ Academic planning or advising (1226)

❏ Academic success resources (1227)

❏ Academic success strategies (e.g., study skills, time management) (1228)

❏ Alcohol awareness and safety (1229)

❏ Basic needs (including housing, food, transportation, and childcare, among other topics) (1230)

❏ Campus activities and involvement (1231)

❏ Campus history and traditions (1232)

❏ Campus policies and community standards (1233)

- ❏ Campus resources (1234)
- ❏ Campus safety (1235)
- ❏ Campus tour (1236)
- ❏ Career exploration or preparation (1237)
- ❏ Commuter issues (1238)
- ❏ Course registration procedures (1239)
- ❏ Critical thinking (1240)
- ❏ Discipline-specific content (1241)
- ❏ Diversity/equity/inclusion issues (1242)
- ❏ Financial information, including financial aid and scholarships (1243)
- ❏ Financial literacy (1244)
- ❏ Global learning (1245)
- ❏ Health and wellness (1246)
- ❏ Information literacy (1247)
- ❏ Library literacy (1248)
- ❏ Navigating transfer-related policies (1249)
- ❏ Professional trends and issues (1250)
- ❏ Relationship issues (e.g., interpersonal skills, conflict resolution) (1251)
- ❏ Sexual assault and dating violence (1252)
- ❏ School–life balance (1253)
- ❏ Social connections (1254)
- ❏ Undergraduate research (1255)
- ❏ Writing skills (1256)
- ❏ Other, please specify: (1257) _______________________________________________

Q49. As of Fall 2021, in what format(s) is your institution's transfer or college success skills course taught? (Select all that apply.)

- ❏ Face-to-face (40)
- ❏ Virtual (41)
- ❏ Hybrid (including face-to-face and virtual components) (42)

Q114. How has COVID-19 affected the delivery of, planning for, and content covered in your institution's transfer or college success skills courses?

_______________________________________________________________________

_______________________________________________________________________

_______________________________________________________________________

_______________________________________________________________________

Q51. Who teaches the transfer or college success skills course? (Select all that apply).

- ❐  Academic advisors (76)
- ❐  Adjunct faculty (77)
- ❐  Full-time, non-tenure-track faculty (78)
- ❐  Tenure-track faculty (79)
- ❐  Student affairs professionals (80)
- ❐  Graduate students (82)
- ❐  Undergraduate students (83)
- ❐  Other, please specify: (81) _______________________________________________
- ❐  I don't know (84)

Q52. Has your transfer or college success skills course been formally assessed or evaluated within the last four years?

- ❐  Yes (13)
- ❐  No (14)
- ❐  I don't know (15)

*Skip To: Q54 If Q52 = 14*
*Skip To: Q54 If Q52 = 15*

Q53. What type of assessment was conducted? (Select all that apply).

- ❐  Analysis of institutional data (e.g., GPA, retention rates, graduation) (184)
- ❐  Direct assessment of student learning outcomes (185)
- ❐  Focus groups with faculty (186)
- ❐  Focus groups with professional staff (187)
- ❐  Focus groups with students (188)
- ❐  Individual interviews with faculty (189)
- ❐  Individual interviews with orientation staff (190)
- ❐  Individual interviews with students (191)
- ❐  Program review (192)
- ❐  Student course evaluation (193)
- ❐  Survey instrument (194)
- ❐  Other, please specify: (195) _______________________________________________

Q54. In your opinion, considering costs (including staff time and resources) and educational gains, how valuable is your institution's transfer or college student success skills in supporting transfer student success?

- ❐  1 – Low benefit (52)
- ❐  2 (53)
- ❐  3 – Medium benefit (54)

❑ 4 (55)

❑ 5 – High benefit (56)

❑ Unable to judge (57)

End of Block: Specific Transfer Initiatives: Transfer/College Success Skills Course
Start of Block: Specific Transfer Initiatives: Orientation

Q56. Specific Transfer Initiatives: Orientation In this section, we will ask specific questions about orientation specifically for transfer/transfer-intending students at your institution.

Q57. Does your institution offer orientation programming for incoming transfer/transfer-intending students?

❑ Yes (13)

❑ No (14)

❑ I don't know (15)

*Skip To: End of Block If Q57 = 14*
*Skip To: End of Block If Q57 = 15*

Q130. Which best describes the orientation programming your institution offers for incoming transfer/transfer-intending students?

❑ My institution offers an orientation specifically for transfer/transfer-intending students (1)

❑ My institution offers an orientation, but transfer/transfer-intending students attend the same sessions as first-year students (2)

❑ My institution offers an orientation that all incoming students attend, but there are specific programs and sessions for transfers/transfer-intending students (4)

❑ Other, please specify: (5) _______________________________________________________

Q58. Does your institution offer orientation programming for incoming students who transfer outside of the fall semester or quarter (i.e., students who transfer in the winter, spring, or summer semesters or quarters)?

❑ Yes (13)

❑ No (14)

❑ I don't know (15)

Q131. Are incoming transfer/transfer-intending students required to participate in orientation programming at your institution?

❑ Yes (1)

❑ No (2)

❑ I don't know (3)

Q59. What is the approximate percentage of incoming transfer/transfer-intending students who participate in orientation programming at your institution?

❑ Less than 10% (161)

❑ 10–19% (162)

❑ 20–29% (163)

❒ 30–39% (164)

❒ 40–49% (165)

❒ 50–59% (166)

❒ 60–69% (167)

❒ 70–79% (168)

❒ 80–89% (169)

❒ 90–100% (170)

❒ I don't know (172)

Q60. Generally, which of the following types of orientation activities does your institution offer for incoming transfer/transfer-intending students? (Select all that apply.)

❒ Bridge programs (53)

❒ On-campus pre-term activities (46)

❒ Online orientation (47)

❒ Outdoor adventure/wilderness experience (48)

❒ Pre-term advising or registration (49)

❒ Programs for specific student populations (e.g., first-generation students, racially/ethnically minoritized students, etc.) (55)

❒ Spirit camps (52)

❒ Welcome week (50)

❒ Other, please specify: (51) _______________________________________________

Q61. Are incoming transfer/transfer-intending students able to select the orientation programming in which they want to participate?

❒ Yes, but some forms are mandatory (24)

❒ Yes, they can select any and all forms in which they want to participate (25)

❒ No, they do not have a choice (26)

❒ I don't know (27)

Q63. Which of the following activities does your campus' orientation programming include? (Select all that apply.)

❒ Academic advising (293)

❒ College- or university-specific policies (310)

❒ Common reading (i.e., a book or article read before and discussed during orientation) (294)

❒ Community building (295)

❒ Convocations or other celebratory activities or traditions (296)

❒ Discussion about finances (297)

❒ Discussion of personal issues and challenges (298)

❒ Discussions about health and wellness on campus (299)

❒  Discussions about identity, diversity, equity, and/or social justice (300)

❒  Employment opportunities (301)

❒  Introduction to campus facilities (302)

❒  Introduction to campus resources and services (303)

❒  Social engagement opportunities (304)

❒  Placement testing (305)

❒  Registration or course enrollment (306)

❒  Sessions for family members (307)

❒  Structured interaction with faculty (308)

❒  Other, please specify: (309) ___________________________________________

Q62. Which incoming transfer/transfer-intending students, by category, are not required to participate in orientation programming? (Select all that apply.)

❒  All transfer/transfer-intending students are required to participate (627)

❒  Anyone not interested in participating (626)

❒  Adult learners (602)

❒  Formerly or currently incarcerated students (604)

❒  Full-time students (605)

❒  Honors students (606)

❒  Institutionally deemed academically underprepared students (e.g., students enrolled in developmental or remedial courses) (607)

❒  International students (608)

❒  Learning community participants (609)

❒  Non-degree students (629)

❒  Online students (610)

❒  Part-time students (611)

❒  Preprofessional students (e.g., pre-law, pre-med) (612)

❒  Reentry students (613)

❒  Student athletes (614)

❒  Students caring for dependents (615)

❒  Students on probationary status (617)

❒  Students residing within a particular residence hall (618)

❒  Students within specific majors, please list: (620) _______________________________

❒  TRIO participants (621)

❒  Undeclared students (622)

❒  Veterans (623)

❒  Visiting students (630)

❒  Other, please specify: (624) _______________________________________________

❒  I don't know (625)

Q115. How has COVID-19 affected the delivery of, planning for, and content covered in your institution's orientation programming for incoming transfer/transfer-intending students?

_______________________________________________________________________
_______________________________________________________________________
_______________________________________________________________________
_______________________________________________________________________

Q110. Which campus unit directly administers orientation programming for incoming transfer/transfer-intending students? (Select all that apply.)

❒  Academic affairs office (1)

❒  Academic department(s), please list: (4)_______________________________________

❒  College or school (e.g., College of Liberal Arts) (5)

❒  Transfer program office (6)

❒  Student affairs/student services office (7)

❒  University college (8)

Q64. Has your orientation programming been formally assessed or evaluated within the last four years?

❒  Yes (22)

❒  No (23)

❒  I don't know (24)

*Skip To: Q66 If Q64 = 23*
*Skip To: Q66 If Q64 = 24*

Q65. What type of assessment was conducted? (Select all that apply).

❒  Analysis of institutional data (e.g., GPA, retention rates, graduation) (148)

❒  Direct assessment of student learning outcomes (149)

❒  Evaluation of student orientation leaders (160)

❒  Focus groups with faculty (150)

❒  Focus groups with professional staff (151)

❒  Focus groups with students (152)

❒  Individual interviews with faculty (153)

❒  Individual interviews with orientation staff (154)

❒  Individual interviews with students (155)

❒  Program review (156)

❒  Student evaluation (157)

❒  Survey instrument (158)

❒  Other, please specify: (159)_______________________________________

Q66. In your opinion, considering costs (including staff time and resources) and educational gains, how beneficial is your institution's orientation programming in supporting transfer student success?

- ☐ 1 – Low benefit (46)
- ☐ 2 (47)
- ☐ 3 – Medium benefit (48)
- ☐ 4 (49)
- ☐ 5 – High benefit (50)
- ☐ Unable to judge (51)

End of Block: Specific Transfer Initiatives: Orientation
Start of Block: Specific Transfer Initiatives: Advising

Q67. Specific Transfer Initiatives: Academic Advising In this section, we will ask specific questions about academic advising for transfer/transfer-intending students at your institution.

Q68. Does your institution offer academic advising to transfer/transfer-intending students?

- ☐ Yes (40)
- ☐ No (41)
- ☐ I don't know (42)

*Skip To: End of Block If Q68 = 41*
*Skip To: End of Block If Q68 = 42*

Q132. When are incoming transfer/transfer-intending students at your institution first offered academic advising services?

- ☐ Before they are admitted to the institution (1)
- ☐ After students have confirmed their acceptance at the institution (2)
- ☐ During orientation (3)
- ☐ Other, please specify: (4) _______________________________________________

Q70. Are incoming transfer/transfer-intending students at your institution required to participate in academic advising?

- ☐ Yes (172)
- ☐ No (173)
- ☐ I don't know (174)

Q69. What is the approximate percentage of incoming transfer/transfer-intending students who participate in academic advising at your institution?

- ☐ 10% or less (124)
- ☐ 11–20% (125)
- ☐ 21–30% (126)
- ☐ 31–40% (127)
- ☐ 41–50% (128)

- ❑  51–60% (129)
- ❑  61–70% (130)
- ❑  71–80% (131)
- ❑  81–90% (132)
- ❑  91–100% (133)
- ❑  I don't know (134)

Q71. Which of the following groups of incoming transfer/transfer-intending students are not required to participate in academic advising? (Select all that apply.)

- ❑  All transfers/transfer-intending students are required to participate (580)
- ❑  Anyone not interested in participating (605)
- ❑  Adult learners (581)
- ❑  Formerly or currently incarcerated students (583)
- ❑  Full-time students (584)
- ❑  Honors students (585)
- ❑  Institutionally deemed academically underprepared students (e.g., students enrolled in developmental or remedial courses) (586)
- ❑  International students (587)
- ❑  Learning community participants (588)
- ❑  Non-degree students (607)
- ❑  Online students (589)
- ❑  Part-time students (590)
- ❑  Preprofessional students (e.g., pre-law, pre-med) (591)
- ❑  Reentry students (592)
- ❑  Student athletes (593)
- ❑  Students caring for dependents (594)
- ❑  Students on probationary status (596)
- ❑  Students residing within a particular residence hall (597)
- ❑  Students within specific majors, please list: (599) _______________________________________
- ❑  TRIO participants (600)
- ❑  Undeclared students (601)
- ❑  Veterans (602)
- ❑  Visiting Students (606)
- ❑  Other, please specify: (603) _______________________________________
- ❑  I don't know (604)

Q111. At your institution, are incoming transfer/transfer-intending students assigned an advisor?

- ❏ Yes (1)
- ❏ No (2)
- ❏ I don't know (3)

*Skip To: Q72 If Q111 = 1*
*Skip To: Q137 If Q111 = 3*
*Skip To: Q137 If Q111 = 2*

Q72. At your institution, how frequently are transfer/transfer-intending students required to meet with their assigned advisor during their first year?

- ❏ Only once, during the first term (34)
- ❏ Once during each term for the entire first year (35)
- ❏ Two or more times each term for the entire first year (36)
- ❏ Transfer/transfer-intending students are not required to meet with their assigned advisor (37)
- ❏ Other, please specify: (38) _______________________________________________
- ❏ I don't know (39)

Q73. At your institution, how frequently are transfer/transfer-intending students required to meet with their assigned advisor after their first year?

- ❏ Once during each term (29)
- ❏ Once during the academic year (30)
- ❏ Two or more times each term (31)
- ❏ Transfer/transfer-intending students are not required to meet with their assigned advisor after their first year (32)
- ❏ Transfer/transfer-intending students must meet with an advisor, but this individual may not be their assigned advisor (35)
- ❏ Other, please specify: (33) _______________________________________________
- ❏ I don't know (34)

*Skip To: Q74 If Q73 = 29*
*Skip To: Q74 If Q73 = 30*
*Skip To: Q74 If Q73 = 31*
*Skip To: Q74 If Q73 = 32*
*Skip To: Q74 If Q73 = 35*
*Skip To: Q74 If Q73 = 33*
*Skip To: Q74 If Q73 = 34*

Q137. At your institution, how frequently are transfer/transfer-intending students required to meet with an advisor during their first year?

- ❏ Only once, during the first term (34)
- ❏ Once during each term for the entire first year (35)
- ❏ Two or more times each term for the entire first year (36)
- ❏ Transfer/transfer-intending students are not required to meet an advisor (37)

❑ Other, please specify: (38)_______________________________________________

❑ I don't know (39)

Q138. At your institution, how frequently are transfer/transfer-intending students required to meet with an advisor after their first year?

❑ Once during each term (29)

❑ Once during the academic year (30)

❑ Two or more times each term (31)

❑ Transfer/transfer-intending students are not required to meet an advisor after their first year (32)

❑ Other, please specify: (33) _______________________________________________

❑ I don't know (34)

Q74. How long has your institution provided targeted advising services and initiatives for transfer/transfer-intending students?

❑ 2 years or less (40)

❑ 3–5 years (41)

❑ 6–10 years (42)

❑ 11–15 years (43)

❑ 16–20 years (44)

❑ More than 20 years (45)

❑ I don't know (46)

Q75. Which campus units directly administer academic advising for transfer/transfer-intending students? (Select all that apply.)

❑ Academic affairs central office (60)

❑ Academic department(s), please specify: (61)_______________________________

❑ College or school (e.g., College of Liberal Arts) (62)

❑ Transfer program office (63)

❑ Student affairs/student services office (64)

❑ University college (65)

❑ Other, please specify: (66)_______________________________________________

Q76. Which of the following parties serve as academic advisors for transfer/transfer-intending students? (Select all that apply.)

❑ Professionally trained advisors (40)

❑ Faculty (41)

❑ College/university counselors (42)

❑ Staff at other institutions (43)

❑ Undergraduate peer mentors (44)

❑ Other, please specify: (45) _______________________________________________

Q133. At your institution, do the parties that serve as academic advisors for transfer/transfer-intending students receive training about student transfer?

☐ Yes, all advisors for transfer/transfer-intending students are required to undergo training about student transfer (1)

☐ Yes, but only interested advisors receive training about student transfer (2)

☐ No, advisors do not receive training about student transfer (3)

Q100. What forms of academic advising does your institution offer to transfer/transfer-intending students? (Select all that apply.)

☐ One-on-one advising (i.e., students meet individually with advisors) (1)

☐ Group advising (i.e., multiple students meet with an advisor(s) concurrently) (2)

☐ Peer advising (i.e., select and trained peers meet with students and provide advising) (3)

☐ Online or distance advising (5)

☐ Other, please specify: (4) _______________________________________________________

Q78. Does your institution use early warning/academic alert systems for transfer/transfer-intending students?

☐ Yes (43)

☐ No (44)

☐ I don't know (45)

*Skip To: Q82 If Q78 = 44*
*Skip To: Q82 If Q78 = 45*

Q79. Please indicate the selection that best describes the early warning/academic alert system for transfer/transfer-intending students that is most prevalent at your institution.

☐ An early warning tool that is entirely technology-based (such as a learner analytics platform that mines data to determine which students are at-risk and subsequently guides intervention) (20)

☐ An early warning system that is entirely human-based and relies on faculty, staff, and/or students observing behavior and then notifying someone so outreach can occur (such as a faculty referral system) (21)

☐ A hybrid approach that utilizes technology- and human-based approaches (22)

☐ Unable to judge (23)

Q80. Which employees at your institution participate in some aspect of early alert/academic warning systems for transfer/transfer-intending students? (Select all that apply.)

☐ Academic advisors (104)

☐ Academic support personnel (105)

☐ Athletic department staff (106)

☐ Counseling/health services staff (107)

☐ Faculty/instructors (108)

☐ Information technology staff (109)

☐ Peer mentors (110)

☐ Residence life staff (111)

❏ Student affairs staff (112)

❏ Other, please specify: (113) _______________________________________________

Q81. Which of the following describes the type of intervention that occurs? (Select all that apply.)

❏ Students are contacted by phone, letter, or electronic means (e.g., email and/or text "nudges") (40)

❏ Students are contacted in person (41)

❏ Students are informed about opportunities to seek assistance (42)

❏ Students are required by individual faculty members, another unit, or the institution to obtain assistance (43)

❏ Students' families are notified (with student waiver of privacy rights) (44)

❏ Other, please specify: (45) _______________________________________________

Q82. Do transfer/transfer-intending students at your institution participate in Guided Pathways?

❏ Yes (13)

❏ No (14)

❏ I don't know (15)

Q83. Do transfer/transfer-intending students at your institution participate in meta majors?

❏ Yes (13)

❏ No (14)

❏ I don't know (15)

Q116. How has COVID-19 affected the delivery, coordination, and planning of advising services for transfer/transfer-intending students at your institution?

_______________________________________________________________

_______________________________________________________________

_______________________________________________________________

_______________________________________________________________

Q84. On your campus, how coordinated is academic advising for transfer/transfer-intending students? (Select the most appropriate answer.)

❏ 1 – Totally decentralized, no coordination between any departments or units in transfer-year initiatives (82)

❏ 2 (83)

❏ 3 (84)

❏ 4 (85)

❏ 5 – Totally centralized, all transfer-year initiatives are coordinated by a single director or office (86)

❏ Unable to judge (87)

Q85. Please identify the activities and processes related to academic advising in which your institution is currently engaged. (Select all that apply.)

❏ Campuswide assessment and planning (94)

❏ Evaluation and continuous improvement of advising (95)

- ❑ Leadership and change management (96)
- ❑ Ongoing professional development and training for advisors (97)
- ❑ Process mapping (98)
- ❑ Structure redesign (99)
- ❑ Technology and data governance and management (100)
- ❑ Technology selection (open response) (101) _______________________________________
- ❑ Other, please specify: (102) _______________________________________
- ❑ My institution is not currently engaged in any activities or processes related to academic advising (103)

Q86. Has academic advising for transfer/transfer-intending students been formally assessed or evaluated in the last four years?

- ❑ Yes (19)
- ❑ No (20)
- ❑ I don't know (21)

*Skip To: Q89 If Q86 = 20*
*Skip To: Q89 If Q86 = 21*


Q87. What type of assessment was conducted? (Select all that apply.)

- ❑ Analysis of institutional data (e.g., GPA, retention rates, graduation) (172)
- ❑ Direct assessment of student learning outcomes (173)
- ❑ Focus groups with faculty (174)
- ❑ Focus groups with professional staff (175)
- ❑ Focus groups with students (176)
- ❑ Individual interviews with faculty (177)
- ❑ Individual interviews with orientation staff (178)
- ❑ Individual interviews with students (179)
- ❑ Program review (180)
- ❑ Student course evaluation (181)
- ❑ Survey instrument (182)
- ❑ Other, please specify: (183)_______________________________________
- ❑ I don't know (184)

Q88. Select the outcome(s) that were measured using the assessment methods indicated in the previous question. (Select all that apply.)

- ❑ Academic planning (1225)
- ❑ Academic success strategies (1226)
- ❑ Analytical, critical-thinking, or problem-solving skills (1227)
- ❑ Career exploration and/or preparation (1228)

- ☐ Civic engagement (1229)
- ☐ Common transfer-year experience (1230)
- ☐ Connection with the institution or campus (1231)
- ☐ Developmental education, remediation, and/or review (1232)
- ☐ Digital literacy (1233)
- ☐ Discipline-specific knowledge (1234)
- ☐ Financial literacy (1235)
- ☐ Gateway course completion (1236)
- ☐ Graduate or professional school preparation (e.g., premed, prelaw) (1237)
- ☐ Health and wellness (1238)
- ☐ Information literacy (1239)
- ☐ Integrative and applied learning (1240)
- ☐ Intercultural competence, diversity skills, or engaging with different perspectives (1241)
- ☐ Introduction to a major, discipline, or career path (1242)
- ☐ Introduction to institutional-specific academic expectations (1243)
- ☐ Introduction to the liberal arts (1244)
- ☐ Knowledge of institution or campus resources and services (1245)
- ☐ Major exploration (1246)
- ☐ On-time graduation rates (i.e., 4-year or 6-year graduation rate for transfers) (1247)
- ☐ Oral communication skills (1248)
- ☐ Persistence of transfer students (1249)
- ☐ Personal exploration or development (1250)
- ☐ Project planning, teamwork, or management skills (1251)
- ☐ Retention of transfer students (1252)
- ☐ Social support networks (e.g., friendships) (1253)
- ☐ Student–faculty interaction (1254)
- ☐ Writing skills (1255)
- ☐ Other, please specify: (1256) _______________________________________________

Q89. In your opinion, considering costs (including staff time and resources) and educational gains, how beneficial are your institution's advising practices in supporting transfer student success?

- ☐ 1 – Low benefit (52)
- ☐ 2 (53)
- ☐ 3 – Medium benefit (54)
- ☐ 4 (55)
- ☐ 5 – High benefit (56)
- ☐ Unable to judge (57)

End of Block: Specific Transfer Initiatives: Advising
Start of Block: Information from Survey

Q96. Information from Survey

Q127. The National Resource Center for The First-Year Experience and Students in Transition plans to conduct a follow-up study in which we will gather and analyze transfer/college student success course syllabi from a national sample of institutions. If your institution offers such a course, please provide the contact information of the person on your campus in the best position to provide an example syllabus from your campus.

Full name, email address, and title of contact:

_______________________________________________________________________________

Q97. It is our practice to make available specific and general information gathered from this survey. In general, findings from the survey are reported in aggregate, but we may identify individual institutions that have agreed to allow their responses to be shared. Please select your preference:

❒  You may share my school's name and survey responses (13)

❒  You may share my school's name as a participant in the survey, but you may not share my survey responses in connection with my school's name (14)

❒  Please do not share my school's name (15)

Q98. We intend to produce research reports based on analyses of the information gathered from this survey. Would you like to be informed when research reports are made available?

❒  Yes (8)

❒  No (9)

# Appendix B: Subset of Institutions Participating in the 2021 National Survey of Transfer Student Initiatives[1]

| Institution | City | State |
| --- | --- | --- |
| Amberton University | Garland | Texas |
| American InterContinental University | Chandler | Arizona |
| Ameritech College of Healthcare | Draper | Utah |
| Anne Arundel Community College | Arnold | Maryland |
| Ashland University | Ashland | Ohio |
| Baldwin Wallace University | Berea | Ohio |
| Brazosport College | Lake Jackson | Texas |
| Calvin University | Grand Rapids | Michigan |
| Capella University | Minneapolis | Minnesota |
| Carroll Community College | Westminster | Maryland |
| Central Ohio Technical College | Newark | Ohio |
| Champion Christian College | Hot Springs National Park | Arkansas |
| Cleary University | Howell | Michigan |
| College of Coastal Georgia | Brunswick | Georgia |
| College of the Marshall Islands | Majuro | Republic of the Marshall Islands |
| Columbia Basin College | Pasco | Washington |
| Cornell College | Mount Vernon | Iowa |
| East Mississippi Community College | Mayhew | Mississippi |
| El Paso Community College | El Paso | Texas |
| Elgin Community College | Elgin | Illinois |
| Fordham University | New York | New York |
| Furman University | Greenville | South Carolina |

*Table continues on page 76*

---

[1] This is a partial list ($n$ = 84) of the institutional affiliations of the respondents to the National Survey of Transfer Student Initiatives ($N$ = 169). Institutions could opt out of identification as a survey respondent.

*Table continued from page 75*

| Institution | City | State |
| --- | --- | --- |
| Gardner-Webb University | Boiling Springs | North Carolina |
| Georgian Court University | Lakewood | New Jersey |
| Highland Community College | Freeport | Illinois |
| Houston Community College System | Houston | Texas |
| Illinois State University | Normal | Illinois |
| Jacksonville State University | Jacksonville | Alabama |
| John A. Logan College | Carterville | Illinois |
| John Carroll University | University Heights | Ohio |
| Keuka College | Keuka Park | New York |
| Knox College | Galesburg | Illinois |
| Louisiana State University Shreveport | Shreveport | Louisiana |
| Loyola Marymount University | Los Angeles | California |
| Lubbock Christian University | Lubbock | Texas |
| Mitchell Community College | Statesville | North Carolina |
| Monroe Community College | Rochester | New York |
| Montgomery County Community College | Blue Bell | Pennsylvania |
| Muskingum University | New Concord | Ohio |
| Neumann University | Aston | Pennsylvania |
| North Dakota State University | Fargo | North Dakota |
| North Iowa Area Community College | Mason City | Iowa |
| Northern Illinois University | DeKalb | Illinois |
| Northwood Technical College | Rice Lake | Wisconsin |
| Onondaga Community College | Syracuse | New York |
| Pasadena City College | Pasadena | California |
| Penn Commercial Business/Technical School | Washington | Pennsylvania |
| Pittsburg State University | Pittsburg | Kansas |
| Portland State University | Portland | Oregon |
| Renton Technical College | Renton | Washington |
| Robert Morris University | Moon Township | Pennsylvania |
| Rowan College South Jersey | Vineland | New Jersey |
| Saint Francis University | Loretto | Pennsylvania |
| Saint Louis University | Saint Louis | Missouri |
| Saint Mary's of Minnesota | Winona | Minnesota |
| Salve Regina University | Newport | Rhode Island |
| Sandhills Community College | Pinehurst | North Carolina |
| Seattle University | Seattle | Washington |
| Sinclair Community College | Dayton | Ohio |
| South Suburban College | South Holland | Illinois |
| Southern Methodist University | Dallas | Texas |

*Table continues on page 77*

*Table continued from page 76*

| Institution | City | State |
| --- | --- | --- |
| Southern State Community College | Hillsboro | Ohio |
| St. Lawrence University | Canton | New York |
| Texas Woman's University | Denton | Texas |
| University of Arkansas Community College at Batesville | Batesville | Arkansas |
| University of California, San Diego | La Jolla | California |
| University of Kansas | Lawrence | Kansas |
| University of Lynchburg | Lynchburg | Virginia |
| University of Mobile | Mobile | Alabama |
| University of New England | Biddeford | Maine |
| University of Phoenix | Phoenix | Arizona |
| University of Tennessee Southern | Pulaski | Tennessee |
| University of Texas at Austin | Austin | Texas |
| University of Texas at Dallas | Richardson | Texas |
| University of Tulsa | Tulsa | Oklahoma |
| University of Vermont | Burlington | Vermont |
| Ursuline College | Pepper Pike | Ohio |
| Valencia College | Orlando | Florida |
| Victor Valley Community College | Victorville | California |
| Virginia Commonwealth University | Richmond | Virginia |
| Virginia Highlands Community College | Abingdon | Virginia |
| West Kentucky Community and Technical College | Paducah | Kentucky |
| Western Governors University | Salt Lake City | Utah |
| Western Nebraska Community College | Scottsbluff | Nebraska |
| Wichita State University | Wichita | Kansas |

# Appendix C: Response Frequencies from the 2021 National Survey of Transfer Student Initiatives

| Survey question/responses | Institutional type | | | | Institution control | | | | Number of undergraduates enrolled | | | | | | | | | | | | Total | |
| --- | --- | --- | --- | --- | --- | --- | --- | --- | --- | --- | --- | --- | --- | --- | --- | --- | --- | --- | --- | --- | --- | --- |
| | Two-year | | Four-year | | Public | | Private | | Under 1,000 | | 1,000-4,999 | | 5,999-9,999 | | 10,000-19,999 | | 20,000 and above | | | | | |
| | Freq. | % | Freq | % | Freq. | % | Freq. | % | Freq. | % | Freq. | % | Freq. | % | Freq. | % | Freq. | % | Freq. | % | Freq. | % |
| Q14. Are transfer or transfer-intending students included in your institution's strategic plan? | | | | | | | | | | | | | | | | | | | | | | |
| Yes | 47 | 87.0% | 64 | 66.7% | 67 | 85.9% | 44 | 62.0% | 10 | 62.5% | 49 | 71.0% | 16 | 69.9% | 17 | 85.0% | 20 | 90.9% | 112 | 74.7% | | |
| No | 4 | 7.4% | 22 | 22.9% | 6 | 7.7% | 19 | 26.8% | 4 | 25.0% | 13 | 18.8% | 5 | 21.7% | 1 | 5.0% | 2 | 9.1% | 25 | 16.7% | | |
| I don't know | 3 | 5.6% | 10 | 10.4% | 5 | 6.4% | 8 | 11.3% | 2 | 12.5% | 7 | 10.1% | 2 | 8.7% | 2 | 10.0% | 0 | 0.0% | 13 | 8.7% | | |
| Total | 54 | 100.0% | 96 | 100.0% | 78 | 100.0% | 71 | 100.0% | 16 | 100.0% | 69 | 100.0% | 23 | 100.0% | 20 | 100.0% | 22 | 100.0% | 150 | 100.0% | | |
| Q101. Does your institution have specific goals associated with equity and transfer/transfer-intending students? | | | | | | | | | | | | | | | | | | | | | | |
| Yes | 42 | 77.8% | 50 | 52.1% | 55 | 70.5% | 37 | 52.1% | 9 | 56.3% | 41 | 59.4% | 12 | 52.2% | 15 | 75.0% | 15 | 68.2% | 92 | 61.3% | | |
| No | 9 | 16.7% | 37 | 38.5% | 18 | 23.1% | 27 | 38.0% | 5 | 31.3% | 26 | 37.7% | 6 | 26.1% | 4 | 20.0% | 5 | 22.7% | 46 | 30.7% | | |
| I don't know | 3 | 5.6% | 9 | 9.4% | 5 | 6.4% | 7 | 9.9% | 2 | 12.5% | 2 | 2.9% | 5 | 21.7% | 1 | 5.0% | 2 | 9.1% | 12 | 8.0% | | |
| Total | 54 | 100.0% | 96 | 100.0% | 78 | 100.0% | 71 | 100.0% | 16 | 100.0% | 69 | 100.0% | 23 | 100.0% | 20 | 100.0% | 22 | 100.0% | 150 | 100.0% | | |

*Table continues on page 80*

*Table continued from page 79*

| | Institutional type | | | | Institution control | | | | Number of undergraduates enrolled | | | | | | | | | | | | Total | |
|---|---|---|---|---|---|---|---|---|---|---|---|---|---|---|---|---|---|---|---|---|---|---|---|
| | Two-year | | Four-year | | Public | | Private | | Under 1,000 | | 1,000-4,999 | | 5,999-9,999 | | 10,000-19,999 | | 20,000 and above | | | | | |
| Survey question/responses | Freq. | % | Freq | % | Freq. | % | Freq. | % | Freq. | % | Freq. | % | Freq. | % | Freq. | % | Freq. | % | Freq. | % | | |
| Q15. In your opinion, how committed is your institution currently to prioritizing transfer student success? | | | | | | | | | | | | | | | | | | | | | | |
| Not committed at all | 0 | 0.0% | 1 | 1.0% | 0 | 0.0% | 1 | 1.4% | 0 | 0.0% | 0 | 0.0% | 1 | 4.3% | 0 | 0.0% | 0 | 0.0% | 1 | 0.7% | | |
| Between not committed - moderately committed | 2 | 3.7% | 8 | 8.3% | 5 | 6.4% | 5 | 7.0% | 0 | 0.0% | 6 | 8.7% | 2 | 8.7% | 1 | 5.0% | 1 | 4.5% | 10 | 6.7% | | |
| Moderately committed | 14 | 25.9% | 32 | 33.3% | 23 | 29.5% | 22 | 31.0% | 5 | 31.3% | 24 | 34.8% | 3 | 13.0% | 6 | 30.0% | 7 | 31.8% | 45 | 30.0% | | |
| Between moderately committed - highly committed | 17 | 31.5% | 26 | 27.1% | 22 | 28.2% | 21 | 29.6% | 6 | 37.5% | 15 | 21.7% | 10 | 43.5% | 5 | 25.0% | 7 | 31.8% | 43 | 28.7% | | |
| Highly committed | 21 | 38.9% | 28 | 29.2% | 28 | 35.9% | 21 | 29.6% | 5 | 31.3% | 23 | 33.3% | 7 | 30.4% | 8 | 40.0% | 7 | 31.8% | 50 | 33.3% | | |
| Unable to judge | 0 | 0.0% | 0 | 0.0% | 0 | 0.0% | 1 | 1.4% | 0 | 0.0% | 1 | 1.4% | 0 | 0.0% | 0 | 0.0% | 0 | 0.0% | 1 | 0.7% | | |
| Total | 54 | 100.0% | 96 | 100.0% | 78 | 100.0% | 71 | 100.0% | 16 | 100.0% | 69 | 100.0% | 23 | 100.0% | 20 | 100.0% | 22 | 100.0% | 150 | 100.0% | | |
| Q18. Does your institution offer success programs, policies, or practices specifically or intentionally geared toward transfer/transfer-intending students? | | | | | | | | | | | | | | | | | | | | | | |
| Yes | 47 | 87.0% | 62 | 65.3% | 66 | 84.6% | 43 | 61.4% | 9 | 56.3% | 47 | 69.1% | 17 | 73.9% | 19 | 95.0% | 18 | 81.8% | 110 | 73.8% | | |
| No | 5 | 9.3% | 31 | 32.6% | 9 | 11.5% | 26 | 37.1% | 7 | 43.8% | 18 | 26.5% | 6 | 26.1% | 1 | 5.0% | 3 | 13.6% | 35 | 23.5% | | |
| I don't know | 2 | 3.7% | 2 | 2.1% | 3 | 3.8% | 1 | 1.4% | 0 | 0.0% | 3 | 4.4% | 0 | 0.0% | 0 | 0.0% | 1 | 4.5% | 4 | 2.7% | | |
| Total | 54 | 100.0% | 95 | 100.0% | 78 | 100.0% | 70 | 100.0% | 16 | 100.0% | 68 | 100.0% | 23 | 100.0% | 20 | 100.0% | 22 | 100.0% | 149 | 100.0% | | |
| Q25. If your institution does not offer any transfer initiatives, indicate the reason(s) why: (Select all that apply.) | | | | | | | | | | | | | | | | | | | | | | |
| Lack of expertise | 1 | 16.7% | 6 | 18.2% | 2 | 18.2% | 5 | 18.5% | 1 | 14.3% | 2 | 10.0% | 3 | 50.0% | 0 | 0.0% | 1 | 25.0% | 7 | 18.4% | | |
| Lack of funding | 1 | 16.7% | 13 | 39.4% | 4 | 36.4% | 10 | 37.0% | 1 | 14.3% | 6 | 30.0% | 5 | 83.3% | 0 | 0.0% | 1 | 25.0% | 14 | 36.8% | | |
| Lack of staff or faculty buy-in | 2 | 33.3% | 9 | 27.3% | 4 | 36.4% | 7 | 25.9% | 0 | 0.0% | 6 | 30.0% | 5 | 83.3% | 0 | 0.0% | 0 | 0.0% | 11 | 28.9% | | |
| Limited time | 2 | 33.3% | 11 | 33.3% | 4 | 36.4% | 9 | 33.3% | 5 | 71.4% | 8 | 40.0% | 3 | 50.0% | 0 | 0.0% | 0 | 0.0% | 13 | 34.2% | | |
| Not an institutional priority | 3 | 50.0% | 10 | 30.3% | 4 | 36.4% | 9 | 33.3% | 2 | 28.6% | 6 | 30.0% | 4 | 66.7% | 0 | 0.0% | 1 | 25.0% | 13 | 34.2% | | |

*Table continues on page 81*

*Table continued from page 80*

| Survey question/responses | Institutional type | | | | Institution control | | | | Number of undergraduates enrolled | | | | | | | | | | | | Total | |
|---|---|---|---|---|---|---|---|---|---|---|---|---|---|---|---|---|---|---|---|---|---|---|
| | Two-year | | Four-year | | Public | | Private | | Under 1,000 | | 1,000-4,999 | | 5,999-9,999 | | 10,000-19,999 | | 20,000 and above | | | | | |
| | Freq. | % | Freq | % | Freq. | % | Freq. | % | Freq. | % | Freq. | % | Freq. | % | Freq. | % | Freq. | % | Freq. | % | | |
| Not a large enough population of transfer/transfer-intending students | 2 | 33.3% | 13 | 39.4% | 4 | 36.4% | 13 | 48.1% | 4 | 57.1% | 9 | 45.0% | 1 | 16.7% | 0 | 0.0% | 0 | 0.0% | 14 | 36.8% | | |
| Other, please specify | 0 | 0.0% | 11 | 33.3% | 1 | 9.1% | 8 | 29.6% | 2 | 28.6% | 6 | 30.0% | 0 | 0.0% | 1 | 100.0% | 2 | 50.0% | 11 | 28.9% | | |
| Total | 6 | 100.0% | 33 | 100.0% | 11 | 100.0% | 27 | 100.0% | 7 | 100.0% | 20 | 100.0% | 28 | 100.0% | 1 | 100.0% | 4 | 100.0% | 38 | 100.0% | | |

Q19. Which of the following transfer student success programs, policies, and practices does your institution offer specifically or intentionally for transfer/transfer-intending students? (Select all that apply.)

| Survey question/responses | Two-year | | Four-year | | Public | | Private | | Under 1,000 | | 1,000-4,999 | | 5,999-9,999 | | 10,000-19,999 | | 20,000 and above | | Total | |
|---|---|---|---|---|---|---|---|---|---|---|---|---|---|---|---|---|---|---|---|---|
| | Freq. | % | Freq | % | Freq. | % | Freq. | % | Freq. | % | Freq. | % | Freq. | % | Freq. | % | Freq. | % | Freq. | % |
| Academic advising | 42 | 91.3% | 58 | 89.2% | 57 | 90.5% | 42 | 89.4% | 11 | 100.0% | 42 | 87.5% | 16 | 94.1% | 17 | 94.4% | 14 | 82.4% | 100 | 90.1% |
| Academic program maps | 34 | 73.9% | 40 | 61.5% | 47 | 74.6% | 27 | 57.4% | 7 | 63.6% | 32 | 66.7% | 11 | 64.7% | 12 | 66.7% | 13 | 76.5% | 75 | 67.6% |
| Academic coaching or mentoring | 24 | 52.2% | 38 | 58.5% | 36 | 57.1% | 26 | 55.3% | 8 | 72.7% | 20 | 41.7% | 11 | 64.7% | 9 | 50.0% | 15 | 88.2% | 63 | 56.8% |
| Articulation and/or admissions agreements | 42 | 91.3% | 55 | 84.6% | 58 | 92.1% | 38 | 80.9% | 11 | 100.0% | 37 | 77.1% | 16 | 94.1% | 17 | 94.4% | 16 | 94.1% | 97 | 87.4% |
| Awarding of experiential learning credits (e.g., prior-learning assessments, credit "badges," and/or CLEP) | 25 | 54.3% | 28 | 43.1% | 31 | 49.2% | 22 | 46.8% | 8 | 72.7% | 24 | 50.0% | 9 | 52.9% | 6 | 33.3% | 7 | 41.2% | 54 | 48.6% |
| Bridge programs | 12 | 26.1% | 11 | 16.9% | 17 | 27.0% | 6 | 12.8% | 2 | 18.2% | 7 | 14.6% | 7 | 41.2% | 5 | 27.8% | 2 | 11.8% | 23 | 20.7% |
| Campus-based event (e.g., common reading experiences, dinners, fairs) | 21 | 45.7% | 25 | 38.5% | 31 | 49.2% | 15 | 31.9% | 3 | 27.3% | 16 | 33.0% | 11 | 64.7% | 7 | 38.9% | 10 | 58.8% | 47 | 42.3% |
| Career exploration | 34 | 73.9% | 33 | 50.8% | 44 | 69.8% | 23 | 48.9% | 7 | 63.6% | 24 | 50.0% | 15 | 88.2% | 10 | 55.6% | 12 | 70.6% | 68 | 61.3% |
| Career planning | 29 | 63.0% | 35 | 53.8% | 36 | 57.1% | 27 | 57.4% | 9 | 81.8% | 22 | 45.8% | 14 | 82.4% | 8 | 44.4% | 11 | 64.7% | 64 | 57.7% |
| Communication or publications (e.g., social media, newsletters, emails, brochures) | 24 | 52.2% | 33 | 50.8% | 37 | 58.7% | 20 | 42.6% | 7 | 63.6% | 19 | 39.6% | 12 | 70.6% | 9 | 50.0% | 11 | 64.7% | 58 | 52.3% |

*Table continues on page 82*

*Table continued from page 81*

| Survey question/responses | Institutional type | | | | Institution control | | | | Number of undergraduates enrolled | | | | | | | | | | | | Total | |
|---|---|---|---|---|---|---|---|---|---|---|---|---|---|---|---|---|---|---|---|---|---|---|
| | Two-year | | Four-year | | Public | | Private | | Under 1,000 | | 1,000-4,999 | | 5,999-9,999 | | 10,000-19,999 | | 20,000 and above | | | | | |
| | Freq. | % | Freq | % | Freq. | % | Freq. | % | Freq. | % | Freq. | % | Freq. | % | Freq. | % | Freq. | % | Freq. | % | | |
| Course-specific support for classes with high dropout, fail, or withdraw rates (e.g., supplemental instruction) | 21 | 45.7% | 12 | 18.5% | 26 | 41.3% | 7 | 14.9% | 1 | 9.1% | 12 | 25.0% | 9 | 52.9% | 7 | 38.9% | 5 | 29.4% | 34 | 30.6% | | |
| Credit-bearing course (e.g., transfer seminar) | 3 | 6.5% | 10 | 15.4% | 5 | 7.9% | 8 | 17.0% | 3 | 27.3% | 7 | 14.6% | 0 | 0.0% | 2 | 11.1% | 2 | 11.8% | 14 | 12.6% | | |
| Cultural enrichment activities (e.g., plays, musical events, multicultural fairs) | 23 | 50.0% | 16 | 24.6% | 28 | 44.4% | 11 | 23.4% | 2 | 18.2% | 14 | 29.2% | 11 | 64.7% | 5 | 27.8% | 8 | 47.1% | 40 | 36.0% | | |
| Early alert systems | 34 | 73.9% | 31 | 47.7% | 41 | 65.1% | 23 | 48.9% | 7 | 63.6% | 28 | 58.3% | 13 | 76.5% | 6 | 33.3% | 11 | 64.7% | 65 | 58.6% | | |
| Equal Opportunity Program (EOP) | 12 | 26.1% | 10 | 15.4% | 14 | 22.2% | 8 | 17.0% | 3 | 27.3% | 7 | 14.6% | 5 | 29.4% | 5 | 27.8% | 3 | 17.6% | 23 | 20.7% | | |
| Faculty or staff mentors | 13 | 28.3% | 26 | 40.0% | 18 | 28.6% | 21 | 44.7% | 6 | 54.5% | 15 | 31.3% | 7 | 41.2% | 8 | 44.4% | 4 | 23.5% | 40 | 36.0% | | |
| Financial aid (e.g., transfer scholarships, loans) | 28 | 60.9% | 44 | 67.7% | 39 | 61.9% | 33 | 70.2% | 10 | 90.9% | 29 | 60.4% | 13 | 76.5% | 11 | 61.1% | 10 | 58.8% | 73 | 65.8% | | |
| Financial planning, coaching, and information | 15 | 32.6% | 15 | 23.1% | 20 | 31.7% | 10 | 21.3% | 2 | 18.2% | 9 | 18.8% | 7 | 41.2% | 5 | 27.8% | 8 | 47.1% | 31 | 27.9% | | |
| Guided pathways | 37 | 80.4% | 31 | 47.7% | 48 | 76.2% | 20 | 42.6% | 4 | 36.4% | 30 | 62.5% | 10 | 58.8% | 13 | 72.2% | 12 | 70.6% | 69 | 62.2% | | |
| Honors societies (e.g., Tau Sigma, Phi Theta Kappa, etc.) | 38 | 82.6% | 25 | 38.5% | 47 | 74.6% | 16 | 34.0% | 3 | 27.3% | 26 | 54.2% | 14 | 82.4% | 8 | 44.4% | 12 | 70.6% | 63 | 56.8% | | |
| Informational sessions about navigating transfer (including admission, policies, and more) | 36 | 78.3% | 42 | 64.6% | 50 | 79.4% | 28 | 59.6% | 7 | 63.6% | 31 | 64.6% | 14 | 82.4% | 14 | 77.8% | 13 | 76.5% | 79 | 71.2% | | |
| Internships or co-ops | 24 | 52.2% | 23 | 35.4% | 29 | 46.0% | 18 | 38.3% | 6 | 54.5% | 16 | 33.3% | 12 | 70.6% | 5 | 27.8% | 9 | 52.9% | 48 | 43.2% | | |
| Leadership development | 19 | 41.3% | 18 | 27.7% | 27 | 42.9% | 10 | 21.3% | 4 | 36.4% | 10 | 20.8% | 9 | 52.9% | 7 | 38.9% | 8 | 47.1% | 38 | 34.2% | | |
| Learning communities (i.e., students take two or more linked courses as a group) | 9 | 19.6% | 9 | 13.8% | 13 | 20.6% | 5 | 10.6% | 1 | 9.1% | 4 | 8.3% | 4 | 23.5% | 5 | 27.8% | 4 | 23.5% | 18 | 16.2% | | |

*Table continues on page 83*

Table continued from page 82

| Survey question/responses | Institutional type | | | | Institution control | | | | Number of undergraduates enrolled | | | | | | | | | | | | Total | |
|---|---|---|---|---|---|---|---|---|---|---|---|---|---|---|---|---|---|---|---|---|---|---|
| | Two-year | | Four-year | | Public | | Private | | Under 1,000 | | 1,000-4,999 | | 5,999-9,999 | | 10,000-19,999 | | 20,000 and above | | | | | |
| | Freq. | % | Freq | % | Freq. | % | Freq. | % | Freq. | % | Freq. | % | Freq. | % | Freq. | % | Freq. | % | Freq. | % |
| Major exploration and selection | 21 | 45.7% | 21 | 32.3% | 26 | 41.3% | 16 | 34.0% | 3 | 27.3% | 13 | 27.1% | 11 | 64.7% | 7 | 38.9% | 8 | 47.1% | 42 | 37.8% |
| Mentoring from others outside of the institution (e.g., peers at other institutions, alumni, and more) | 6 | 13.0% | 8 | 12.3% | 8 | 12.7% | 6 | 12.8% | 3 | 27.3% | 2 | 4.2% | 3 | 17.6% | 2 | 11.1% | 5 | 29.4% | 15 | 13.5% |
| Next-steps enrollment checklist (i.e., details about to-do items students must complete before enrollment) | 21 | 45.7% | 40 | 61.5% | 35 | 55.6% | 26 | 55.3% | 6 | 54.5% | 21 | 43.8% | 9 | 52.9% | 14 | 77.8% | 12 | 70.6% | 62 | 55.9% |
| Off-campus event (e.g., retreat, outdoor adventure) | 10 | 21.7% | 8 | 12.3% | 13 | 20.6% | 5 | 10.6% | 3 | 27.3% | 5 | 10.4% | 4 | 23.5% | 5 | 27.8% | 2 | 11.8% | 19 | 17.7% |
| Opportunities to co-teach or assist in teaching a class | 1 | 2.2% | 6 | 9.2% | 5 | 7.9% | 2 | 4.3% | 2 | 18.2% | 0 | 0.0% | 1 | 5.9% | 0 | 0.0% | 12 | 70.6% | 8 | 7.2% |
| Orientation (institution-wide) | 24 | 40.0% | 50 | 76.9% | 39 | 61.9% | 34 | 72.3% | 8 | 72.7% | 30 | 62.5% | 13 | 76.5% | 11 | 61.1% | 12 | 70.6% | 74 | 66.7% |
| Peer mentoring across institutions (e.g., transfer students at four-year institutions mentoring students at partner community colleges) | 4 | 8.7% | 6 | 9.2% | 5 | 7.9% | 5 | 10.6% | 1 | 9.1% | 3 | 6.3% | 4 | 23.5% | 1 | 5.6% | 1 | 5.9% | 10 | 9.0% |
| Peer mentoring by transfers/transfer-intending students (i.e., transfer/transfer-intending students mentoring other students at the same institution) | 4 | 8.7% | 8 | 12.3% | 9 | 14.3% | 3 | 6.4% | 0 | 0.0% | 3 | 6.3% | 2 | 11.8% | 3 | 16.7% | 4 | 23.5% | 12 | 10.8% |
| Peer mentoring by undergraduate students (i.e., undergraduate students mentoring transfers/transfer-intending students at the same institution) | 4 | 8.7% | 15 | 23.1% | 10 | 15.9% | 9 | 19.1% | 2 | 18.2% | 3 | 6.3% | 5 | 29.4% | 6 | 33.3% | 3 | 17.0% | 19 | 17.1% |

Table continues on page 84

*Table continued from page 83*

| Survey question/responses | Institutional type | | | | Institution control | | | | Number of undergraduates enrolled | | | | | | | | | | | | Total | |
| --- | --- | --- | --- | --- | --- | --- | --- | --- | --- | --- | --- | --- | --- | --- | --- | --- | --- | --- | --- | --- | --- | --- |
| | Two-year | | Four-year | | Public | | Private | | Under 1,000 | | 1,000-4,999 | | 5,999-9,999 | | 10,000-19,999 | | 20,000 and above | | | | | |
| | Freq. | % | Freq | % | Freq. | % | Freq. | % | Freq. | % | Freq. | % | Freq. | % | Freq. | % | Freq. | % | Freq. | % |
| Practica or other supervised practice experiences | 4 | 8.7% | 12 | 18.5% | 6 | 9.5% | 10 | 21.3% | 5 | 45.5% | 5 | 10.4% | 3 | 17.6% | 2 | 11.1% | 2 | 11.8% | 17 | 15.3% |
| Regional institutional partnerships that include joint transfer programs and/or staff positions | 17 | 37.0% | 14 | 21.5% | 23 | 36.5% | 8 | 17.0% | 1 | 9.1% | 11 | 22.9% | 5 | 29.4% | 7 | 38.9% | 7 | 41.2% | 31 | 27.9% |
| Residence life—transfer live on-campus requirement | 2 | 4.3% | 11 | 16.9% | 5 | 7.9% | 8 | 17.0% | 3 | 27.3% | 4 | 8.3% | 2 | 11.8% | 2 | 11.1% | 2 | 11.8% | 13 | 11.7% |
| Residence life — transfer-specific living-learning community | 1 | 2.2% | 10 | 15.4% | 6 | 9.5% | 5 | 10.6% | 2 | 18.2% | 3 | 6.3% | 2 | 11.8% | 2 | 11.1% | 3 | 17.6% | 12 | 10.8% |
| Residence life—transfer-specific residential curriculum | 0 | 0.0% | 3 | 4.6% | 1 | 1.6% | 2 | 4.3% | 0 | 0.0% | 1 | 2.1% | 0 | 0.0% | 1 | 5.6% | 1 | 5.9% | 3 | 2.7% |
| Service-learning or community service | 14 | 30.4% | 22 | 33.8% | 21 | 33.3% | 15 | 31.9% | 3 | 27.3% | 12 | 25.0% | 8 | 47.1% | 7 | 38.9% | 7 | 41.2% | 37 | 33.3% |
| Signature course (i.e., introductory academic credit-bearing course on various interdisciplinary topics) | 12 | 26.1% | 18 | 27.7% | 16 | 25.4% | 14 | 29.8% | 4 | 36.4% | 9 | 18.8% | 6 | 35.3% | 6 | 33.3% | 5 | 29.4% | 30 | 27.0% |
| Standardized policies for awarding of transfer credit | 27 | 58.7% | 48 | 73.8% | 40 | 63.5% | 34 | 72.3% | 7 | 63.6% | 27 | 56.3% | 14 | 82.4% | 13 | 72.2% | 14 | 82.4% | 75 | 67.6% |
| Statewide articulation agreements | 33 | 71.7% | 30 | 46.2% | 46 | 73.0% | 16 | 34.0% | 6 | 54.5% | 21 | 43.8% | 12 | 70.6% | 12 | 66.7% | 11 | 64.7% | 62 | 55.9% |
| Student government (e.g., designated transfer student representative or council) | 11 | 23.9% | 18 | 27.7% | 18 | 28.6% | 11 | 23.4% | 3 | 27.3% | 8 | 16.7% | 6 | 35.3% | 7 | 38.9% | 6 | 35.3% | 30 | 27.0% |
| Study abroad | 15 | 32.6% | 23 | 35.4% | 21 | 33.3% | 17 | 36.2% | 5 | 45.5% | 10 | 20.8% | 10 | 58.8% | 7 | 38.9% | 6 | 35.3% | 38 | 34.2% |
| Targeted admissions recruitment of transfer students | 14 | 30.4% | 49 | 75.4% | 30 | 47.6% | 33 | 70.2% | 8 | 72.7% | 25 | 52.1% | 9 | 52.9% | 13 | 72.2% | 9 | 52.9% | 64 | 57.7% |

*Table continues on page 85*

*Table continued from page 84*

| Survey question/responses | Institutional type | | | | Institution control | | | | Number of undergraduates enrolled | | | | | | | | | | Total | |
|---|---|---|---|---|---|---|---|---|---|---|---|---|---|---|---|---|---|---|---|---|
| | Two-year | | Four-year | | Public | | Private | | Under 1,000 | | 1,000-4,999 | | 5,999-9,999 | | 10,000-19,999 | | 20,000 and above | | | |
| | Freq. | % | Freq | % | Freq. | % | Freq. | % | Freq. | % | Freq. | % | Freq. | % | Freq. | % | Freq. | % | Freq. | % |
| Transfer fairs (e.g., admissions fairs) | 37 | 80.4% | 34 | 52.3% | 49 | 77.8% | 22 | 46.8% | 4 | 36.4% | 28 | 58.3% | 13 | 76.5% | 16 | 88.9% | 10 | 58.8% | 71 | 64.0% |
| Transfer/college student success skills course | 19 | 41.3% | 21 | 32.3% | 29 | 46.0% | 11 | 23.4% | 4 | 36.4% | 11 | 22.9% | 8 | 47.1% | 8 | 44.4% | 10 | 58.8% | 41 | 36.9% |
| Transfer planning guide (i.e., how-to, things to consider) | 20 | 43.5% | 18 | 27.7% | 28 | 44.4% | 10 | 21.3% | 0 | 0.0% | 13 | 27.1% | 10 | 58.8% | 6 | 33.3% | 9 | 52.9% | 38 | 34.2% |
| Transfer student center | 15 | 32.6% | 9 | 13.8% | 20 | 31.7% | 4 | 8.5% | 0 | 0.0% | 5 | 10.4% | 6 | 35.3% | 6 | 33.3% | 7 | 41.2% | 24 | 21.6% |
| Transfer student organization(s) | 3 | 6.5% | 14 | 21.5% | 11 | 17.5% | 6 | 12.8% | 1 | 9.1% | 3 | 6.3% | 2 | 11.8% | 4 | 22.2% | 7 | 41.2% | 17 | 15.3% |
| Undergraduate research | 14 | 30.4% | 20 | 30.8% | 22 | 34.9% | 12 | 25.5% | 3 | 27.3% | 10 | 20.8% | 8 | 47.1% | 8 | 44.4% | 5 | 29.4% | 34 | 30.6% |
| Other, please specify | 1 | 2.2% | 5 | 7.7% | 3 | 4.8% | 3 | 6.4% | 0 | 0.0% | 1 | 2.1% | 3 | 17.6% | 1 | 5.6% | 1 | 5.9% | 6 | 5.4% |
| Total | 46 | 100.0% | 65 | 100.0% | 63 | 100.0% | 47 | 100.0% | 11 | 100.0% | 48 | 100.0% | 17 | 100.0% | 18 | 100.0% | 17 | 100.0% | 111 | 100.0% |

Q17. Which of the following objectives are associated with the transfer-specific programs, policies, and practices available to transfer/transfer-intending students on your campus? (Select all that apply.)

| Survey question/responses | Two-year | | Four-year | | Public | | Private | | Under 1,000 | | 1,000-4,999 | | 5,999-9,999 | | 10,000-19,999 | | 20,000 and above | | Total | |
|---|---|---|---|---|---|---|---|---|---|---|---|---|---|---|---|---|---|---|---|---|
| Academic planning | 41 | 89.1% | 54 | 83.1% | 57 | 90.5% | 38 | 80.9% | 7 | 63.6% | 42 | 87.5% | 16 | 94.1% | 17 | 94.4% | 14 | 82.4% | 96 | 86.5% |
| Academic success strategies | 27 | 45.0% | 43 | 66.2% | 40 | 63.5% | 30 | 63.8% | 6 | 54.5% | 30 | 62.5% | 12 | 70.6% | 10 | 55.6% | 13 | 76.5% | 71 | 64.0% |
| Analytical, critical-thinking, or problem-solving skills | 21 | 45.7% | 22 | 33.8% | 27 | 42.9% | 16 | 34.0% | 5 | 45.5% | 16 | 33.3% | 12 | 70.6% | 4 | 22.2% | 7 | 41.2% | 44 | 39.6% |
| Career exploration and/or preparation | 30 | 65.2% | 36 | 55.4% | 39 | 61.9% | 26 | 55.3% | 8 | 72.7% | 25 | 52.1% | 13 | 76.5% | 9 | 50.0% | 11 | 64.7% | 66 | 59.5% |
| Civic engagement | 10 | 21.7% | 12 | 18.5% | 15 | 23.8% | 7 | 14.9% | 4 | 36.4% | 8 | 16.7% | 5 | 29.4% | 4 | 22.2% | 2 | 11.8% | 23 | 20.7% |
| Common transfer-year experience | 8 | 17.4% | 17 | 26.2% | 15 | 23.8% | 10 | 21.3% | 2 | 18.2% | 8 | 16.7% | 4 | 23.5% | 7 | 38.9% | 5 | 29.4% | 26 | 23.4% |
| Connection with the institution or campus | 16 | 34.8% | 34 | 52.3% | 30 | 47.6% | 20 | 42.6% | 4 | 36.4% | 15 | 31.3% | 11 | 64.7% | 10 | 55.6% | 11 | 64.7% | 51 | 45.9% |
| Developmental education, remediation, and/or review | 17 | 37.0% | 6 | 9.2% | 20 | 31.7% | 3 | 6.4% | 2 | 18.2% | 9 | 18.8% | 5 | 29.4% | 6 | 33.3% | 2 | 11.8% | 24 | 21.6% |

*Table continues on page 86*

*Table continued from page 85*

| Survey question/responses | Institutional type | | | | Institution control | | | | Number of undergraduates enrolled | | | | | | | | | | | | Total | |
| --- | --- | --- | --- | --- | --- | --- | --- | --- | --- | --- | --- | --- | --- | --- | --- | --- | --- | --- | --- | --- | --- | --- |
| | Two-year | | Four-year | | Public | | Private | | Under 1,000 | | 1,000-4,999 | | 5,999-9,999 | | 10,000-19,999 | | 20,000 and above | | | | | |
| | Freq. | % | Freq | % | Freq. | % | Freq. | % | Freq. | % | Freq. | % | Freq. | % | Freq. | % | Freq. | % | Freq. | % | Freq. | % |
| Digital literacy | 19 | 41.3% | 14 | 21.5% | 25 | 39.7% | 8 | 17.0% | 1 | 9.1% | 11 | 22.9% | 10 | 58.8% | 7 | 38.9% | 5 | 29.4% | 34 | 30.6% |
| Discipline-specific knowledge | 20 | 43.5% | 19 | 29.2% | 24 | 38.1% | 15 | 31.9% | 6 | 54.5% | 16 | 33.3% | 9 | 52.9% | 4 | 22.2% | 5 | 29.4% | 40 | 36.0% |
| Financial literacy | 20 | 43.5% | 17 | 26.2% | 26 | 41.3% | 11 | 23.4% | 5 | 45.5% | 11 | 22.9% | 11 | 64.7% | 5 | 27.8% | 6 | 35.3% | 38 | 34.2% |
| Gateway course completion | 26 | 56.5% | 13 | 20.0% | 34 | 54.0% | 5 | 10.6% | 2 | 18.2% | 15 | 31.3% | 10 | 58.8% | 7 | 38.9% | 6 | 35.3% | 40 | 36.0% |
| Global education | 8 | 17.4% | 16 | 24.6% | 13 | 20.6% | 11 | 23.4% | 3 | 27.3% | 10 | 20.8% | 6 | 35.3% | 5 | 27.8% | 1 | 5.9% | 25 | 22.5% |
| Graduate or professional school preparation (e.g., pre-med, pre-law) | 4 | 8.7% | 16 | 24.6% | 9 | 14.3% | 11 | 23.4% | 2 | 18.2% | 5 | 10.4% | 5 | 29.4% | 3 | 16.7% | 5 | 29.4% | 20 | 18.0% |
| Health and wellness | 19 | 41.3% | 24 | 36.9% | 27 | 42.9% | 16 | 34.0% | 7 | 63.6% | 15 | 31.3% | 9 | 52.9% | 6 | 33.3% | 7 | 41.2% | 44 | 39.6% |
| Information literacy | 18 | 39.1% | 19 | 29.2% | 25 | 39.7% | 12 | 25.5% | 4 | 36.4% | 12 | 25.0% | 9 | 52.9% | 6 | 33.3% | 6 | 35.3% | 37 | 33.3% |
| Integrative and applied learning | 12 | 26.1% | 16 | 24.6% | 16 | 25.4% | 12 | 25.5% | 4 | 36.4% | 11 | 22.9% | 8 | 47.1% | 4 | 22.2% | 2 | 11.8% | 29 | 26.1% |
| Intercultural competence, diversity skills, or engaging with different perspectives | 20 | 43.5% | 25 | 38.5% | 29 | 46.0% | 16 | 34.0% | 4 | 36.4% | 15 | 31.3% | 11 | 64.7% | 7 | 38.9% | 9 | 52.9% | 46 | 41.4% |
| Introduction to a major, discipline, or career path | 14 | 30.4% | 24 | 36.9% | 19 | 30.2% | 19 | 40.4% | 5 | 45.5% | 16 | 33.3% | 7 | 41.2% | 4 | 22.2% | 7 | 41.2% | 39 | 35.1% |
| Introduction to institutional-specific academic expectations | 22 | 47.8% | 36 | 55.4% | 34 | 54.0% | 23 | 48.9% | 5 | 45.5% | 22 | 45.8% | 11 | 64.7% | 8 | 44.4% | 12 | 70.6% | 58 | 52.3% |
| Introduction to the liberal arts | 10 | 21.7% | 19 | 29.2% | 13 | 20.6% | 16 | 34.0% | 3 | 27.3% | 13 | 27.1% | 7 | 41.2% | 3 | 16.7% | 3 | 17.6% | 29 | 26.1% |
| Integration of learning and reflection | 8 | 17.4% | 24 | 36.9% | 16 | 25.4% | 16 | 34.0% | 3 | 27.3% | 12 | 25.0% | 7 | 41.2% | 5 | 27.8% | 6 | 35.3% | 33 | 29.7% |
| Knowledge of institution or campus resources and services | 22 | 47.8% | 46 | 70.8% | 37 | 58.7% | 30 | 63.8% | 7 | 63.6% | 29 | 60.4% | 10 | 58.8% | 11 | 61.1% | 11 | 64.7% | 68 | 61.3% |
| Leadership skill development | 13 | 28.3% | 24 | 36.9% | 24 | 38.1% | 13 | 27.7% | 5 | 45.5% | 9 | 18.8% | 7 | 41.2% | 6 | 33.3% | 11 | 64.7% | 38 | 34.2% |

*Table continues on page 87*

*Table continued from page 86*

| Survey question/responses | Institutional type | | | | Institution control | | | | Number of undergraduates enrolled | | | | | | | | | | | | Total | |
|---|---|---|---|---|---|---|---|---|---|---|---|---|---|---|---|---|---|---|---|---|---|---|
| | Two-year | | Four-year | | Public | | Private | | Under 1,000 | | 1,000-4,999 | | 5,999-9,999 | | 10,000-19,999 | | 20,000 and above | | | | | |
| | Freq. | % | Freq | % | Freq. | % | Freq. | % | Freq. | % | Freq. | % | Freq. | % | Freq. | % | Freq. | % | Freq. | % | | |
| Library science education | 5 | 10.9% | 11 | 16.9% | 7 | 11.1% | 9 | 19.1% | 2 | 18.2% | 5 | 10.4% | 5 | 29.4% | 3 | 16.7% | 1 | 5.9% | 16 | 14.4% | | |
| Major exploration | 22 | 47.8% | 24 | 36.9% | 28 | 44.4% | 18 | 38.3% | 2 | 18.2% | 19 | 39.6% | 12 | 70.6% | 7 | 38.9% | 6 | 35.3% | 46 | 41.4% | | |
| On-time graduation rates (i.e., 4-year or 6-year graduation rate for transfers) | 14 | 30.4% | 34 | 52.3% | 26 | 41.3% | 22 | 46.8% | 3 | 27.3% | 15 | 31.3% | 12 | 70.6% | 9 | 50.0% | 10 | 58.8% | 49 | 44.1% | | |
| Oral communication skills | 27 | 58.7% | 17 | 26.2% | 32 | 50.8% | 11 | 23.4% | 5 | 45.5% | 16 | 33.3% | 11 | 64.7% | 5 | 27.8% | 7 | 41.2% | 44 | 39.6% | | |
| Persistence of transfer/transfer-intending students | 24 | 52.2% | 25 | 38.5% | 34 | 54.0% | 15 | 31.9% | 5 | 45.5% | 16 | 33.3% | 11 | 64.7% | 7 | 38.9% | 11 | 64.7% | 50 | 45.0% | | |
| Personal exploration or development | 16 | 34.8% | 19 | 29.2% | 24 | 38.1% | 11 | 23.4% | 3 | 27.3% | 11 | 22.9% | 7 | 41.2% | 5 | 27.8% | 10 | 58.8% | 36 | 32.4% | | |
| Project planning, teamwork, or management skills | 8 | 17.4% | 12 | 18.5% | 13 | 20.6% | 7 | 14.9% | 3 | 27.3% | 4 | 8.3% | 5 | 29.4% | 4 | 22.2% | 5 | 29.4% | 21 | 18.9% | | |
| Research skill building | 10 | 21.7% | 17 | 26.2% | 16 | 25.4% | 11 | 23.4% | 4 | 36.4% | 6 | 12.5% | 8 | 47.1% | 6 | 33.3% | 4 | 23.5% | 28 | 25.2% | | |
| Retention of transfer/transfer-intending students | 22 | 47.8% | 31 | 47.7% | 34 | 54.0% | 19 | 40.4% | 3 | 27.3% | 18 | 37.5% | 13 | 76.5% | 7 | 38.9% | 13 | 76.5% | 54 | 48.6% | | |
| Social support networks (e.g., peer connections and friendships) | 9 | 19.6% | 30 | 46.2% | 21 | 33.3% | 18 | 38.3% | 4 | 36.4% | 10 | 20.8% | 8 | 47.1% | 7 | 38.9% | 11 | 64.7% | 40 | 36.0% | | |
| Student-faculty interaction | 20 | 43.5% | 34 | 52.3% | 31 | 49.2% | 22 | 46.8% | 9 | 81.8% | 17 | 35.4% | 11 | 64.7% | 9 | 50.0% | 8 | 47.1% | 54 | 48.6% | | |
| Writing skills | 27 | 58.7% | 28 | 43.1% | 36 | 57.1% | 19 | 40.4% | 7 | 63.6% | 20 | 41.7% | 12 | 70.6% | 8 | 44.4% | 9 | 52.9% | 56 | 50.5% | | |
| Other, please specify | 0 | 0.0% | 4 | 6.2% | 1 | 1.6% | 3 | 6.4% | 0 | 0.0% | 1 | 2.1% | 2 | 11.8% | 1 | 5.6% | 0 | 0.0% | 4 | 3.6% | | |
| My institution has not identified objectives for initiatives available to transfer/transfer-intending students | 1 | 2.2% | 4 | 6.2% | 3 | 4.8% | 2 | 4.3% | 0 | 0.0% | 2 | 4.2% | 0 | 0.0% | 2 | 11.1% | 1 | 5.9% | 5 | 4.5% | | |
| Total | 46 | 100.0% | 65 | 100.0% | 89 | 100.0% | 47 | 100.0% | 11 | 100.0% | 48 | 100.0% | 17 | 100.0% | 18 | 100.0% | 17 | 100.0% | 111 | 100.0% | | |

*Table continues on page 88*

*Table continued from page 87*

| Survey question/responses | Institutional type | | | | Institution control | | | | Number of undergraduates enrolled | | | | | | | | | | | | Total | |
| --- | --- | --- | --- | --- | --- | --- | --- | --- | --- | --- | --- | --- | --- | --- | --- | --- | --- | --- | --- | --- | --- | --- |
| | Two-year | | Four-year | | Public | | Private | | Under 1,000 | | 1,000-4,999 | | 5,999-9,999 | | 10,000-19,999 | | 20,000 and above | | | | | |
| | Freq. | % | Freq | % | Freq. | % | Freq. | % | Freq. | % | Freq. | % | Freq. | % | Freq. | % | Freq. | % | Freq. | % | | |
| Q23. You indicated that the following transfer-specific programs, policies, and practices are available at your institution. In your opinion, which of these are most important to transfer/transfer-intending student success? (Academic Advising) | | | | | | | | | | | | | | | | | | | | | | |
| Academic advising | 36 | 85.7% | 52 | 89.7% | 51 | 89.5% | 36 | 85.7% | 10 | 90.9% | 35 | 83.3% | 16 | 100.0% | 16 | 94.1% | 11 | 78.6% | 88 | 88.0% | | |
| Total | 42 | 100.0% | 58 | 100.0% | 57 | 100.0% | 42 | 100.0% | 11 | 100.0% | 42 | 100.0% | 16 | 100.0% | 17 | 100.0% | 14 | 100.0% | 100 | 100.0% | | |
| Q23. You indicated that the following transfer-specific programs, policies, and practices are available at your institution. In your opinion, which of these are most important to transfer/transfer-intending student success? (Academic program maps) | | | | | | | | | | | | | | | | | | | | | | |
| Academic program maps | 25 | 73.5% | 21 | 52.5% | 34 | 72.3% | 12 | 44.4% | 2 | 28.6% | 17 | 53.1% | 10 | 90.9% | 6 | 50.0% | 12 | 92.3% | 47 | 62.7% | | |
| Total | 34 | 100.0% | 40 | 100.0% | 47 | 100.0% | 27 | 100.0% | 7 | 100.0% | 32 | 100.0% | 11 | 100.0% | 12 | 100.0% | 13 | 100.0% | 75 | 100.0% | | |
| Q23. You indicated that the following transfer-specific programs, policies, and practices are available at your institution. In your opinion, which of these are most important to transfer/transfer-intending student success? (Academic coaching or mentoring) | | | | | | | | | | | | | | | | | | | | | | |
| Academic coaching or mentoring | 13 | 54.2% | 17 | 44.7% | 18 | 50.0% | 12 | 46.2% | 3 | 37.5% | 13 | 65.0% | 7 | 63.6% | 4 | 44.4% | 4 | 26.7% | 31 | 49.2% | | |
| Total | 24 | 100.0% | 38 | 100.0% | 36 | 100.0% | 26 | 100.0% | 8 | 100.0% | 20 | 100.0% | 11 | 100.0% | 9 | 100.0% | 15 | 100.0% | 63 | 100.0% | | |
| Q23. You indicated that the following transfer-specific programs, policies, and practices are available at your institution. In your opinion, which of these are most important to transfer/transfer-intending student success? (Articulation and/or admissions agreements) | | | | | | | | | | | | | | | | | | | | | | |
| Articulation and/or admissions agreements | 35 | 83.3% | 25 | 45.5% | 44 | 75.9% | 15 | 39.5% | 3 | 27.3% | 22 | 59.5% | 13 | 81.3% | 10 | 58.8% | 11 | 68.8% | 59 | 60.8% | | |
| Total | 42 | 100.0% | 55 | 100.0% | 58 | 100.0% | 38 | 100.0% | 11 | 100.0% | 37 | 100.0% | 16 | 100.0% | 17 | 100.0% | 16 | 100.0% | 97 | 100.0% | | |
| Q23. You indicated that the following transfer-specific programs, policies, and practices are available at your institution. In your opinion, which of these are most important to transfer/transfer-intending student success? (Awarding of experiential learning credits (e.g., prior-learning assessments, credit "badges," and/or CLEP)) | | | | | | | | | | | | | | | | | | | | | | |
| Awarding of experiential learning credits (e.g., prior-learning assessments, credit "badges," and/or CLEP) | 5 | 20.0% | 10 | 35.7% | 8 | 25.8% | 7 | 31.8% | 1 | 12.5% | 6 | 25.0% | 3 | 33.3% | 2 | 33.3% | 3 | 42.9% | 15 | 27.8% | | |
| Total | 25 | 100.0% | 28 | 100.0% | 31 | 100.0% | 22 | 100.0% | 8 | 100.0% | 24 | 100.0% | 9 | 100.0% | 6 | 100.0% | 7 | 100.0% | 54 | 100.0% | | |

*Table continues on page 89*

*Table continued from page 88*

| Survey question/responses | Institutional type | | | | Institution control | | | | Number of undergraduates enrolled | | | | | | | | | | Total | |
|---|---|---|---|---|---|---|---|---|---|---|---|---|---|---|---|---|---|---|---|---|
| | Two-year | | Four-year | | Public | | Private | | Under 1,000 | | 1,000-4,999 | | 5,999-9,999 | | 10,000-19,999 | | 20,000 and above | | | |
| | Freq. | % | Freq | % | Freq. | % | Freq. | % | Freq. | % | Freq. | % | Freq. | % | Freq. | % | Freq. | % | Freq. | % |
| Q23. You indicated that the following transfer-specific programs, policies, and practices are available at your institution. In your opinion, which of these are most important to transfer/transfer-intending student success? (Bridge programs) | | | | | | | | | | | | | | | | | | | | |
| Bridge programs | 6 | 50.0% | 5 | 45.5% | 9 | 52.9% | 2 | 33.3% | 1 | 50.0% | 3 | 42.9% | 6 | 85.7% | 0 | 0.0% | 1 | 50.0% | 11 | 47.8% |
| Total | 12 | 100.0% | 11 | 100.0% | 17 | 100.0% | 6 | 100.0% | 2 | 100.0% | 7 | 100.0% | 7 | 100.0% | 5 | 100.0% | 2 | 100.0% | 23 | 100.0% |
| Q23. You indicated that the following transfer-specific programs, policies, and practices are available at your institution. In your opinion, which of these are most important to transfer/transfer-intending student success? (Campus-based event (e.g., common reading experiences, dinners, fairs)) | | | | | | | | | | | | | | | | | | | | |
| Campus-based event (e.g., common reading experiences, dinners, fairs) | 3 | 14.3% | 4 | 16.0% | 6 | 19.4% | 1 | 6.7% | 1 | 33.3% | 1 | 6.3% | 3 | 27.3% | 1 | 14.3% | 1 | 10.0% | 7 | 14.9% |
| Total | 21 | 100.0% | 25 | 100.0% | 31 | 100.0% | 15 | 100.0% | 3 | 100.0% | 16 | 100.0% | 11 | 100.0% | 7 | 100.0% | 10 | 100.0% | 47 | 100.0% |
| Q23. You indicated that the following transfer-specific programs, policies, and practices are available at your institution. In your opinion, which of these are most important to transfer/transfer-intending student success? (Career exploration) | | | | | | | | | | | | | | | | | | | | |
| Career exploration | 15 | 44.1% | 11 | 33.3% | 19 | 43.2% | 7 | 30.4% | 2 | 28.6% | 9 | 37.5% | 7 | 46.7% | 3 | 30.0% | 5 | 41.7% | 26 | 38.2% |
| Total | 34 | 100.0% | 33 | 100.0% | 44 | 100.0% | 23 | 100.0% | 7 | 100.0% | 24 | 100.0% | 15 | 100.0% | 10 | 100.0% | 12 | 100.0% | 68 | 100.0% |
| Q23. You indicated that the following transfer-specific programs, policies, and practices are available at your institution. In your opinion, which of these are most important to transfer/transfer-intending student success? (Career planning) | | | | | | | | | | | | | | | | | | | | |
| Career planning | 14 | 48.3% | 18 | 51.4% | 19 | 52.8% | 12 | 44.4% | 6 | 66.7% | 10 | 45.5% | 8 | 57.1% | 2 | 25.0% | 5 | 45.5% | 31 | 48.4% |
| Total | 29 | 100.0% | 35 | 100.0% | 36 | 100.0% | 27 | 100.0% | 9 | 100.0% | 22 | 100.0% | 14 | 100.0% | 8 | 100.0% | 11 | 100.0% | 64 | 100.0% |
| Q23. You indicated that the following transfer-specific programs, policies, and practices are available at your institution. In your opinion, which of these are most important to transfer/transfer-intending student success? (Communication or publications (e.g., social media, newsletters, emails, brochures)) | | | | | | | | | | | | | | | | | | | | |
| Communication or publications (e.g., social media, newsletters, emails, brochures) | 5 | 20.8% | 5 | 15.2% | 8 | 21.6% | 2 | 10.0% | 1 | 14.3% | 1 | 5.3% | 4 | 33.3% | 2 | 22.2% | 2 | 18.2% | 10 | 17.2% |
| Total | 24 | 100.0% | 33 | 100.0% | 37 | 100.0% | 20 | 100.0% | 7 | 100.0% | 19 | 100.0% | 12 | 100.0% | 9 | 100.0% | 11 | 100.0% | 58 | 100.0% |

*Table continues on page 90*

*Table continued from page 89*

| | Institutional type | | | | Institution control | | | | Number of undergraduates enrolled | | | | | | | | | | | Total | |
|---|---|---|---|---|---|---|---|---|---|---|---|---|---|---|---|---|---|---|---|---|---|---|
| | Two-year | | Four-year | | Public | | Private | | Under 1,000 | | 1,000-4,999 | | 5,999-9,999 | | 10,000-19,999 | | 20,000 and above | | | |
| Survey question/responses | Freq. | % | Freq | % | Freq. | % | Freq. | % | Freq. | % | Freq. | % | Freq. | % | Freq. | % | Freq. | % | Freq. | % |
| Q23. You indicated that the following transfer-specific programs, policies, and practices are available at your institution. In your opinion, which of these are most important to transfer/transfer-intending student success? (Course-specific support for classes with high dropout, fail, or withdraw rates (e.g., supplemental instruction)) | | | | | | | | | | | | | | | | | | | | |
| Course-specific support for classes with high dropout, fail, or withdraw rates (e.g., supplemental instruction) | 6 | 28.6% | 5 | 41.7% | 7 | 26.9% | 4 | 57.1% | 0 | 0.0% | 4 | 33.3% | 4 | 44.4% | 1 | 14.3% | 2 | 40.0% | 11 | 32.4% |
| Total | 21 | 100.0% | 12 | 100.0% | 26 | 100.0% | 7 | 100.0% | 1 | 100.0% | 12 | 100.0% | 9 | 100.0% | 7 | 100.0% | 5 | 100.0% | 34 | 100.0% |
| Q23. You indicated that the following transfer-specific programs, policies, and practices are available at your institution. In your opinion, which of these are most important to transfer/transfer-intending student success? (Credit-bearing course (e.g., transfer seminar)) | | | | | | | | | | | | | | | | | | | | |
| Credit-bearing course (e.g., transfer seminar) | 0 | 0.0% | 5 | 50.0% | 1 | 20.0% | 4 | 50.0% | 1 | 33.3% | 3 | 42.9% | 0 | 0.0% | 0 | 0.0% | 1 | 50.0% | 5 | 35.7% |
| Total | 3 | 100.0% | 10 | 100.0% | 5 | 100.0% | 8 | 100.0% | 3 | 100.0% | 7 | 100.0% | 0 | 100.0% | 2 | 100.0% | 2 | 100.0% | 14 | 100.0% |
| Q23. You indicated that the following transfer-specific programs, policies, and practices are available at your institution. In your opinion, which of these are most important to transfer/transfer-intending student success? (Cultural enrichment activities (e.g., plays, musical events, multicultural fairs)) | | | | | | | | | | | | | | | | | | | | |
| Cultural enrichment activities (e.g., plays, musical events, multicultural fairs) | 3 | 13.0% | 1 | 6.3% | 3 | 10.7% | 1 | 9.1% | 1 | 50.0% | 1 | 7.1% | 2 | 18.2% | 0 | 0.0% | 0 | 0.0% | 4 | 10.0% |
| Total | 23 | 100.0% | 16 | 100.0% | 28 | 100.0% | 11 | 100.0% | 2 | 100.0% | 14 | 100.0% | 11 | 100.0% | 5 | 100.0% | 8 | 100.0% | 40 | 100.0% |
| Q23. You indicated that the following transfer-specific programs, policies, and practices are available at your institution. In your opinion, which of these are most important to transfer/transfer-intending student success? (Early alert systems) | | | | | | | | | | | | | | | | | | | | |
| Early alert systems | 16 | 47.1% | 16 | 51.6% | 20 | 48.8% | 11 | 47.8% | 4 | 57.1% | 13 | 46.4% | 7 | 53.8% | 4 | 66.7% | 3 | 27.3% | 31 | 47.7% |
| Total | 34 | 100.0% | 31 | 100.0% | 41 | 100.0% | 23 | 100.0% | 7 | 100.0% | 28 | 100.0% | 13 | 100.0% | 6 | 100.0% | 11 | 100.0% | 65 | 100.0% |
| Q23. You indicated that the following transfer-specific programs, policies, and practices are available at your institution. In your opinion, which of these are most important to transfer/transfer-intending student success? (Equal Opportunity Program (EOP)) | | | | | | | | | | | | | | | | | | | | |
| Equal Opportunity Program (EOP) | 4 | 33.3% | 1 | 10.0% | 5 | 35.7% | 0 | 0.0% | 2 | 66.7% | 1 | 14.3% | 1 | 20.0% | 1 | 20.0% | 1 | 33.3% | 6 | 26.1% |
| Total | 12 | 100.0% | 10 | 100.0% | 14 | 100.0% | 8 | 100.0% | 3 | 100.0% | 7 | 100.0% | 5 | 100.0% | 5 | 100.0% | 3 | 100.0% | 23 | 100.0% |

*Table continues on page 91*

Table continued from page 90

| Survey question/responses | Institutional type | | | | Institution control | | | | Number of undergraduates enrolled | | | | | | | | | | | | Total | |
| --- | --- | --- | --- | --- | --- | --- | --- | --- | --- | --- | --- | --- | --- | --- | --- | --- | --- | --- | --- | --- | --- | --- |
| | Two-year | | Four-year | | Public | | Private | | Under 1,000 | | 1,000-4,999 | | 5,999-9,999 | | 10,000-19,999 | | 20,000 and above | | | | | |
| | Freq. | % | Freq | % | Freq. | % | Freq. | % | Freq. | % | Freq. | % | Freq. | % | Freq. | % | Freq. | % | Freq. | % | Freq. | % |
| Q23. You indicated that the following transfer-specific programs, policies, and practices are available at your institution. In your opinion, which of these are most important to transfer/transfer-intending student success? (Faculty or staff mentors) | | | | | | | | | | | | | | | | | | | | | | |
| Faculty or staff mentors | 5 | 38.5% | 18 | 69.2% | 8 | 44.4% | 15 | 71.4% | 5 | 83.3% | 8 | 53.3% | 4 | 57.1% | 4 | 50.0% | 3 | 75.0% | 24 | 60.0% | | |
| Total | 13 | 100.0% | 26 | 100.0% | 18 | 100.0% | 21 | 100.0% | 6 | 100.0% | 15 | 100.0% | 7 | 100.0% | 8 | 100.0% | 4 | 100.0% | 40 | 100.0% | | |
| Q23. You indicated that the following transfer-specific programs, policies, and practices are available at your institution. In your opinion, which of these are most important to transfer/transfer-intending student success? (Financial aid (e.g., transfer scholarships, loans)) | | | | | | | | | | | | | | | | | | | | | | |
| Financial aid (e.g., transfer scholarships, loans) | 15 | 53.6% | 34 | 77.3% | 25 | 64.1% | 24 | 72.7% | 8 | 80.0% | 17 | 58.6% | 9 | 69.2% | 10 | 90.9% | 6 | 60.0% | 50 | 68.5% | | |
| Total | 28 | 100.0% | 44 | 100.0% | 39 | 100.0% | 33 | 100.0% | 10 | 100.0% | 29 | 100.0% | 13 | 100.0% | 11 | 100.0% | 10 | 100.0% | 73 | 100.0% | | |
| Q23. You indicated that the following transfer-specific programs, policies, and practices are available at your institution. In your opinion, which of these are most important to transfer/transfer-intending student success? (Financial planning, coaching, and information) | | | | | | | | | | | | | | | | | | | | | | |
| Financial planning, coaching, and information | 8 | 53.3% | 5 | 33.3% | 11 | 55.0% | 2 | 20.0% | 0 | 0.0% | 4 | 44.4% | 4 | 57.1% | 2 | 40.0% | 3 | 37.5% | 13 | 41.9% | | |
| Total | 15 | 100.0% | 15 | 100.0% | 20 | 100.0% | 10 | 100.0% | 2 | 100.0% | 9 | 100.0% | 7 | 100.0% | 5 | 100.0% | 8 | 100.0% | 31 | 100.0% | | |
| Q23. You indicated that the following transfer-specific programs, policies, and practices are available at your institution. In your opinion, which of these are most important to transfer/transfer-intending student success? (Guided pathways) | | | | | | | | | | | | | | | | | | | | | | |
| Guided pathways | 26 | 70.3% | 13 | 41.9% | 32 | 66.7% | 7 | 35.0% | 2 | 50.0% | 19 | 63.3% | 7 | 70.0% | 5 | 38.5% | 7 | 58.3% | 40 | 58.0% | | |
| Total | 37 | 100.0% | 31 | 100.0% | 48 | 100.0% | 20 | 100.0% | 4 | 100.0% | 30 | 100.0% | 10 | 100.0% | 13 | 100.0% | 12 | 100.0% | 69 | 100.0% | | |
| Q23. You indicated that the following transfer-specific programs, policies, and practices are available at your institution. In your opinion, which of these are most important to transfer/transfer-intending student success? (Honors societies (e.g., Tau Sigma, Phi Theta Kappa, etc.)) | | | | | | | | | | | | | | | | | | | | | | |
| Honors societies (e.g., Tau Sigma, Phi Theta Kappa, etc.) | 13 | 34.2% | 7 | 28.0% | 15 | 31.9% | 5 | 31.3% | 2 | 66.7% | 10 | 38.5% | 6 | 42.9% | 1 | 12.5% | 1 | 8.3% | 20 | 31.7% | | |
| Total | 38 | 100.0% | 25 | 100.0% | 47 | 100.0% | 16 | 100.0% | 3 | 100.0% | 26 | 100.0% | 14 | 100.0% | 8 | 100.0% | 12 | 100.0% | 63 | 100.0% | | |

Table continues on page 92

*Table continued from page 91*

| Survey question/responses | Institutional type | | | | Institution control | | | | Number of undergraduates enrolled | | | | | | | | | | | | Total | |
|---|---|---|---|---|---|---|---|---|---|---|---|---|---|---|---|---|---|---|---|---|---|---|
| | Two-year | | Four-year | | Public | | Private | | Under 1,000 | | 1,000-4,999 | | 5,999-9,999 | | 10,000-19,999 | | 20,000 and above | | | | | |
| | Freq. | % | Freq | % | Freq. | % | Freq. | % | Freq. | % | Freq. | % | Freq. | % | Freq. | % | Freq. | % | Freq. | % | | |
| Q23. You indicated that the following transfer-specific programs, policies, and practices are available at your institution. In your opinion, which of these are most important to transfer/transfer-intending student success? (Informational sessions about navigating transfer (including admission, policies, and more)) | | | | | | | | | | | | | | | | | | | | | | |
| Informational sessions about navigating transfer (including admission, policies, and more) | 14 | 38.9% | 17 | 40.5% | 18 | 36.0% | 13 | 46.4% | 3 | 42.9% | 12 | 38.7% | 5 | 35.7% | 5 | 35.7% | 6 | 46.2% | 31 | 39.2% | | |
| Total | 36 | 100.0% | 42 | 100.0% | 50 | 100.0% | 28 | 100.0% | 7 | 100.0% | 31 | 100.0% | 14 | 100.0% | 14 | 100.0% | 13 | 100.0% | 79 | 100.0% | | |
| Q23. You indicated that the following transfer-specific programs, policies, and practices are available at your institution. In your opinion, which of these are most important to transfer/transfer-intending student success? (Internships or co-ops) | | | | | | | | | | | | | | | | | | | | | | |
| Internships or co-ops | 6 | 25.0% | 8 | 34.8% | 7 | 24.1% | 7 | 38.9% | 3 | 50.0% | 4 | 25.0% | 5 | 41.7% | 1 | 20.0% | 1 | 11.1% | 14 | 29.2% | | |
| Total | 24 | 100.0% | 23 | 100.0% | 29 | 100.0% | 18 | 100.0% | 6 | 100.0% | 16 | 100.0% | 12 | 100.0% | 5 | 100.0% | 9 | 100.0% | 48 | 100.0% | | |
| Q23. You indicated that the following transfer-specific programs, policies, and practices are available at your institution. In your opinion, which of these are most important to transfer/transfer-intending student success? (Leadership development) | | | | | | | | | | | | | | | | | | | | | | |
| Leadership development | 4 | 21.1% | 4 | 22.2% | 6 | 22.2% | 2 | 20.0% | 3 | 75.0% | 2 | 20.0% | 3 | 33.3% | 0 | 0.0% | 1 | 12.5% | 9 | 23.7% | | |
| Total | 19 | 100.0% | 18 | 100.0% | 27 | 100.0% | 10 | 100.0% | 4 | 100.0% | 10 | 100.0% | 9 | 100.0% | 7 | 100.0% | 8 | 100.0% | 38 | 100.0% | | |
| Q23. You indicated that the following transfer-specific programs, policies, and practices are available at your institution. In your opinion, which of these are most important to transfer/transfer-intending student success? (Learning communities (i.e., students take two or more linked courses as a group)) | | | | | | | | | | | | | | | | | | | | | | |
| Learning communities (i.e., students take two or more linked courses as a group) | 2 | 22.2% | 4 | 44.4% | 5 | 38.5% | 1 | 20.0% | 0 | 0.0% | 0 | 0.0% | 2 | 50.0% | 1 | 20.0% | 3 | 75.0% | 6 | 33.3% | | |
| Total | 9 | 100.0% | 9 | 100.0% | 13 | 100.0% | 5 | 100.0% | 1 | 100.0% | 4 | 100.0% | 4 | 100.0% | 5 | 100.0% | 4 | 100.0% | 18 | 100.0% | | |
| Q23. You indicated that the following transfer-specific programs, policies, and practices are available at your institution. In your opinion, which of these are most important to transfer/transfer-intending student success? (Major exploration and selection) | | | | | | | | | | | | | | | | | | | | | | |
| Major exploration and selection | 13 | 61.9% | 7 | 33.3% | 15 | 57.7% | 5 | 31.3% | 1 | 33.3% | 8 | 61.5% | 5 | 45.5% | 2 | 28.6% | 4 | 50.0% | 20 | 47.6% | | |
| Total | 21 | 100.0% | 21 | 100.0% | 26 | 100.0% | 16 | 100.0% | 3 | 100.0% | 13 | 100.0% | 11 | 100.0% | 7 | 100.0% | 8 | 100.0% | 42 | 100.0% | | |

*Table continues on page 93*

*Table continued from page 92*



| Survey question/responses | Institutional type | | | | Institution control | | | | Number of undergraduates enrolled | | | | | | | | | | | | Total | |
|---|---|---|---|---|---|---|---|---|---|---|---|---|---|---|---|---|---|---|---|---|---|---|
| | Two-year | | Four-year | | Public | | Private | | Under 1,000 | | 1,000-4,999 | | 5,999-9,999 | | 10,000-19,999 | | 20,000 and above | | | |
| | Freq. | % | Freq | % | Freq. | % | Freq. | % | Freq. | % | Freq. | % | Freq. | % | Freq. | % | Freq. | % | Freq. | % |
| Q23. You indicated that the following transfer-specific programs, policies, and practices are available at your institution. In your opinion, which of these are most important to transfer/transfer-intending student success? (Mentoring from others outside of the institution (e.g., peers at other institutions, alumni, and more)) | | | | | | | | | | | | | | | | | | | | |
| Mentoring from others outside of the institution (e.g., peers at other institutions, alumni, and more) | 2 | 33.3% | 0 | 0.0% | 2 | 25.0% | 0 | 0.0% | 0 | 0.0% | 0 | 0.0% | 0 | 0.0% | 0 | 0.0% | 2 | 40.0% | 2 | 13.3% |
| Total | 6 | 100.0% | 8 | 100.0% | 8 | 100.0% | 6 | 100.0% | 3 | 100.0% | 2 | 100.0% | 3 | 100.0% | 2 | 100.0% | 5 | 100.0% | 15 | 100.0% |
| Q23. You indicated that the following transfer-specific programs, policies, and practices are available at your institution. In your opinion, which of these are most important to transfer/transfer-intending student success? (Next-steps enrollment checklist (i.e., details about to-do items students must complete before enrollment)) | | | | | | | | | | | | | | | | | | | | |
| Next-steps enrollment checklist (i.e., details about to-do items students must complete before enrollment) | 7 | 33.3% | 16 | 40.0% | 15 | 42.9% | 8 | 30.8% | 0 | 0.0% | 8 | 38.1% | 4 | 44.4% | 7 | 50.0% | 4 | 33.3% | 23 | 37.1% |
| Total | 21 | 100.0% | 40 | 100.0% | 35 | 100.0% | 26 | 100.0% | 6 | 100.0% | 21 | 100.0% | 9 | 100.0% | 14 | 100.0% | 12 | 100.0% | 62 | 100.0% |
| Q23. You indicated that the following transfer-specific programs, policies, and practices are available at your institution. In your opinion, which of these are most important to transfer/transfer-intending student success? (Off-campus event (e.g., retreat, outdoor adventure)) | | | | | | | | | | | | | | | | | | | | |
| Off-campus event (e.g., retreat, outdoor adventure) | 2 | 20.0% | 0 | 0.0% | 2 | 15.4% | 0 | 0.0% | 1 | 33.3% | 0 | 0.0% | 1 | 25.0% | 0 | 0.0% | 0 | 0.0% | 2 | 10.5% |
| Total | 10 | 100.0% | 8 | 100.0% | 13 | 100.0% | 5 | 100.0% | 3 | 100.0% | 5 | 100.0% | 4 | 100.0% | 5 | 100.0% | 2 | 100.0% | 19 | 100.0% |
| Q23. You indicated that the following transfer-specific programs, policies, and practices are available at your institution. In your opinion, which of these are most important to transfer/transfer-intending student success? (Opportunities to co-teach or assist in teaching a class) | | | | | | | | | | | | | | | | | | | | |
| Opportunities to co-teach or assist in teaching a class | 0 | 0.0% | 1 | 16.7% | 1 | 20.0% | 0 | 0.0% | 0 | 0.0% | 0 | 0.0% | 0 | 0.0% | 0 | 0.0% | 1 | 8.3% | 1 | 12.5% |
| Total | 1 | 100.0% | 6 | 100.0% | 5 | 100.0% | 2 | 100.0% | 2 | 100.0% | 0 | 100.0% | 1 | 100.0% | 0 | 100.0% | 12 | 100.0% | 8 | 100.0% |
| Q23. You indicated that the following transfer-specific programs, policies, and practices are available at your institution. In your opinion, which of these are most important to transfer/transfer-intending student success? (Orientation (institution-wide)) | | | | | | | | | | | | | | | | | | | | |
| Orientation (institution-wide) | 9 | 37.5% | 25 | 50.0% | 18 | 46.2% | 15 | 44.1% | 4 | 50.0% | 12 | 40.0% | 6 | 46.2% | 5 | 45.5% | 7 | 58.3% | 34 | 45.9% |
| Total | 24 | 100.0% | 50 | 100.0% | 39 | 100.0% | 34 | 100.0% | 8 | 100.0% | 30 | 100.0% | 13 | 100.0% | 11 | 100.0% | 12 | 100.0% | 74 | 100.0% |

*Table continues on page 94*

*Table continued from page 93*

| Survey question/responses | Institutional type | | | | Institution control | | | | Number of undergraduates enrolled | | | | | | | | | | | | Total | |
|---|---|---|---|---|---|---|---|---|---|---|---|---|---|---|---|---|---|---|---|---|---|---|
| | Two-year | | Four-year | | Public | | Private | | Under 1,000 | | 1,000-4,999 | | 5,999-9,999 | | 10,000-19,999 | | 20,000 and above | | | | | |
| | Freq. | % | Freq | % | Freq. | % | Freq. | % | Freq. | % | Freq. | % | Freq. | % | Freq. | % | Freq. | % | Freq. | % | Freq. | % |
| Q23. You indicated that the following transfer-specific programs, policies, and practices are available at your institution. In your opinion, which of these are most important to transfer/transfer-intending student success? (Peer mentoring across Peer mentoring across institutions (e.g., transfer students at four-year institutions mentoring students at partner community colleges)) | | | | | | | | | | | | | | | | | | | | | | |
| Peer mentoring across institutions (e.g., transfer students at four-year institutions mentoring students at partner community colleges) | 2 | 50.0% | 0 | 0.0% | 2 | 40.0% | 0 | 0.0% | 0 | 0.0% | 1 | 33.3% | 1 | 25.0% | 0 | 0.0% | 0 | 0.0% | 2 | 20.0% | | |
| Total | 4 | 100.0% | 6 | 100.0% | 5 | 100.0% | 5 | 100.0% | 1 | 100.0% | 3 | 100.0% | 4 | 100.0% | 1 | 100.0% | 1 | 100.0% | 10 | 100.0% | | |
| Q23. You indicated that the following transfer-specific programs, policies, and practices are available at your institution. In your opinion, which of these are most important to transfer/transfer-intending student success? (Peer mentoring by transfers/transfer-intending students (i.e., transfer/transfer-intending students mentoring other students at the same institution)) | | | | | | | | | | | | | | | | | | | | | | |
| Peer mentoring by transfers/transfer-intending students (i.e., transfer/transfer-intending students mentoring other students at the same institution) | 3 | 75.0% | 4 | 50.0% | 6 | 66.7% | 1 | 33.3% | 0 | 0.0% | 2 | 66.7% | 1 | 50.0% | 2 | 66.7% | 2 | 50.0% | 7 | 58.3% | | |
| Total | 4 | 100.0% | 8 | 100.0% | 9 | 100.0% | 3 | 100.0% | 0 | 100.0% | 3 | 100.0% | 2 | 100.0% | 3 | 100.0% | 4 | 100.0% | 12 | 100.0% | | |
| Q23. You indicated that the following transfer-specific programs, policies, and practices are available at your institution. In your opinion, which of these are most important to transfer/transfer-intending student success? (Peer mentoring by undergraduate students (i.e., undergraduate students mentoring transfers/transfer-intending students at the same institution)) | | | | | | | | | | | | | | | | | | | | | | |
| Peer mentoring by undergraduate students (i.e., undergraduate students mentoring transfers/transfer-intending students at the same institution) | 1 | 25.0% | 3 | 20.0% | 2 | 20.0% | 2 | 22.2% | 0 | 0.0% | 2 | 66.7% | 0 | 0.0% | 1 | 16.7% | 1 | 33.3% | 4 | 21.1% | | |
| Total | 4 | 100.0% | 15 | 100.0% | 10 | 100.0% | 9 | 100.0% | 2 | 100.0% | 3 | 100.0% | 5 | 100.0% | 6 | 100.0% | 3 | 100.0% | 19 | 100.0% | | |
| Q23. You indicated that the following transfer-specific programs, policies, and practices are available at your institution. In your opinion, which of these are most important to transfer/transfer-intending student success? (Practica or other supervised practice experiences) | | | | | | | | | | | | | | | | | | | | | | |
| Practica or other supervised practice experiences | 1 | 25.0% | 2 | 16.7% | 1 | 16.7% | 2 | 20.0% | 3 | 60.0% | 1 | 20.0% | 0 | 0.0% | 0 | 0.0% | 0 | 0.0% | 4 | 23.5% | | |

*Table continues on page 95*

*Table continued from page 94*

| Survey question/responses | Institutional type | | | | Institution control | | | | Number of undergraduates enrolled | | | | | | | | | | | | Total | |
| | Two-year | | Four-year | | Public | | Private | | Under 1,000 | | 1,000-4,999 | | 5,999-9,999 | | 10,000-19,999 | | 20,000 and above | | | |
| | Freq. | % | Freq | % | Freq. | % | Freq. | % | Freq. | % | Freq. | % | Freq. | % | Freq. | % | Freq. | % | Freq. | % |
|---|---|---|---|---|---|---|---|---|---|---|---|---|---|---|---|---|---|---|---|---|
| Total | 4 | 100.0% | 12 | 100.0% | 6 | 100.0% | 10 | 100.0% | 5 | 100.0% | 5 | 100.0% | 3 | 100.0% | 2 | 100.0% | 2 | 100.0% | 17 | 100.0% |

Q23. You indicated that the following transfer-specific programs, policies, and practices are available at your institution. In your opinion, which of these are most important to transfer/transfer-intending student success? (Regional institutional partnerships that include joint transfer programs and/or staff positions)

| Survey question/responses | Two-year | | Four-year | | Public | | Private | | Under 1,000 | | 1,000-4,999 | | 5,999-9,999 | | 10,000-19,999 | | 20,000 and above | | Total | |
| | Freq. | % | Freq | % | Freq. | % | Freq. | % | Freq. | % | Freq. | % | Freq. | % | Freq. | % | Freq. | % | Freq. | % |
|---|---|---|---|---|---|---|---|---|---|---|---|---|---|---|---|---|---|---|---|---|
| Regional institutional partnerships that include joint transfer programs and/or staff positions | 5 | 29.4% | 6 | 42.9% | 8 | 34.8% | 3 | 37.5% | 0 | 0.0% | 3 | 27.3% | 1 | 20.0% | 3 | 42.9% | 4 | 57.1% | 11 | 35.5% |
| Total | 17 | 100.0% | 14 | 100.0% | 23 | 100.0% | 8 | 100.0% | 1 | 100.0% | 11 | 100.0% | 5 | 100.0% | 7 | 100.0% | 7 | 100.0% | 31 | 100.0% |

Q23. You indicated that the following transfer-specific programs, policies, and practices are available at your institution. In your opinion, which of these are most important to transfer/transfer-intending student success? (Residence life—transfer live on-campus requirement)

| Survey question/responses | Two-year | | Four-year | | Public | | Private | | Under 1,000 | | 1,000-4,999 | | 5,999-9,999 | | 10,000-19,999 | | 20,000 and above | | Total | |
| | Freq. | % | Freq | % | Freq. | % | Freq. | % | Freq. | % | Freq. | % | Freq. | % | Freq. | % | Freq. | % | Freq. | % |
|---|---|---|---|---|---|---|---|---|---|---|---|---|---|---|---|---|---|---|---|---|
| Residence life—transfer live on-campus requirement | 1 | 50.0% | 4 | 36.4% | 4 | 80.0% | 1 | 12.5% | 1 | 33.3% | 1 | 25.0% | 0 | 0.0% | 1 | 50.0% | 0 | 0.0% | 5 | 38.5% |
| Total | 2 | 100.0% | 11 | 100.0% | 5 | 100.0% | 8 | 100.0% | 3 | 100.0% | 4 | 100.0% | 2 | 100.0% | 2 | 100.0% | 2 | 100.0% | 13 | 100.0% |

Q23. You indicated that the following transfer-specific programs, policies, and practices are available at your institution. In your opinion, which of these are most important to transfer/transfer-intending student success? (Residence life — transfer-specific living-learning community)

| Survey question/responses | Two-year | | Four-year | | Public | | Private | | Under 1,000 | | 1,000-4,999 | | 5,999-9,999 | | 10,000-19,999 | | 20,000 and above | | Total | |
| | Freq. | % | Freq | % | Freq. | % | Freq. | % | Freq. | % | Freq. | % | Freq. | % | Freq. | % | Freq. | % | Freq. | % |
|---|---|---|---|---|---|---|---|---|---|---|---|---|---|---|---|---|---|---|---|---|
| Residence life — transfer-specific living-learning community | 0 | 0.0% | 5 | 50.0% | 4 | 66.7% | 1 | 20.0% | 1 | 50.0% | 1 | 33.3% | 1 | 50.0% | 0 | 0.0% | 0 | 0.0% | 6 | 50.0% |
| Total | 1 | 100.0% | 10 | 100.0% | 6 | 100.0% | 5 | 100.0% | 2 | 100.0% | 3 | 100.0% | 2 | 100.0% | 2 | 100.0% | 3 | 100.0% | 12 | 100.0% |

Q23. You indicated that the following transfer-specific programs, policies, and practices are available at your institution. In your opinion, which of these are most important to transfer/transfer-intending student success? (Residence life—transfer specific residential curriculum)

| Survey question/responses | Two-year | | Four-year | | Public | | Private | | Under 1,000 | | 1,000-4,999 | | 5,999-9,999 | | 10,000-19,999 | | 20,000 and above | | Total | |
| | Freq. | % | Freq | % | Freq. | % | Freq. | % | Freq. | % | Freq. | % | Freq. | % | Freq. | % | Freq. | % | Freq. | % |
|---|---|---|---|---|---|---|---|---|---|---|---|---|---|---|---|---|---|---|---|---|
| Residence life—transfer-specific residential curriculum | 0 | 0.0% | 0 | 0.0% | 0 | 0.0% | 0 | 0.0% | 0 | 0.0% | 0 | 0.0% | 0 | 0.0% | 0 | 0.0% | 0 | 0.0% | 0 | 0.0% |
| Total | 0 | 0.0% | 3 | 100.0% | 1 | 100.0% | 2 | 100.0% | 0 | 0.0% | 1 | 100.0% | 0 | 0.0% | 1 | 100.0% | 1 | 100.0% | 3 | 100.0% |

Q23. You indicated that the following transfer-specific programs, policies, and practices are available at your institution. In your opinion, which of these are most important to transfer/transfer-intending student success? (Service-learning or community service)

| Survey question/responses | Two-year | | Four-year | | Public | | Private | | Under 1,000 | | 1,000-4,999 | | 5,999-9,999 | | 10,000-19,999 | | 20,000 and above | | Total | |
| | Freq. | % | Freq | % | Freq. | % | Freq. | % | Freq. | % | Freq. | % | Freq. | % | Freq. | % | Freq. | % | Freq. | % |
|---|---|---|---|---|---|---|---|---|---|---|---|---|---|---|---|---|---|---|---|---|
| Service-learning or community service | 3 | 21.4% | 5 | 22.7% | 6 | 28.6% | 2 | 13.3% | 2 | 66.7% | 2 | 16.7% | 1 | 12.5% | 1 | 14.3% | 2 | 28.6% | 8 | 21.6% |

*Table continues on page 96*

*Table continued from page 95*

| | Institutional type | | | | Institution control | | | | Number of undergraduates enrolled | | | | | | | | | | Total | |
| Survey question/responses | Two-year | | Four-year | | Public | | Private | | Under 1,000 | | 1,000-4,999 | | 5,999-9,999 | | 10,000-19,999 | | 20,000 and above | | | |
| | Freq. | % | Freq | % | Freq. | % | Freq. | % | Freq. | % | Freq. | % | Freq. | % | Freq. | % | Freq. | % | Freq. | % |
|---|---|---|---|---|---|---|---|---|---|---|---|---|---|---|---|---|---|---|---|---|
| Total | 14 | 100.0% | 22 | 100.0% | 21 | 100.0% | 15 | 100.0% | 3 | 100.0% | 12 | 100.0% | 8 | 100.0% | 7 | 100.0% | 7 | 100.0% | 37 | 100.0% |
| Q23. You indicated that the following transfer-specific programs, policies, and practices are available at your institution. In your opinion, which of these are most important to transfer/transfer-intending student success? (Signature course (i.e., introductory academic credit-bearing course on various interdisciplinary topics)) | | | | | | | | | | | | | | | | | | | | |
| Signature course (i.e., introductory academic credit-bearing course on various interdisciplinary topics) | 0 | 0.0% | 4 | 22.2% | 1 | 6.3% | 3 | 21.4% | 1 | 25.0% | 1 | 11.1% | 0 | 0.0% | 0 | 0.0% | 2 | 40.0% | 4 | 13.3% |
| Total | 12 | 100.0% | 18 | 100.0% | 16 | 100.0% | 14 | 100.0% | 4 | 100.0% | 9 | 100.0% | 6 | 100.0% | 6 | 100.0% | 5 | 100.0% | 30 | 100.0% |
| Q23. You indicated that the following transfer-specific programs, policies, and practices are available at your institution. In your opinion, which of these are most important to transfer/transfer-intending student success? (Standardized policies for awarding of transfer credit) | | | | | | | | | | | | | | | | | | | | |
| Standardized policies for awarding of transfer credit | 10 | 37.0% | 34 | 70.8% | 19 | 47.5% | 24 | 70.6% | 5 | 71.4% | 15 | 55.6% | 6 | 42.9% | 8 | 61.5% | 9 | 64.3% | 43 | 57.3% |
| Total | 27 | 100.0% | 48 | 100.0% | 40 | 100.0% | 34 | 100.0% | 7 | 100.0% | 27 | 100.0% | 14 | 100.0% | 13 | 100.0% | 14 | 100.0% | 75 | 100.0% |
| Q23. You indicated that the following transfer-specific programs, policies, and practices are available at your institution. In your opinion, which of these are most important to transfer/transfer-intending student success? (Statewide articulation agreements) | | | | | | | | | | | | | | | | | | | | |
| Statewide articulation agreements | 18 | 54.5% | 14 | 46.7% | 25 | 54.3% | 7 | 43.8% | 2 | 33.3% | 13 | 61.9% | 7 | 58.3% | 3 | 25.0% | 7 | 63.6% | 32 | 51.6% |
| Total | 33 | 100.0% | 30 | 100.0% | 46 | 100.0% | 16 | 100.0% | 6 | 100.0% | 21 | 100.0% | 12 | 100.0% | 12 | 100.0% | 11 | 100.0% | 62 | 100.0% |
| Q23. You indicated that the following transfer-specific programs, policies, and practices are available at your institution. In your opinion, which of these are most important to transfer/transfer-intending student success? (Student government (e.g., designated transfer student representative or council)) | | | | | | | | | | | | | | | | | | | | |
| Student government (e.g., designated transfer student representative or council) | 0 | 0.0% | 3 | 16.7% | 2 | 11.1% | 1 | 9.1% | 0 | 0.0% | 1 | 12.5% | 0 | 0.0% | 0 | 0.0% | 2 | 33.3% | 3 | 10.0% |
| Total | 11 | 100.0% | 18 | 100.0% | 18 | 100.0% | 11 | 100.0% | 3 | 100.0% | 8 | 100.0% | 6 | 100.0% | 7 | 100.0% | 6 | 100.0% | 30 | 100.0% |
| Q23. You indicated that the following transfer-specific programs, policies, and practices are available at your institution. In your opinion, which of these are most important to transfer/transfer-intending student success? (Study abroad) | | | | | | | | | | | | | | | | | | | | |
| Study abroad | 4 | 26.7% | 3 | 13.0% | 4 | 19.0% | 3 | 17.6% | 1 | 20.0% | 3 | 30.0% | 3 | 30.0% | 0 | 0.0% | 0 | 0.0% | 7 | 18.4% |
| Total | 15 | 100.0% | 23 | 100.0% | 21 | 100.0% | 17 | 100.0% | 5 | 100.0% | 10 | 100.0% | 10 | 100.0% | 7 | 100.0% | 6 | 100.0% | 38 | 100.0% |

*Table continues on page 97*

Table continued from page 96

| Survey question/responses | Institutional type | | | | Institution control | | | | Number of undergraduates enrolled | | | | | | | | | | | | Total | |
| --- | --- | --- | --- | --- | --- | --- | --- | --- | --- | --- | --- | --- | --- | --- | --- | --- | --- | --- | --- | --- | --- | --- |
| | Two-year | | Four-year | | Public | | Private | | Under 1,000 | | 1,000-4,999 | | 5,999-9,999 | | 10,000-19,999 | | 20,000 and above | | | | | |
| | Freq. | % | Freq | % | Freq. | % | Freq. | % | Freq. | % | Freq. | % | Freq. | % | Freq. | % | Freq. | % | Freq. | % | Freq. | % |
| Q23. You indicated that the following transfer-specific programs, policies, and practices are available at your institution. In your opinion, which of these are most important to transfer/transfer-intending student success? (Targeted admissions recruitment of transfer students) | | | | | | | | | | | | | | | | | | | | | | |
| Targeted admissions recruitment of transfer students | 4 | 28.6% | 17 | 34.7% | 12 | 40.0% | 9 | 27.3% | 2 | 25.0% | 4 | 16.0% | 6 | 66.7% | 7 | 53.8% | 2 | 22.2% | 21 | 32.8% | | |
| Total | 14 | 100.0% | 49 | 100.0% | 30 | 100.0% | 33 | 100.0% | 8 | 100.0% | 25 | 100.0% | 9 | 100.0% | 13 | 100.0% | 9 | 100.0% | 64 | 100.0% | | |
| Q23. You indicated that the following transfer-specific programs, policies, and practices are available at your institution. In your opinion, which of these are most important to transfer/transfer-intending student success? (Transfer fairs (e.g., admissions fairs)) | | | | | | | | | | | | | | | | | | | | | | |
| Transfer fairs (e.g., admissions fairs) | 18 | 48.6% | 8 | 23.5% | 21 | 42.9% | 5 | 22.7% | 1 | 25.0% | 12 | 42.9% | 8 | 61.5% | 3 | 18.8% | 2 | 20.0% | 26 | 36.6% | | |
| Total | 37 | 100.0% | 34 | 100.0% | 49 | 100.0% | 22 | 100.0% | 4 | 100.0% | 28 | 100.0% | 13 | 100.0% | 16 | 100.0% | 10 | 100.0% | 71 | 100.0% | | |
| Q23. You indicated that the following transfer-specific programs, policies, and practices are available at your institution. In your opinion, which of these are most important to transfer/transfer-intending student success? (Transfer/college student success skills course) | | | | | | | | | | | | | | | | | | | | | | |
| Transfer/college student success skills course | 7 | 36.8% | 9 | 42.9% | 11 | 37.9% | 5 | 45.5% | 3 | 75.0% | 4 | 36.4% | 3 | 37.5% | 2 | 25.0% | 4 | 40.0% | 16 | 39.0% | | |
| Total | 19 | 100.0% | 21 | 100.0% | 29 | 100.0% | 11 | 100.0% | 4 | 100.0% | 11 | 100.0% | 8 | 100.0% | 8 | 100.0% | 10 | 100.0% | 41 | 100.0% | | |
| Q23. You indicated that the following transfer-specific programs, policies, and practices are available at your institution. In your opinion, which of these are most important to transfer/transfer-intending student success? (Transfer planning guide (i.e., how-to, things to consider)) | | | | | | | | | | | | | | | | | | | | | | |
| Transfer planning guide (i.e., how-to, things to consider) | 10 | 50.0% | 9 | 50.0% | 14 | 50.0% | 5 | 50.0% | 0 | 0.0% | 4 | 30.8% | 7 | 70.0% | 4 | 66.7% | 4 | 44.4% | 19 | 50.0% | | |
| Total | 20 | 100.0% | 18 | 100.0% | 28 | 100.0% | 10 | 100.0% | 0 | 0.0% | 13 | 100.0% | 10 | 100.0% | 6 | 100.0% | 9 | 100.0% | 38 | 100.0% | | |
| Q23. You indicated that the following transfer-specific programs, policies, and practices are available at your institution. In your opinion, which of these are most important to transfer/transfer-intending student success? (Transfer student center) | | | | | | | | | | | | | | | | | | | | | | |
| Transfer student center | 11 | 73.3% | 6 | 66.7% | 16 | 80.0% | 1 | 25.0% | 0 | 0.0% | 3 | 60.0% | 4 | 66.7% | 4 | 66.7% | 6 | 85.7% | 17 | 70.8% | | |
| Total | 15 | 100.0% | 9 | 100.0% | 20 | 100.0% | 4 | 100.0% | 0 | 0.0% | 5 | 100.0% | 6 | 100.0% | 6 | 100.0% | 7 | 100.0% | 24 | 100.0% | | |

Table continues on page 98

*Table continued from page 97*

| Survey question/responses | Institutional type | | | | Institution control | | | | Number of undergraduates enrolled | | | | | | | | | | | | Total | |
| --- | --- | --- | --- | --- | --- | --- | --- | --- | --- | --- | --- | --- | --- | --- | --- | --- | --- | --- | --- | --- | --- | --- |
| | Two-year | | Four-year | | Public | | Private | | Under 1,000 | | 1,000-4,999 | | 5,999-9,999 | | 10,000-19,999 | | 20,000 and above | | | | | |
| | Freq. | % | Freq | % | Freq. | % | Freq. | % | Freq. | % | Freq. | % | Freq. | % | Freq. | % | Freq. | % | Freq. | % | | |
| Q23. You indicated that the following transfer-specific programs, policies, and practices are available at your institution. In your opinion, which of these are most important to transfer/transfer-intending student success? (Transfer student organization(s)) | | | | | | | | | | | | | | | | | | | | | | |
| Transfer student organization(s) | 1 | 33.3% | 3 | 21.4% | 3 | 27.3% | 1 | 16.7% | 0 | 0.0% | 1 | 33.3% | 1 | 50.0% | 0 | 0.0% | 2 | 28.6% | 4 | 23.5% | | |
| Total | 3 | 100.0% | 14 | 100.0% | 11 | 100.0% | 6 | 100.0% | 1 | 100.0% | 3 | 100.0% | 2 | 11.8% | 4 | 22.2% | 7 | 41.2% | 17 | 100.0% | | |
| Q23. You indicated that the following transfer-specific programs, policies, and practices are available at your institution. In your opinion, which of these are most important to transfer/transfer-intending student success? (Undergraduate research) | | | | | | | | | | | | | | | | | | | | | | |
| Undergraduate research | 3 | 21.4% | 3 | 15.0% | 4 | 18.2% | 2 | 16.7% | 1 | 33.3% | 2 | 20.0% | 2 | 25.0% | 1 | 12.5% | 0 | 0.0% | 6 | 17.6% | | |
| Total | 14 | 100.0% | 20 | 100.0% | 22 | 100.0% | 12 | 100.0% | 3 | 100.0% | 10 | 100.0% | 8 | 100.0% | 8 | 100.0% | 5 | 100.0% | 34 | 100.0% | | |
| Q23. You indicated that the following transfer-specific programs, policies, and practices are available at your institution. In your opinion, which of these are most important to transfer/transfer-intending student success? (Other, please specify) | | | | | | | | | | | | | | | | | | | | | | |
| Other, please specify | 0 | 0.0% | 3 | 60.0% | 1 | 33.3% | 2 | 66.7% | 0 | 0.0% | 0 | 0.0% | 2 | 66.7% | 1 | 100.0% | 0 | 0.0% | 3 | 50.0% | | |
| Total | 1 | 100.0% | 5 | 100.0% | 3 | 100.0% | 3 | 100.0% | 0 | 0.0% | 1 | 100.0% | 3 | 100.0% | 1 | 100.0% | 1 | 100.0% | 6 | 100.0% | | |
| Q24. How long has your institution provided targeted programs, policies, and practices for transfer/transfer-intending students? | | | | | | | | | | | | | | | | | | | | | | |
| 1 year or less | 1 | 2.2% | 0 | 0.0% | 1 | 1.6% | 0 | 0.0% | 0 | 0.0% | 1 | 2.1% | 0 | 0.0% | 0 | 0.0% | 0 | 0.0% | 1 | 0.9% | | |
| 2-5 years | 7 | 15.2% | 12 | 18.5% | 10 | 15.9% | 9 | 19.1% | 2 | 18.2% | 11 | 22.9% | 3 | 17.6% | 3 | 16.7% | 1 | 5.9% | 20 | 18.0% | | |
| 6-10 years | 11 | 23.9% | 15 | 23.1% | 18 | 28.6% | 8 | 17.0% | 2 | 18.2% | 10 | 20.8% | 3 | 17.6% | 5 | 27.8% | 6 | 35.3% | 26 | 23.4% | | |
| 11-15 years | 8 | 17.4% | 4 | 6.2% | 9 | 14.3% | 3 | 6.4% | 1 | 9.1% | 7 | 14.6% | 1 | 5.9% | 2 | 11.1% | 1 | 5.9% | 12 | 10.8% | | |
| 16-20 years | 3 | 6.5% | 6 | 9.2% | 2 | 3.2% | 6 | 12.8% | 2 | 18.2% | 2 | 4.2% | 2 | 11.8% | 0 | 0.0% | 2 | 11.8% | 8 | 7.2% | | |
| More than 20 years | 8 | 17.4% | 16 | 24.6% | 13 | 20.6% | 11 | 23.4% | 4 | 36.4% | 8 | 16.7% | 3 | 17.6% | 4 | 22.2% | 5 | 29.4% | 24 | 21.6% | | |
| I don't know | 8 | 17.4% | 12 | 18.5% | 10 | 15.9% | 10 | 21.3% | 0 | 0.0% | 9 | 18.8% | 5 | 29.4% | 4 | 22.2% | 2 | 11.8% | 20 | 18.0% | | |
| Total | 46 | 100.0% | 65 | 100.0% | 63 | 100.0% | 47 | 100.0% | 11 | 100.0% | 48 | 100.0% | 17 | 100.0% | 18 | 100.0% | 17 | 100.0% | 111 | 100.0% | | |
| Q92. Is your institution considering or developing any future initiatives specifically or intentionally geared toward transfer students? | | | | | | | | | | | | | | | | | | | | | | |
| Yes | 28 | 59.6% | 48 | 54.5% | 39 | 56.5% | 37 | 56.9% | 9 | 56.3% | 36 | 59.0% | 9 | 45.0% | 9 | 47.4% | 14 | 73.7% | 77 | 57.0% | | |

*Table continues on page 99*

*Table continued from page 98*

| Survey question/responses | Institutional type | | | | Institution control | | | | Number of undergraduates enrolled | | | | | | | | | | | | Total | |
| --- | --- | --- | --- | --- | --- | --- | --- | --- | --- | --- | --- | --- | --- | --- | --- | --- | --- | --- | --- | --- | --- | --- |
| | Two-year | | Four-year | | Public | | Private | | Under 1,000 | | 1,000-4,999 | | 5,999-9,999 | | 10,000-19,999 | | 20,000 and above | | | | | |
| | Freq. | % | Freq | % | Freq. | % | Freq. | % | Freq. | % | Freq. | % | Freq. | % | Freq. | % | Freq. | % | Freq. | % | Freq. | % |
| No | 10 | 21.3% | 19 | 21.6% | 13 | 18.8% | 15 | 23.1% | 4 | 25.0% | 16 | 26.2% | 5 | 25.0% | 2 | 10.5% | 1 | 5.3% | | | 28 | 20.7% |
| I don't know | 9 | 19.1% | 21 | 23.8% | 17 | 24.6% | 13 | 20.0% | 3 | 18.8% | 9 | 14.7% | 6 | 30.0% | 8 | 42.1% | 4 | 21.1% | | | 30 | 22.2% |
| Total | 47 | 100.0% | 88 | 100.0% | 69 | 100.0% | 65 | 100.0% | 16 | 100.0% | 61 | 100.0% | 20 | 100.0% | 19 | 100.0% | 19 | 100.0% | | | 135 | 100.0% |
| Q94. Select the objectives(s) that will be measured in the upcoming initiative(s) you described: | | | | | | | | | | | | | | | | | | | | | | |
| Academic planning | 17 | 60.7% | 32 | 66.7% | 25 | 64.1% | 24 | 64.9% | 6 | 66.7% | 23 | 63.9% | 8 | 88.9% | 5 | 55.6% | 7 | 50.0% | | | 49 | 63.6% |
| Academic success strategies | 8 | 28.6% | 20 | 41.7% | 13 | 33.3% | 15 | 40.5% | 5 | 55.6% | 10 | 27.8% | 5 | 55.6% | 3 | 33.3% | 5 | 35.7% | | | 28 | 36.4% |
| Analytical, critical-thinking, or problem-solving skills | 2 | 7.1% | 6 | 12.5% | 2 | 5.1% | 6 | 16.2% | 2 | 22.2% | 4 | 11.1% | 2 | 22.2% | 0 | 0.0% | 0 | 0.0% | | | 8 | 10.4% |
| Career exploration and/or preparation | 8 | 28.6% | 16 | 33.3% | 12 | 30.8% | 12 | 32.4% | 1 | 11.1% | 11 | 30.6% | 4 | 44.4% | 2 | 22.2% | 6 | 42.9% | | | 24 | 31.2% |
| Civic engagement | 0 | 0.0% | 3 | 6.3% | 0 | 0.0% | 3 | 8.1% | 0 | 0.0% | 2 | 5.6% | 1 | 11.1% | 0 | 0.0% | 0 | 0.0% | | | 3 | 3.9% |
| Common transfer-year experience | 7 | 25.0% | 10 | 20.8% | 9 | 23.1% | 8 | 21.6% | 2 | 22.2% | 7 | 19.4% | 4 | 44.4% | 2 | 22.2% | 2 | 14.3% | | | 17 | 22.1% |
| Connection with the institution or campus | 12 | 42.9% | 18 | 37.5% | 18 | 46.2% | 12 | 32.4% | 3 | 33.3% | 13 | 36.1% | 3 | 33.3% | 3 | 33.3% | 8 | 57.1% | | | 30 | 39.0% |
| Developmental education, remediation, and/or review | 4 | 14.3% | 4 | 8.3% | 4 | 10.3% | 4 | 10.8% | 0 | 0.0% | 6 | 16.7% | 2 | 22.2% | 0 | 0.0% | 0 | 0.0% | | | 8 | 10.4% |
| Digital literacy | 2 | 7.1% | 2 | 4.2% | 2 | 5.1% | 2 | 5.4% | 1 | 11.1% | 2 | 5.6% | 1 | 11.1% | 0 | 0.0% | 0 | 0.0% | | | 4 | 5.2% |
| Discipline-specific knowledge | 3 | 10.7% | 4 | 8.3% | 4 | 10.3% | 3 | 8.1% | 0 | 0.0% | 4 | 11.1% | 2 | 22.2% | 1 | 11.1% | 0 | 0.0% | | | 7 | 9.1% |
| Financial literacy | 0 | 0.0% | 10 | 20.8% | 3 | 7.7% | 7 | 18.9% | 1 | 11.1% | 3 | 8.3% | 2 | 22.2% | 1 | 11.1% | 3 | 21.4% | | | 10 | 13.0% |
| Gateway course completion | 6 | 21.4% | 9 | 18.8% | 7 | 17.9% | 8 | 21.6% | 0 | 0.0% | 5 | 13.9% | 6 | 66.7% | 2 | 22.2% | 2 | 14.3% | | | 15 | 19.5% |
| Graduate or professional school preparation (e.g., pre-med, pre-law) | 0 | 0.0% | 4 | 8.3% | 1 | 2.6% | 3 | 8.1% | 0 | 0.0% | 2 | 5.6% | 0 | 0.0% | 0 | 0.0% | 2 | 14.3% | | | 4 | 5.2% |
| Health and wellness | 3 | 10.7% | 7 | 14.6% | 5 | 12.8% | 5 | 13.5% | 2 | 22.2% | 3 | 8.3% | 1 | 11.1% | 1 | 11.1% | 3 | 21.4% | | | 10 | 13.0% |

*Table continues on page 100*

*Table continued from page 99*

| Survey question/responses | Institutional type | | | | Institution control | | | | Number of undergraduates enrolled | | | | | | | | | | | | Total | |
| --- | --- | --- | --- | --- | --- | --- | --- | --- | --- | --- | --- | --- | --- | --- | --- | --- | --- | --- | --- | --- | --- | --- |
| | Two-year | | Four-year | | Public | | Private | | Under 1,000 | | 1,000-4,999 | | 5,999-9,999 | | 10,000-19,999 | | 20,000 and above | | | | | |
| | Freq. | % | Freq | % | Freq. | % | Freq. | % | Freq. | % | Freq. | % | Freq. | % | Freq. | % | Freq. | % | Freq. | % | | |
| Information literacy | 0 | 0.0% | 4 | 8.3% | 1 | 2.6% | 3 | 8.1% | 0 | 0.0% | 2 | 5.6% | 0 | 0.0% | 0 | 0.0% | 2 | 14.3% | 4 | 5.2% | | |
| Integrative and applied learning | 2 | 7.1% | 3 | 6.3% | 2 | 5.1% | 3 | 8.1% | 1 | 11.1% | 3 | 8.3% | 0 | 0.0% | 0 | 0.0% | 1 | 7.1% | 5 | 6.5% | | |
| Intercultural competence, diversity skills, or engaging with different perspectives | 5 | 17.9% | 5 | 10.4% | 6 | 15.4% | 4 | 10.8% | 0 | 0.0% | 6 | 16.7% | 2 | 22.2% | 0 | 0.0% | 2 | 14.3% | 10 | 13.0% | | |
| Introduction to a major, discipline, or career path | 8 | 28.6% | 10 | 20.8% | 9 | 23.1% | 9 | 24.3% | 2 | 22.2% | 7 | 19.4% | 4 | 44.4% | 3 | 33.3% | 2 | 14.3% | 18 | 23.4% | | |
| Introduction to institutional-specific academic expectations | 6 | 21.4% | 12 | 25.0% | 9 | 23.1% | 9 | 24.3% | 2 | 22.2% | 7 | 19.4% | 4 | 44.4% | 0 | 0.0% | 5 | 35.7% | 18 | 23.4% | | |
| Introduction to the liberal arts | 1 | 3.6% | 4 | 8.3% | 1 | 2.6% | 4 | 10.8% | 2 | 22.2% | 2 | 5.6% | 1 | 11.1% | 0 | 0.0% | 0 | 0.0% | 5 | 6.5% | | |
| Knowledge of institution or campus resources and services | 10 | 35.7% | 19 | 39.6% | 16 | 41.0% | 13 | 35.1% | 2 | 22.2% | 14 | 38.9% | 5 | 55.6% | 2 | 22.2% | 6 | 42.9% | 29 | 37.7% | | |
| Major exploration | 5 | 17.9% | 10 | 20.8% | 6 | 15.4% | 9 | 24.3% | 2 | 22.2% | 9 | 25.0% | 1 | 11.1% | 1 | 11.1% | 2 | 14.3% | 15 | 19.5% | | |
| On-time graduation rates (i.e., 4-year or 6-year graduation rate for transfers) | 13 | 46.4% | 23 | 47.9% | 20 | 51.3% | 16 | 43.2% | 2 | 22.2% | 14 | 38.9% | 6 | 66.7% | 4 | 44.4% | 10 | 71.4% | 36 | 46.8% | | |
| Oral communication skills | 1 | 3.6% | 1 | 2.1% | 1 | 2.6% | 1 | 2.7% | 0 | 0.0% | 2 | 5.6% | 0 | 0.0% | 0 | 0.0% | 0 | 0.0% | 2 | 2.6% | | |
| Persistence of transfer/transfer-intending students | 15 | 53.6% | 26 | 54.2% | 23 | 59.0% | 18 | 48.6% | 5 | 55.6% | 17 | 47.2% | 4 | 44.4% | 5 | 55.6% | 10 | 71.4% | 41 | 53.2% | | |
| Personal exploration or development | 4 | 14.3% | 7 | 14.6% | 8 | 20.5% | 3 | 8.1% | 0 | 0.0% | 5 | 13.9% | 0 | 0.0% | 1 | 11.1% | 5 | 35.7% | 11 | 14.3% | | |
| Project planning, teamwork, or management skills | 1 | 3.6% | 1 | 2.1% | 1 | 2.6% | 1 | 2.7% | 0 | 0.0% | 1 | 2.8% | 0 | 0.0% | 0 | 0.0% | 1 | 7.1% | 2 | 2.6% | | |
| Retention of transfer students | 16 | 57.1% | 31 | 64.6% | 24 | 61.5% | 23 | 62.2% | 4 | 44.4% | 20 | 55.6% | 6 | 66.7% | 5 | 55.6% | 12 | 85.7% | 47 | 61.0% | | |

*Table continues on page 101*

*Table continued from page 100*

| Survey question/responses | Institutional type | | | | Institution control | | | | Number of undergraduates enrolled | | | | | | | | | | | | | Total | |
|---|---|---|---|---|---|---|---|---|---|---|---|---|---|---|---|---|---|---|---|---|---|---|---|
| | Two-year | | Four-year | | Public | | Private | | Under 1,000 | | 1,000-4,999 | | 5,999-9,999 | | 10,000-19,999 | | 20,000 and above | | | | | | | |
| | Freq. | % | Freq | % | Freq. | % | Freq. | % | Freq. | % | Freq. | % | Freq. | % | Freq. | % | Freq. | % | Freq. | % |
| Social support networks (e.g., peer connections and friendships) | 2 | 7.1% | 8 | 16.7% | 5 | 12.8% | 5 | 13.5% | 0 | 0.0% | 6 | 16.7% | 1 | 11.1% | 1 | 11.1% | 2 | 14.3% | 10 | 13.0% |
| Student-faculty interaction | 7 | 25.0% | 10 | 20.8% | 10 | 25.6% | 7 | 18.9% | 1 | 11.1% | 8 | 22.2% | 3 | 33.3% | 1 | 11.1% | 4 | 28.6% | 17 | 22.1% |
| Writing skills | 2 | 7.1% | 4 | 8.3% | 2 | 5.1% | 4 | 10.8% | 1 | 11.1% | 3 | 8.3% | 1 | 11.1% | 0 | 0.0% | 1 | 7.1% | 6 | 7.8% |
| Other, please specify | 3 | 10.7% | 2 | 4.2% | 4 | 10.3% | 1 | 2.7% | 0 | 0.0% | 3 | 8.3% | 0 | 0.0% | 1 | 11.1% | 1 | 7.1% | 5 | 6.5% |
| My institution has not identified objectives for initiatives available to transfer/transfer-intending students | 3 | 10.7% | 4 | 8.3% | 4 | 10.3% | 3 | 8.1% | 2 | 22.2% | 3 | 8.3% | 0 | 0.0% | 0 | 0.0% | 3 | 21.4% | 8 | 10.4% |
| Total | 28 | 100.0% | 48 | 100.0% | 39 | 100.0% | 37 | 100.0% | 9 | 100.0% | 36 | 100.0% | 9 | 100.0% | 9 | 100.0% | 14 | 100.0% | 77 | 100.0% |

Q28. On your campus, how coordinated are transfer initiatives? (Select the most appropriate answer.)

| Survey question/responses | Two-year | | Four-year | | Public | | Private | | Under 1,000 | | 1,000-4,999 | | 5,999-9,999 | | 10,000-19,999 | | 20,000 and above | | Total | |
|---|---|---|---|---|---|---|---|---|---|---|---|---|---|---|---|---|---|---|---|---|
| Totally decentralized, no coordination between any departments or units associated with transfer initiatives | 3 | 6.0% | 5 | 5.4% | 2 | 2.7% | 5 | 7.2% | 2 | 12.5% | 2 | 3.1% | 2 | 9.1% | 1 | 5.3% | 0 | 0.0% | 7 | 4.9% |
| Mostly decentralized, little coordination | 6 | 12.0% | 18 | 19.4% | 16 | 21.9% | 8 | 11.6% | 2 | 12.5% | 6 | 9.2% | 8 | 36.4% | 4 | 21.1% | 4 | 19.0% | 24 | 16.8% |
| Somewhere between decentralized/centralized, no to all coordinated | 19 | 38.0% | 37 | 39.8% | 31 | 42.5% | 25 | 36.2% | 5 | 31.3% | 27 | 41.5% | 6 | 27.3% | 7 | 36.8% | 11 | 52.4% | 56 | 39.2% |
| Almost all centralized, almost all coordinated | 16 | 32.0% | 24 | 25.8% | 18 | 24.7% | 22 | 31.9% | 6 | 37.5% | 23 | 35.4% | 4 | 18.2% | 4 | 21.1% | 4 | 19.0% | 41 | 28.7% |
| Totally centralized, all transfer-oriented initiatives are coordinated by a single director or office | 5 | 10.0% | 7 | 7.5% | 5 | 6.8% | 7 | 10.1% | 1 | 6.3% | 5 | 7.7% | 2 | 9.1% | 2 | 10.5% | 2 | 9.5% | 12 | 8.4% |
| Unable to judge | 1 | 2.0% | 2 | 2.2% | 1 | 1.4% | 2 | 2.9% | 0 | 0.0% | 2 | 3.1% | 0 | 0.0% | 1 | 5.3% | 0 | 0.0% | 3 | 2.1% |

*Table continues on page 102*

*Table continued from page 101*

| Survey question/responses | Institutional type | | | | Institution control | | | | Number of undergraduates enrolled | | | | | | | | | | | | Total | |
|---|---|---|---|---|---|---|---|---|---|---|---|---|---|---|---|---|---|---|---|---|---|---|
| | Two-year | | Four-year | | Public | | Private | | Under 1,000 | | 1,000-4,999 | | 5,999-9,999 | | 10,000-19,999 | | 20,000 and above | | | |
| | Freq. | % | Freq | % | Freq. | % | Freq. | % | Freq. | % | Freq. | % | Freq. | % | Freq. | % | Freq. | % | Freq. | % |
| Total | 50 | 100.0% | 93 | 100.0% | 73 | 100.0% | 69 | 100.0% | 16 | 100.0% | 65 | 100.0% | 22 | 100.0% | 19 | 100.0% | 21 | 100.0% | 143 | 100.0% |

Q29. Which units on your campus participate in the coordination of transfer-related initiatives? (Select all that apply.)

| Survey question/responses | Two-year Freq. | % | Four-year Freq | % | Public Freq. | % | Private Freq. | % | Under 1,000 Freq. | % | 1,000-4,999 Freq. | % | 5,999-9,999 Freq. | % | 10,000-19,999 Freq. | % | 20,000 and above Freq. | % | Total Freq. | % |
|---|---|---|---|---|---|---|---|---|---|---|---|---|---|---|---|---|---|---|---|---|
| Academic advising | 46 | 92.0% | 75 | 80.6% | 65 | 89.0% | 55 | 79.7% | 14 | 87.5% | 54 | 83.1% | 20 | 90.9% | 18 | 94.7% | 15 | 71.4% | 121 | 84.6% |
| Academic affairs office | 29 | 58.0% | 56 | 60.2% | 40 | 54.8% | 44 | 63.8% | 14 | 87.5% | 34 | 52.3% | 14 | 63.6% | 11 | 57.9% | 12 | 57.1% | 85 | 59.4% |
| Academic department (s), please specify | 19 | 38.0% | 25 | 26.9% | 27 | 37.0% | 17 | 24.6% | 1 | 6.3% | 23 | 35.4% | 8 | 36.4% | 5 | 26.3% | 7 | 33.3% | 44 | 30.8% |
| Admissions office | 20 | 40.0% | 81 | 87.1% | 40 | 54.8% | 60 | 87.0% | 14 | 87.5% | 45 | 69.2% | 13 | 59.1% | 14 | 73.7% | 15 | 71.4% | 101 | 70.6% |
| Career services | 20 | 40.0% | 23 | 24.7% | 24 | 32.9% | 19 | 27.5% | 3 | 18.8% | 18 | 27.7% | 12 | 54.5% | 5 | 26.3% | 5 | 23.8% | 43 | 30.1% |
| Center for teaching excellence | 3 | 6.0% | 9 | 9.7% | 6 | 8.2% | 6 | 8.7% | 1 | 6.3% | 5 | 7.7% | 3 | 13.6% | 2 | 10.5% | 1 | 4.8% | 12 | 8.4% |
| Enrollment management | 12 | 24.0% | 51 | 54.8% | 28 | 38.4% | 34 | 49.3% | 5 | 31.3% | 27 | 41.5% | 8 | 36.4% | 12 | 63.2% | 11 | 52.4% | 63 | 44.1% |
| Financial aid office | 17 | 34.0% | 46 | 49.5% | 25 | 34.2% | 37 | 53.6% | 9 | 56.3% | 27 | 41.5% | 9 | 40.9% | 10 | 52.6% | 8 | 38.1% | 63 | 44.1% |
| First-year experience/transfer-year experience office | 11 | 22.0% | 17 | 18.3% | 14 | 19.2% | 14 | 20.3% | 1 | 6.3% | 11 | 16.9% | 7 | 31.8% | 5 | 26.3% | 4 | 19.0% | 28 | 19.6% |
| Institutional research office | 13 | 26.0% | 18 | 19.4% | 17 | 23.3% | 14 | 20.3% | 2 | 12.5% | 13 | 20.0% | 4 | 18.2% | 5 | 26.3% | 7 | 33.3% | 31 | 21.7% |
| Library services | 5 | 10.0% | 12 | 12.9% | 7 | 9.6% | 10 | 14.5% | 1 | 6.3% | 11 | 16.9% | 3 | 13.6% | 1 | 5.3% | 1 | 4.8% | 17 | 11.9% |
| Orientation | 10 | 20.0% | 55 | 59.1% | 28 | 38.4% | 37 | 53.6% | 9 | 56.3% | 28 | 43.1% | 10 | 45.5% | 9 | 47.4% | 10 | 47.6% | 66 | 46.2% |
| Registrar or transfer evaluation coordinator | 14 | 28.0% | 64 | 68.8% | 30 | 41.1% | 48 | 69.6% | 10 | 62.5% | 38 | 58.5% | 9 | 40.9% | 12 | 63.2% | 10 | 47.6% | 79 | 55.2% |
| Residence life or housing | 1 | 2.0% | 23 | 24.7% | 6 | 8.2% | 18 | 26.1% | 3 | 18.8% | 11 | 16.9% | 5 | 22.7% | 5 | 26.3% | 1 | 4.8% | 25 | 17.5% |
| Student activities and leadership | 7 | 14.0% | 13 | 14.0% | 12 | 16.4% | 8 | 11.6% | 1 | 6.3% | 8 | 12.3% | 4 | 18.2% | 4 | 21.1% | 3 | 14.3% | 20 | 14.0% |
| Student affairs office | 14 | 28.0% | 30 | 32.3% | 20 | 27.4% | 24 | 34.8% | 5 | 31.3% | 22 | 33.8% | 8 | 36.4% | 5 | 26.3% | 5 | 23.8% | 45 | 31.5% |
| Student success center | 13 | 26.0% | 32 | 34.4% | 18 | 24.7% | 27 | 39.1% | 5 | 31.3% | 21 | 32.3% | 10 | 45.5% | 5 | 26.3% | 4 | 19.0% | 45 | 31.5% |

*Table continues on page 103*

*Table continued from page 102.*

| Survey question/responses | Institutional type | | | | Institution control | | | | Number of undergraduates enrolled | | | | | | | | | | | | Total | |
|---|---|---|---|---|---|---|---|---|---|---|---|---|---|---|---|---|---|---|---|---|---|---|
| | Two-year | | Four-year | | Public | | Private | | Under 1,000 | | 1,000-4,999 | | 5,999-9,999 | | 10,000-19,999 | | 20,000 and above | | | |
| | Freq. | % | Freq | % | Freq. | % | Freq. | % | Freq. | % | Freq. | % | Freq. | % | Freq. | % | Freq. | % | Freq. | % |
| Transfer center | 15 | 30.0% | 8 | 8.6% | 21 | 28.8% | 2 | 2.9% | 1 | 6.3% | 5 | 7.7% | 3 | 13.6% | 5 | 26.3% | 9 | 42.9% | 23 | 16.1% |
| Other, please specify | 4 | 8.0% | 7 | 7.5% | 8 | 11.0% | 3 | 4.3% | 1 | 6.3% | 5 | 7.7% | 1 | 4.5% | 1 | 5.3% | 3 | 14.3% | 11 | 7.7% |
| I don't know | 0 | 0.0% | 0 | 0.0% | 0 | 0.0% | 0 | 0.0% | 0 | 0.0% | 0 | 0.0% | 0 | 0.0% | 0 | 0.0% | 0 | 0.0% | 0 | 0.0% |
| Total | 50 | 100.0% | 93 | 100.0% | 73 | 100.0% | 69 | 100.0% | 16 | 100.0% | 65 | 100.0% | 22 | 100.0% | 19 | 100.0% | 21 | 100.0% | 143 | 100.0% |

Q30. Which of the following organizational structures does your institution offer to coordinate the transfer experience? (Select all that apply).

| Survey question/responses | Two-year | | Four-year | | Public | | Private | | Under 1,000 | | 1,000-4,999 | | 5,999-9,999 | | 10,000-19,999 | | 20,000 and above | | Total | |
|---|---|---|---|---|---|---|---|---|---|---|---|---|---|---|---|---|---|---|---|---|
| | Freq. | % | Freq | % | Freq. | % | Freq. | % | Freq. | % | Freq. | % | Freq. | % | Freq. | % | Freq. | % | Freq. | % |
| Cross-institutional transfer team (e.g., team inclusive of various institutions) | 9 | 18.0% | 16 | 17.2% | 14 | 19.2% | 11 | 15.9% | 1 | 6.3% | 11 | 16.9% | 5 | 22.7% | 2 | 10.5% | 7 | 33.3% | 26 | 18.2% |
| Transfer center/designated space on campus | 16 | 32.0% | 11 | 11.8% | 22 | 30.1% | 5 | 7.2% | 0 | 0.0% | 9 | 13.8% | 5 | 22.7% | 4 | 21.1% | 9 | 42.9% | 27 | 18.9% |
| Transfer curriculum committee | 6 | 12.0% | 4 | 4.3% | 6 | 8.2% | 4 | 5.8% | 1 | 6.3% | 2 | 3.1% | 5 | 22.7% | 0 | 0.0% | 2 | 9.5% | 10 | 7.0% |
| Transfer program committee, task force, or advisory board | 4 | 8.0% | 22 | 23.7% | 11 | 15.1% | 15 | 21.7% | 3 | 18.8% | 9 | 13.8% | 5 | 22.7% | 3 | 15.8% | 6 | 28.6% | 26 | 18.2% |
| Transfer program office (e.g., transfer-year experience program) | 10 | 20.0% | 14 | 15.1% | 13 | 17.8% | 11 | 15.9% | 3 | 18.8% | 9 | 13.8% | 3 | 13.6% | 4 | 21.1% | 6 | 28.6% | 25 | 17.5% |
| Other campuswide transfer coordination, please describe | 6 | 12.0% | 16 | 17.2% | 10 | 13.7% | 12 | 17.4% | 2 | 12.5% | 12 | 18.5% | 1 | 4.5% | 5 | 26.3% | 2 | 9.5% | 22 | 15.4% |
| My institution does not have any organizational structures to coordinate transfer experiences. | 18 | 36.0% | 37 | 39.8% | 26 | 35.6% | 28 | 40.6% | 9 | 56.3% | 27 | 41.5% | 9 | 40.9% | 5 | 26.3% | 4 | 19.0% | 54 | 37.8% |
| Total | 50 | 100.0% | 93 | 100.0% | 73 | 100.0% | 69 | 100.0% | 16 | 100.0% | 65 | 100.0% | 22 | 100.0% | 19 | 100.0% | 21 | 100.0% | 143 | 100.0% |

Q121. Does your institution have a transfer programs office?

| Survey question/responses | Two-year | | Four-year | | Public | | Private | | Under 1,000 | | 1,000-4,999 | | 5,999-9,999 | | 10,000-19,999 | | 20,000 and above | | Total | |
|---|---|---|---|---|---|---|---|---|---|---|---|---|---|---|---|---|---|---|---|---|
| | Freq. | % | Freq | % | Freq. | % | Freq. | % | Freq. | % | Freq. | % | Freq. | % | Freq. | % | Freq. | % | Freq. | % |
| Yes | 22 | 44.0% | 21 | 22.6% | 30 | 41.1% | 13 | 18.8% | 0 | 0.0% | 18 | 27.7% | 7 | 31.8% | 6 | 31.6% | 12 | 57.1% | 43 | 30.1% |
| No | 28 | 56.0% | 71 | 76.3% | 43 | 58.9% | 55 | 79.7% | 16 | 100.0% | 47 | 72.3% | 15 | 68.2% | 12 | 63.2% | 9 | 42.9% | 99 | 69.2% |
| I don't know | 0 | 0.0% | 1 | 1.1% | 0 | 0.0% | 1 | 1.4% | 0 | 0.0% | 0 | 0.0% | 0 | 0.0% | 1 | 5.3% | 0 | 0.0% | 1 | 0.7% |

*Table continues on page 104*

Table continues on page 104

*Table continued from page 103*

| Survey question/responses | Two-year | | Four-year | | Public | | Private | | Under 1,000 | | 1,000-4,999 | | 5,999-9,999 | | 10,000-19,999 | | 20,000 and above | | Total | |
|---|---|---|---|---|---|---|---|---|---|---|---|---|---|---|---|---|---|---|---|---|
| | Freq. | % | Freq | % | Freq. | % | Freq. | % | Freq. | % | Freq. | % | Freq. | % | Freq. | % | Freq. | % | Freq. | % |
| Total | 50 | 100.0% | 93 | 100.0% | 73 | 100.0% | 69 | 100.0% | 16 | 100.0% | 65 | 100.0% | 22 | 100.0% | 19 | 100.0% | 21 | 100.0% | 143 | 100.0% |
| Q31. Which of the following describe the institutional division(s) where transfer-specific services are housed at your institution? (Select all that apply.) | | | | | | | | | | | | | | | | | | | | |
| Academic affairs central office | 6 | 28.6% | 11 | 52.4% | 9 | 31.0% | 8 | 61.5% | 0 | 0.0% | 9 | 52.9% | 2 | 28.6% | 3 | 50.0% | 3 | 25.0% | 17 | 40.5% |
| Academic department(s), please specify | 4 | 19.0% | 1 | 4.8% | 5 | 17.2% | 0 | 0.0% | 0 | 0.0% | 2 | 11.8% | 2 | 28.6% | 0 | 0.0% | 1 | 8.3% | 5 | 11.9% |
| College or school (e.g., College of Liberal Arts) | 0 | 0.0% | 1 | 4.8% | 0 | 0.0% | 1 | 7.7% | 0 | 0.0% | 0 | 0.0% | 1 | 14.3% | 0 | 0.0% | 0 | 0.0% | 1 | 2.4% |
| Enrollment management central office | 3 | 14.3% | 8 | 38.1% | 6 | 20.7% | 5 | 38.5% | 0 | 0.0% | 3 | 17.6% | 3 | 42.9% | 3 | 50.0% | 2 | 16.7% | 11 | 26.2% |
| Student affairs central office | 4 | 19.0% | 7 | 33.3% | 6 | 20.7% | 5 | 38.5% | 0 | 0.0% | 3 | 17.6% | 1 | 14.3% | 2 | 33.3% | 5 | 41.7% | 11 | 26.2% |
| Other, please specify | 7 | 33.3% | 4 | 19.0% | 10 | 34.5% | 1 | 7.7% | 0 | 0.0% | 5 | 29.4% | 1 | 14.3% | 1 | 16.7% | 4 | 33.3% | 11 | 26.2% |
| Total | 21 | 100.0% | 21 | 100.0% | 29 | 100.0% | 13 | 100.0% | 0 | 100.0% | 17 | 100.0% | 7 | 100.0% | 6 | 100.0% | 12 | 100.0% | 42 | 100.0% |
| Q122. Is this position solely dedicated to transfer programs and initiatives on a full-time basis (approximately 40 hours per week), or does it include other duties and responsibilities? | | | | | | | | | | | | | | | | | | | | |
| Yes, the position is solely focused on transfer | 8 | 38.1% | 7 | 33.3% | 13 | 44.8% | 2 | 15.4% | 0 | 0.0% | 2 | 11.8% | 2 | 28.6% | 3 | 50.0% | 8 | 66.7% | 15 | 35.7% |
| No, the position oversees other populations/initiatives, as well | 12 | 57.1% | 12 | 57.1% | 15 | 51.7% | 9 | 69.2% | 0 | 0.0% | 14 | 82.4% | 4 | 57.1% | 2 | 33.3% | 4 | 33.3% | 24 | 57.1% |
| I don't know | 1 | 4.8% | 2 | 9.5% | 1 | 3.4% | 2 | 15.4% | 0 | 0.0% | 1 | 5.9% | 1 | 14.3% | 1 | 16.7% | 0 | 0.0% | 3 | 7.1% |
| Total | 21 | 100.0% | 21 | 100.0% | 29 | 100.0% | 13 | 100.0% | 0 | 100.0% | 17 | 100.0% | 7 | 100.0% | 6 | 100.0% | 12 | 100.0% | 42 | 100.0% |
| Q123. Is the person responsible for transfer programs and initiatives have another position on campus? | | | | | | | | | | | | | | | | | | | | |
| Yes | 6 | 28.6% | 4 | 19.0% | 7 | 24.1% | 3 | 23.1% | 0 | 0.0% | 7 | 41.2% | 1 | 14.3% | 1 | 16.7% | 1 | 8.3% | 10 | 23.8% |
| No | 14 | 66.7% | 15 | 71.4% | 21 | 72.4% | 8 | 84.6% | 0 | 0.0% | 9 | 52.9% | 5 | 71.4% | 4 | 66.7% | 11 | 91.7% | 29 | 69.0% |
| I don't know | 1 | 4.8% | 2 | 9.5% | 1 | 3.4% | 2 | 15.4% | 0 | 0.0% | 1 | 5.9% | 1 | 14.3% | 1 | 16.7% | 0 | 0.0% | 3 | 7.1% |
| Total | 21 | 100.0% | 21 | 100.0% | 29 | 100.0% | 13 | 100.0% | 0 | 100.0% | 17 | 100.0% | 7 | 100.0% | 6 | 100.0% | 12 | 100.0% | 42 | 100.0% |

*Table continues on page 105*

The header spans **Institutional type** (Two-year, Four-year), **Institution control** (Public, Private), and **Number of undergraduates enrolled** (Under 1,000; 1,000-4,999; 5,999-9,999; 10,000-19,999; 20,000 and above), plus **Total**.

Table continued from page 104



| | Institutional type | | | | Institution control | | | | Number of undergraduates enrolled | | | | | | | | | | | | Total | |
|---|---|---|---|---|---|---|---|---|---|---|---|---|---|---|---|---|---|---|---|---|---|---|---|
| | Two-year | | Four-year | | Public | | Private | | Under 1,000 | | 1,000-4,999 | | 5,999-9,999 | | 10,000-19,999 | | 20,000 and above | | | | | |
| Survey question/responses | Freq. | % | Freq | % | Freq. | % | Freq. | % | Freq. | % | Freq. | % | Freq. | % | Freq. | % | Freq. | % | Freq. | % |
| Q125. The other role of the person responsible for transfer programs and initiatives is: (Select all that apply.) | | | | | | | | | | | | | | | | | | | | |
| Academic affairs administrator | 0 | 0.0% | 3 | 75.0% | 1 | 14.3% | 2 | 66.7% | 0 | 0.0% | 2 | 28.6% | 0 | 0.0% | 0 | 0.0% | 1 | 100.0% | 3 | 30.0% |
| Adjunct or part-time faculty member | 1 | 16.7% | 1 | 25.0% | 1 | 14.3% | 1 | 33.3% | 0 | 0.0% | 1 | 14.3% | 1 | 100.0% | 0 | 0.0% | 0 | 0.0% | 2 | 20.0% |
| Full-time or tenure track faculty member | 2 | 33.3% | 0 | 0.0% | 2 | 28.6% | 0 | 0.0% | 0 | 0.0% | 2 | 28.6% | 0 | 0.0% | 0 | 0.0% | 0 | 0.0% | 2 | 20.0% |
| Student affairs staff member | 3 | 50.0% | 2 | 50.0% | 3 | 42.9% | 2 | 66.7% | 0 | 0.0% | 4 | 57.1% | 0 | 0.0% | 0 | 0.0% | 0 | 0.0% | 5 | 50.0% |
| Other, please specify | 2 | 33.3% | 0 | 0.0% | 2 | 28.6% | 0 | 0.0% | 0 | 0.0% | 1 | 14.3% | 0 | 0.0% | 0 | 0.0% | 0 | 0.0% | 2 | 20.0% |
| Total | 6 | 100.0% | 4 | 100.0% | 7 | 100.0% | 3 | 100.0% | 0 | 0.0% | 7 | 100.0% | 1 | 100.0% | 0 | 0.0% | 1 | 100.0% | 10 | 100.0% |
| Q37. Which of the following institution-wide efforts include a specific focus on transfer/transfer-intending students? (Select all that apply.) | | | | | | | | | | | | | | | | | | | | |
| Accreditation (e.g., Action Project or Quality Enhancement Plan focused on transfer/transfer-intending students) | 14 | 28.6% | 19 | 20.7% | 19 | 26.4% | 14 | 20.6% | 4 | 25.0% | 13 | 20.3% | 5 | 23.8% | 5 | 26.3% | 7 | 33.3% | 34 | 24.1% |
| Curricular or gateway course redesign | 25 | 51.0% | 17 | 18.5% | 30 | 41.7% | 12 | 17.6% | 2 | 12.5% | 18 | 28.1% | 9 | 42.9% | 5 | 26.3% | 8 | 38.1% | 42 | 29.8% |
| Employment or job-placement study | 5 | 10.2% | 9 | 9.8% | 7 | 9.7% | 7 | 10.3% | 3 | 18.8% | 2 | 3.1% | 4 | 19.0% | 2 | 10.5% | 4 | 19.0% | 15 | 10.6% |
| Enrollment management (e.g., Admissions, Financial Aid, and/or Registrar) | 21 | 42.9% | 67 | 72.8% | 40 | 55.6% | 48 | 70.6% | 9 | 56.3% | 44 | 68.8% | 10 | 47.6% | 13 | 68.4% | 13 | 61.9% | 89 | 63.1% |
| Graduation study | 11 | 22.4% | 12 | 13.0% | 15 | 20.8% | 8 | 11.0% | 1 | 6.3% | 0 | 12.5% | 5 | 23.8% | 3 | 15.8% | 6 | 28.6% | 23 | 16.3% |
| Grant-funded project | 10 | 20.4% | 11 | 12.0% | 14 | 19.4% | 7 | 10.3% | 2 | 12.5% | 12 | 18.8% | 0 | 0.0% | 2 | 10.5% | 6 | 28.6% | 22 | 15.6% |
| Institutional assessment (i.e., analysis of data collected with a specific focus on transfers, including enrollment data) | 21 | 42.9% | 45 | 48.9% | 35 | 48.6% | 31 | 45.6% | 9 | 56.3% | 26 | 40.6% | 11 | 52.4% | 11 | 57.9% | 10 | 47.6% | 67 | 47.5% |

Table continues on page 106

*Table continued from page 105*

| | Institutional type | | | | Institution control | | | | Number of undergraduates enrolled | | | | | | | | | | | | Total | |
|---|---|---|---|---|---|---|---|---|---|---|---|---|---|---|---|---|---|---|---|---|---|---|
| | Two-year | | Four-year | | Public | | Private | | Under 1,000 | | 1,000-4,999 | | 5,999-9,999 | | 10,000-19,999 | | 20,000 and above | | | |
| Survey question/responses | Freq. | % | Freq | % | Freq. | % | Freq. | % | Freq. | % | Freq. | % | Freq. | % | Freq. | % | Freq. | % | Freq. | % |
| Participation in a national survey (e.g., CCSSE, NSSE, SERU) | 22 | 44.9% | 28 | 30.4% | 29 | 40.3% | 21 | 30.9% | 2 | 12.5% | 25 | 39.1% | 13 | 61.9% | 6 | 31.6% | 4 | 19.0% | 50 | 35.5% |
| Pathways programs | 34 | 69.4% | 21 | 22.8% | 41 | 56.9% | 14 | 20.6% | 3 | 18.8% | 23 | 35.9% | 12 | 57.1% | 11 | 57.9% | 7 | 33.3% | 56 | 39.7% |
| Program self-study (i.e., using a set of professional standards, such as CAS standards, to engage in a self-study of transfer-oriented programs) | 6 | 12.2% | 6 | 6.5% | 9 | 12.5% | 3 | 4.4% | 0 | 0.0% | 9 | 14.4% | 0 | 0.0% | 2 | 10.5% | 1 | 4.8% | 12 | 8.5% |
| Retention study | 10 | 20.4% | 39 | 42.4% | 18 | 25.0% | 31 | 45.6% | 7 | 43.8% | 22 | 34.4% | 7 | 33.3% | 6 | 31.6% | 8 | 38.1% | 50 | 35.5% |
| Strategic planning | 21 | 42.9% | 39 | 42.4% | 32 | 44.4% | 28 | 41.2% | 7 | 43.8% | 23 | 35.9% | 11 | 52.4% | 9 | 47.4% | 11 | 52.4% | 61 | 43.3% |
| Student services programming | 23 | 46.9% | 22 | 23.9% | 29 | 40.3% | 16 | 23.5% | 3 | 18.8% | 22 | 34.4% | 7 | 33.3% | 5 | 26.3% | 9 | 42.9% | 46 | 32.6% |
| Transfer advisory council | 2 | 4.1% | 10 | 10.9% | 5 | 6.9% | 7 | 10.3% | 0 | 0.0% | 4 | 6.3% | 3 | 14.3% | 3 | 15.8% | 2 | 9.5% | 12 | 8.5% |
| Other, please specify | 2 | 4.1% | 5 | 5.4% | 5 | 6.9% | 2 | 2.9% | 0 | 0.0% | 3 | 4.7% | 1 | 4.8% | 1 | 5.3% | 2 | 9.5% | 7 | 5.0% |
| My institution is not engaged in any efforts with a specific focus on transfers/transfer-intending students | 1 | 2.0% | 8 | 8.7% | 0 | 0.0% | 8 | 11.8% | 5 | 31.3% | 2 | 3.1% | 0 | 0.0% | 1 | 5.3% | 0 | 0.0% | 8 | 5.7% |
| Total | 49 | 100.0% | 92 | 100.0% | 72 | 100.0% | 68 | 100.0% | 16 | 100.0% | 64 | 100.0% | 21 | 100.0% | 19 | 100.0% | 21 | 100.0% | 141 | 100.0% |
| Q38. Based on your knowledge, how long have your institution-wide efforts included a concerted focus on transfer/transfer-intending students? | | | | | | | | | | | | | | | | | | | | |
| 1 year or less | 1 | 2.1% | 7 | 8.3% | 2 | 2.8% | 6 | 10.0% | 2 | 18.2% | 4 | 6.5% | 1 | 4.8% | 0 | 0.0% | 1 | 4.8% | 8 | 6.0% |
| 2-5 years | 11 | 22.9% | 32 | 38.1% | 19 | 26.4% | 24 | 40.0% | 4 | 36.4% | 22 | 35.5% | 5 | 23.8% | 8 | 44.4% | 5 | 23.8% | 44 | 33.1% |
| 6-10 years | 10 | 20.8% | 13 | 15.5% | 18 | 25.0% | 5 | 8.3% | 0 | 0.0% | 10 | 16.1% | 5 | 23.8% | 4 | 22.2% | 4 | 19.0% | 23 | 17.3% |
| 11-15 years | 7 | 14.6% | 4 | 4.8% | 7 | 9.7% | 4 | 6.7% | 2 | 18.2% | 6 | 9.7% | 1 | 4.8% | 1 | 5.6% | 1 | 4.8% | 11 | 8.3% |
| 16-20 years | 2 | 4.2% | 4 | 4.8% | 3 | 4.2% | 3 | 5.0% | 0 | 0.0% | 2 | 3.2% | 1 | 4.8% | 0 | 0.0% | 3 | 14.3% | 6 | 4.5% |
| More than 20 years | 5 | 10.4% | 14 | 16.7% | 10 | 13.9% | 9 | 15.0% | 3 | 27.3% | 6 | 9.7% | 2 | 9.5% | 3 | 16.7% | 5 | 23.8% | 19 | 14.3% |

*Table continues on page 107*

Table continued from page 106

| Survey question/responses | Institutional type | | | | Institution control | | | | Number of undergraduates enrolled | | | | | | | | | | | | Total | |
| --- | --- | --- | --- | --- | --- | --- | --- | --- | --- | --- | --- | --- | --- | --- | --- | --- | --- | --- | --- | --- | --- | --- |
| | Two-year | | Four-year | | Public | | Private | | Under 1,000 | | 1,000-4,999 | | 5,999-9,999 | | 10,000-19,999 | | 20,000 and above | | | | | |
| | Freq. | % | Freq | % | Freq. | % | Freq. | % | Freq. | % | Freq. | % | Freq. | % | Freq. | % | Freq. | % | Freq. | % | Freq. | % |
| I don't know | 12 | 25.0% | 10 | 11.9% | 13 | 18.1% | 9 | 15.0% | 0 | 0.0% | 12 | 19.4% | 6 | 28.6% | 2 | 11.1% | 2 | 9.5% | 22 | 16.5% |
| Total | 48 | 100.0% | 84 | 100.0% | 72 | 100.0% | 60 | 100.0% | 11 | 100.0% | 62 | 100.0% | 21 | 100.0% | 18 | 100.0% | 21 | 100.0% | 133 | 100.0% |
| **Q40. Does your institution offer a transfer success or college success skills course (that includes a focus on transfer)?** | | | | | | | | | | | | | | | | | | | | | | |
| Yes | 19 | 31.7% | 23 | 25.3% | 26 | 36.6% | 16 | 23.9% | 4 | 25.0% | 18 | 28.6% | 7 | 33.3% | 5 | 26.3% | 9 | 45.0% | 43 | 30.9% |
| No | 28 | 46.7% | 65 | 71.4% | 44 | 62.0% | 48 | 71.6% | 12 | 75.0% | 44 | 69.8% | 13 | 61.9% | 13 | 68.4% | 10 | 50.0% | 92 | 66.2% |
| I don't know | 1 | 1.7% | 3 | 3.3% | 1 | 1.4% | 3 | 4.5% | 0 | 0.0% | 1 | 1.6% | 1 | 4.8% | 1 | 5.3% | 1 | 5.0% | 4 | 2.9% |
| Total | 48 | 100.0% | 91 | 100.0% | 71 | 100.0% | 67 | 100.0% | 16 | 100.0% | 63 | 100.0% | 21 | 100.0% | 19 | 100.0% | 20 | 100.0% | 139 | 100.0% |
| **Q42. Approximately how many years has your institution offered a transfer or college success skills course?** | | | | | | | | | | | | | | | | | | | | | | |
| 2 year or less | 0 | 0.0% | 4 | 17.4% | 1 | 3.8% | 3 | 18.8% | 0 | 0.0% | 1 | 5.6% | 2 | 28.6% | 0 | 0.0% | 1 | 11.1% | 4 | 9.3% |
| 3-5 years | 6 | 31.6% | 7 | 30.4% | 7 | 26.9% | 6 | 37.5% | 1 | 25.0% | 8 | 44.4% | 1 | 14.3% | 3 | 60.0% | 1 | 11.1% | 14 | 32.6% |
| 6-10 years | 7 | 36.8% | 4 | 17.4% | 7 | 26.9% | 4 | 25.0% | 2 | 50.0% | 5 | 27.8% | 1 | 14.3% | 1 | 20.0% | 2 | 22.2% | 11 | 25.6% |
| 11-15 years | 3 | 15.8% | 2 | 8.7% | 4 | 15.4% | 1 | 6.3% | 1 | 25.0% | 2 | 11.1% | 1 | 14.3% | 0 | 0.0% | 1 | 11.1% | 5 | 11.6% |
| 16-20 years | 0 | 0.0% | 1 | 4.3% | 1 | 3.8% | 0 | 0.0% | 0 | 0.0% | 0 | 0.0% | 0 | 0.0% | 1 | 20.0% | 0 | 0.0% | 1 | 2.3% |
| More than 20 years | 3 | 15.8% | 2 | 8.7% | 4 | 15.4% | 1 | 6.3% | 0 | 0.0% | 1 | 5.6% | 2 | 28.6% | 0 | 0.0% | 2 | 22.2% | 5 | 11.6% |
| I don't know | 0 | 0.0% | 3 | 13.0% | 2 | 7.7% | 1 | 6.3% | 0 | 0.0% | 1 | 5.6% | 0 | 0.0% | 0 | 0.0% | 2 | 22.2% | 3 | 7.0% |
| Total | 19 | 100.0% | 23 | 100.0% | 26 | 100.0% | 16 | 100.0% | 4 | 100.0% | 18 | 100.0% | 7 | 100.0% | 5 | 100.0% | 9 | 100.0% | 43 | 100.0% |
| **Q128. Are transfer/transfer-intending students required to take a transfer or college success skills course at your institution?** | | | | | | | | | | | | | | | | | | | | | | |
| Yes, transfer/transfer-intending students are required to take a course at my institution | 11 | 57.9% | 6 | 27.3% | 11 | 42.3% | 6 | 40.0% | 2 | 50.0% | 11 | 64.7% | 2 | 28.6% | 1 | 20.0% | 1 | 11.1% | 17 | 40.5% |

Table continues on page 108

*Table continued from page 107*

| Survey question/responses | Institutional type | | | | Institution control | | | | Number of undergraduates enrolled | | | | | | | | | | | | Total | |
|---|---|---|---|---|---|---|---|---|---|---|---|---|---|---|---|---|---|---|---|---|---|---|
| | Two-year | | Four-year | | Public | | Private | | Under 1,000 | | 1,000-4,999 | | 5,999-9,999 | | 10,000-19,999 | | 20,000 and above | | | |
| | Freq. | % | Freq | % | Freq. | % | Freq. | % | Freq. | % | Freq. | % | Freq. | % | Freq. | % | Freq. | % | Freq. | % |
| No, transfer/transfer-intending students are not required to take a course at my institution | 5 | 26.3% | 12 | 54.5% | 11 | 42.3% | 6 | 40.0% | 1 | 25.0% | 4 | 23.5% | 3 | 42.9% | 3 | 60.0% | 6 | 66.7% | 17 | 40.5% |
| Other, please specify | 3 | 15.8% | 3 | 13.6% | 4 | 15.4% | 2 | 13.3% | 1 | 25.0% | 2 | 11.8% | 1 | 14.3% | 1 | 20.0% | 2 | 22.2% | 7 | 16.7% |
| I don't know | 0 | 0.0% | 1 | 4.5% | 0 | 0.0% | 1 | 6.7% | 0 | 0.0% | 0 | 0.0% | 1 | 14.3% | 0 | 0.0% | 0 | 0.0% | 1 | 2.4% |
| Total | 19 | 100.0% | 22 | 100.0% | 26 | 100.0% | 15 | 100.0% | 4 | 100.0% | 17 | 100.0% | 7 | 100.0% | 5 | 100.0% | 9 | 100.0% | 42 | 100.0% |

Q141. Which transfer/transfer-intending students, by category, are not required to take a transfer or college success skills course at your institution? (Select all that apply.)

| Survey question/responses | Two-year | | Four-year | | Public | | Private | | Under 1,000 | | 1,000-4,999 | | 5,999-9,999 | | 10,000-19,999 | | 20,000 and above | | Total | |
|---|---|---|---|---|---|---|---|---|---|---|---|---|---|---|---|---|---|---|---|---|
| | Freq. | % | Freq | % | Freq. | % | Freq. | % | Freq. | % | Freq. | % | Freq. | % | Freq. | % | Freq. | % | Freq. | % |
| All transfer/transfer-intending students are required to participate | 9 | 47.4% | 6 | 26.1% | 11 | 42.3% | 4 | 25.0% | 1 | 25.0% | 8 | 44.4% | 3 | 42.9% | 0 | 0.0% | 3 | 33.3% | 15 | 34.9% |
| Anyone not interested in participating | 4 | 21.1% | 9 | 39.1% | 9 | 34.6% | 4 | 25.0% | 0 | 0.0% | 3 | 16.7% | 3 | 42.9% | 2 | 40.0% | 5 | 55.6% | 13 | 30.2% |
| Adult learners | 1 | 5.3% | 5 | 21.7% | 4 | 15.4% | 2 | 12.5% | 1 | 25.0% | 1 | 5.6% | 1 | 14.3% | 0 | 0.0% | 3 | 33.3% | 6 | 14.0% |
| Formerly or currently incarcerated students | 1 | 5.3% | 3 | 13.0% | 4 | 15.4% | 0 | 0.0% | 0 | 0.0% | 0 | 0.0% | 1 | 14.3% | 0 | 0.0% | 3 | 33.3% | 4 | 9.3% |
| Full-time students | 1 | 5.3% | 4 | 17.4% | 4 | 15.4% | 1 | 6.3% | 0 | 0.0% | 1 | 5.6% | 1 | 14.3% | 0 | 0.0% | 3 | 33.3% | 5 | 11.6% |
| Honors students | 1 | 5.3% | 3 | 13.0% | 4 | 15.4% | 0 | 0.0% | 0 | 0.0% | 0 | 0.0% | 1 | 14.3% | 0 | 0.0% | 3 | 33.3% | 4 | 9.3% |
| Institutionally-deemed academically underprepared students (e.g., students enrolled in developmental or remedial courses) | 0 | 0.0% | 4 | 17.4% | 3 | 11.5% | 1 | 6.3% | 1 | 25.0% | 0 | 0.0% | 0 | 0.0% | 0 | 0.0% | 3 | 33.3% | 4 | 9.3% |
| International students | 1 | 5.3% | 4 | 17.4% | 4 | 15.4% | 1 | 6.3% | 0 | 0.0% | 0 | 0.0% | 2 | 28.6% | 0 | 0.0% | 3 | 33.3% | 5 | 11.6% |
| Learning community participants | 2 | 10.5% | 3 | 13.0% | 5 | 19.2% | 0 | 0.0% | 0 | 0.0% | 0 | 0.0% | 1 | 14.3% | 1 | 20.0% | 3 | 33.3% | 5 | 11.6% |
| Non-degree students | 6 | 31.6% | 5 | 21.7% | 9 | 34.6% | 2 | 12.5% | 2 | 50.0% | 4 | 22.2% | 1 | 14.3% | 1 | 20.0% | 4 | 44.4% | 12 | 27.9% |
| Online students | 1 | 5.3% | 4 | 17.4% | 4 | 15.4% | 1 | 6.3% | 0 | 0.0% | 1 | 5.6% | 1 | 14.3% | 0 | 0.0% | 3 | 33.3% | 5 | 11.6% |

*Table continues on page 109*

Table continued from page 108



| Survey question/responses | Institutional type | | | | Institution control | | | | Number of undergraduates enrolled | | | | | | | | | | | | Total | |
|---|---|---|---|---|---|---|---|---|---|---|---|---|---|---|---|---|---|---|---|---|---|---|
| | Two-year | | Four-year | | Public | | Private | | Under 1,000 | | 1,000-4,999 | | 5,999-9,999 | | 10,000-19,999 | | 20,000 and above | | | | | |
| | Freq. | % | Freq | % | Freq. | % | Freq. | % | Freq. | % | Freq. | % | Freq. | % | Freq. | % | Freq. | % | Freq. | % | | |
| Part-time students | 1 | 5.3% | 6 | 26.1% | 4 | 15.4% | 3 | 18.8% | 0 | 0.0% | 4 | 22.2% | 0 | 0.0% | 0 | 0.0% | 3 | 33.3% | 7 | 16.3% | | |
| Preprofessional students (e.g., pre-law, pre-med) | 0 | 0.0% | 4 | 17.4% | 3 | 11.5% | 1 | 6.3% | 0 | 0.0% | 1 | 5.6% | 0 | 0.0% | 0 | 0.0% | 3 | 33.3% | 4 | 9.3% | | |
| Reentry students | 3 | 15.8% | 5 | 21.7% | 6 | 23.1% | 2 | 12.5% | 2 | 50.0% | 3 | 16.7% | 1 | 14.3% | 0 | 0.0% | 3 | 33.3% | 9 | 20.9% | | |
| Student athletes | 1 | 5.3% | 4 | 17.4% | 4 | 15.4% | 1 | 6.3% | 0 | 0.0% | 1 | 5.6% | 1 | 14.3% | 0 | 0.0% | 3 | 33.3% | 5 | 11.6% | | |
| Students caring for dependents | 1 | 5.3% | 3 | 13.0% | 4 | 15.4% | 0 | 0.0% | 0 | 0.0% | 0 | 0.0% | 1 | 14.3% | 0 | 0.0% | 3 | 33.3% | 4 | 9.3% | | |
| Students on probationary status | 1 | 5.3% | 4 | 17.4% | 4 | 15.4% | 1 | 6.3% | 1 | 25.0% | 0 | 0.0% | 1 | 14.3% | 0 | 0.0% | 3 | 33.3% | 5 | 11.6% | | |
| Students residing within a particular residence hall | 1 | 5.3% | 3 | 13.0% | 4 | 15.4% | 0 | 0.0% | 0 | 0.0% | 0 | 0.0% | 1 | 14.3% | 0 | 0.0% | 3 | 33.3% | 4 | 9.3% | | |
| Students within specific majors, please list: | 2 | 10.5% | 4 | 17.4% | 5 | 19.2% | 1 | 6.3% | 0 | 0.0% | 2 | 11.1% | 1 | 14.3% | 0 | 0.0% | 3 | 33.3% | 6 | 14.0% | | |
| TRIO participants | 1 | 5.3% | 2 | 8.7% | 3 | 11.5% | 0 | 0.0% | 0 | 0.0% | 0 | 0.0% | 1 | 14.3% | 0 | 0.0% | 2 | 22.2% | 3 | 7.0% | | |
| Undeclared students | 2 | 10.5% | 3 | 13.0% | 5 | 19.2% | 0 | 0.0% | 0 | 0.0% | 0 | 0.0% | 1 | 14.3% | 1 | 20.0% | 3 | 33.3% | 5 | 11.6% | | |
| Veterans | 1 | 5.3% | 3 | 13.0% | 4 | 15.4% | 0 | 0.0% | 0 | 0.0% | 0 | 0.0% | 1 | 14.3% | 0 | 0.0% | 3 | 33.3% | 4 | 9.3% | | |
| Visiting students | 5 | 26.3% | 5 | 21.7% | 8 | 30.8% | 2 | 12.5% | 2 | 50.0% | 3 | 16.7% | 1 | 14.3% | 1 | 20.0% | 4 | 44.4% | 11 | 25.6% | | |
| Other, please specify | 2 | 10.5% | 4 | 17.4% | 3 | 11.5% | 3 | 18.8% | 2 | 50.0% | 1 | 5.6% | 1 | 14.3% | 1 | 20.0% | 2 | 22.2% | 7 | 16.3% | | |
| I don't know | 1 | 5.3% | 2 | 8.7% | 2 | 7.7% | 1 | 6.3% | 0 | 0.0% | 0 | 0.0% | 1 | 14.3% | 1 | 20.0% | 1 | 11.1% | 3 | 7.0% | | |
| Total | 19 | 100.0% | 23 | 100.0% | 26 | 100.0% | 16 | 100.0% | 4 | 100.0% | 18 | 100.0% | 21 | 100.0% | 5 | 100.0% | 9 | 100.0% | 126 | 100.0% | | |
| Q43. What is the approximate percentage of transfer/transfer intending students who take a transfer or college success skills course at your institution? | | | | | | | | | | | | | | | | | | | | | | |
| Less than 10% | 0 | 0.0% | 7 | 30.4% | 4 | 15.4% | 3 | 18.8% | 1 | 25.0% | 0 | 0.0% | 2 | 28.6% | 1 | 20.0% | 3 | 33.3% | 7 | 16.3% | | |
| 10-19% | 1 | 5.3% | 1 | 4.3% | 1 | 3.8% | 1 | 6.3% | 0 | 0.0% | 0 | 0.0% | 1 | 14.3% | 1 | 20.0% | 0 | 0.0% | 2 | 4.7% | | |
| 20-29% | 1 | 5.3% | 2 | 8.7% | 3 | 11.5% | 0 | 0.0% | 0 | 0.0% | 0 | 0.0% | 1 | 14.3% | 0 | 0.0% | 2 | 22.2% | 3 | 7.0% | | |

Table continues on page 110

*Table continued from page 109*

| Survey question/responses | Institutional type | | | | Institution control | | | | Number of undergraduates enrolled | | | | | | | | | | | | Total | |
|---|---|---|---|---|---|---|---|---|---|---|---|---|---|---|---|---|---|---|---|---|---|---|
| | Two-year | | Four-year | | Public | | Private | | Under 1,000 | | 1,000-4,999 | | 5,999-9,999 | | 10,000-19,999 | | 20,000 and above | | | |
| | Freq. | % | Freq | % | Freq. | % | Freq. | % | Freq. | % | Freq. | % | Freq. | % | Freq. | % | Freq. | % | Freq. | % |
| 30-39% | 1 | 5.3% | 0 | 0.0% | 1 | 3.8% | 0 | 0.0% | 0 | 0.0% | 0 | 0.0% | 0 | 0.0% | 0 | 0.0% | 1 | 11.1% | 1 | 2.3% |
| 40-49% | 0 | 0.0% | 0 | 0.0% | 0 | 0.0% | 0 | 0.0% | 0 | 0.0% | 0 | 0.0% | 0 | 0.0% | 0 | 0.0% | 0 | 0.0% | 2 | 4.7% |
| 50-59% | 2 | 10.5% | 0 | 0.0% | 2 | 7.7% | 0 | 0.0% | 0 | 0.0% | 2 | 11.1% | 0 | 0.0% | 0 | 0.0% | 0 | 0.0% | 3 | 7.0% |
| 60-69% | 0 | 0.0% | 0 | 0.0% | 0 | 0.0% | 0 | 0.0% | 0 | 0.0% | 0 | 0.0% | 0 | 0.0% | 0 | 0.0% | 0 | 0.0% | 0 | 0.0% |
| 70-79% | 2 | 10.5% | 1 | 4.3% | 2 | 7.7% | 1 | 6.3% | 1 | 25.0% | 1 | 5.6% | 0 | 0.0% | 1 | 20.0% | 0 | 0.0% | 3 | 7.0% |
| 80-89% | 1 | 5.3% | 2 | 8.7% | 1 | 3.8% | 2 | 12.5% | 1 | 25.0% | 2 | 11.1% | 1 | 14.3% | 0 | 0.0% | 0 | 0.0% | 4 | 9.3% |
| 90-99% | 4 | 21.1% | 4 | 17.4% | 4 | 15.4% | 4 | 25.0% | 0 | 0.0% | 7 | 38.9% | 0 | 0.0% | 0 | 0.0% | 1 | 11.1% | 8 | 18.6% |
| 100% | 3 | 15.8% | 3 | 13.0% | 3 | 11.5% | 3 | 18.8% | 1 | 25.0% | 4 | 22.2% | 1 | 14.3% | 0 | 0.0% | 0 | 0.0% | 6 | 14.0% |
| I don't know | 4 | 21.1% | 3 | 13.0% | 5 | 19.2% | 2 | 12.5% | 0 | 0.0% | 2 | 11.1% | 1 | 14.3% | 2 | 40.0% | 2 | 22.2% | 7 | 16.3% |
| Total | 19 | 100.0% | 23 | 100.0% | 26 | 100.0% | 16 | 100.0% | 4 | 100.0% | 18 | 100.0% | 21 | 100.0% | 5 | 100.0% | 9 | 100.0% | 43 | 100.0% |
| Q44. What is the duration of the transfer or college success skills course? (Select all that apply.) | | | | | | | | | | | | | | | | | | | | |
| Half a term | 11 | 57.9% | 1 | 4.3% | 11 | 42.3% | 1 | 6.3% | 0 | 0.0% | 7 | 38.9% | 2 | 28.6% | 2 | 40.0% | 1 | 11.1% | 12 | 27.9% |
| One quarter | 1 | 5.3% | 3 | 13.0% | 3 | 11.5% | 1 | 6.3% | 0 | 0.0% | 1 | 5.6% | 0 | 0.0% | 1 | 20.0% | 2 | 22.2% | 4 | 9.3% |
| One semester | 9 | 47.4% | 17 | 73.9% | 14 | 53.8% | 12 | 75.0% | 3 | 75.0% | 10 | 55.6% | 5 | 71.4% | 2 | 40.0% | 7 | 77.8% | 27 | 62.8% |
| One year | 0 | 0.0% | 0 | 0.0% | 0 | 0.0% | 0 | 0.0% | 0 | 0.0% | 0 | 0.0% | 0 | 0.0% | 0 | 0.0% | 0 | 0.0% | 0 | 0.0% |
| Other, please specify | 1 | 5.3% | 2 | 8.7% | 1 | 3.8% | 2 | 12.5% | 1 | 25.0% | 1 | 5.6% | 0 | 0.0% | 1 | 20.0% | 0 | 0.0% | 3 | 7.0% |
| I don't know | 0 | 0.0% | 0 | 0.0% | 0 | 0.0% | 0 | 0.0% | 0 | 0.0% | 0 | 0.0% | 0 | 0.0% | 0 | 0.0% | 0 | 0.0% | 0 | 0.0% |
| Total | 19 | 100.0% | 23 | 100.0% | 26 | 100.0% | 16 | 100.0% | 4 | 100.0% | 18 | 100.0% | 7 | 100.0% | 5 | 100.0% | 9 | 100.0% | 43 | 100.0% |
| Q45. How many credits does the transfer or college success skills course carry? | | | | | | | | | | | | | | | | | | | | |
| None | 0 | 0.0% | 2 | 8.7% | 1 | 3.8% | 1 | 6.3% | 0 | 0.0% | 1 | 5.6% | 0 | 0.0% | 0 | 0.0% | 1 | 11.1% | 2 | 4.7% |
| 1 credit | 12 | 63.2% | 12 | 52.2% | 17 | 65.4% | 7 | 43.8% | 1 | 25.0% | 10 | 55.6% | 5 | 71.4% | 4 | 80.0% | 5 | 55.6% | 25 | 58.1% |

*Table continues on page 111*

*Table continued from page 110*

| Survey question/responses | Institutional type | | | | Institution control | | | | Number of undergraduates enrolled | | | | | | | | | | | | Total | |
|---|---|---|---|---|---|---|---|---|---|---|---|---|---|---|---|---|---|---|---|---|---|---|
| | Two-year | | Four-year | | Public | | Private | | Under 1,000 | | 1,000-4,999 | | 5,999-9,999 | | 10,000-19,999 | | 20,000 and above | | | | | |
| | Freq. | % | Freq | % | Freq. | % | Freq. | % | Freq. | % | Freq. | % | Freq. | % | Freq. | % | Freq. | % | Freq. | % | | |
| 2 credits | 1 | 5.3% | 4 | 17.4% | 1 | 3.8% | 4 | 25.0% | 1 | 25.0% | 4 | 22.2% | 0 | 0.0% | 0 | 0.0% | 0 | 0.0% | 5 | 11.6% | | |
| 3 credits | 6 | 31.6% | 4 | 17.4% | 7 | 26.9% | 3 | 18.8% | 1 | 25.0% | 3 | 16.7% | 2 | 28.6% | 1 | 20.0% | 3 | 33.3% | 10 | 23.3% | | |
| 4 credits | 0 | 0.0% | 1 | 4.3% | 0 | 0.0% | 1 | 6.3% | 1 | 25.0% | 0 | 0.0% | 0 | 0.0% | 0 | 0.0% | 0 | 0.0% | 1 | 2.3% | | |
| 5 credits | 0 | 0.0% | 0 | 0.0% | 0 | 0.0% | 0 | 0.0% | 0 | 0.0% | 0 | 0.0% | 0 | 0.0% | 0 | 0.0% | 0 | 0.0% | 0 | 0.0% | | |
| 6 or more credits | 0 | 0.0% | 0 | 0.0% | 0 | 0.0% | 0 | 0.0% | 0 | 0.0% | 0 | 0.0% | 0 | 0.0% | 0 | 0.0% | 0 | 0.0% | 0 | 0.0% | | |
| I don't know | 0 | 0.0% | 0 | 0.0% | 0 | 0.0% | 0 | 0.0% | 0 | 0.0% | 0 | 0.0% | 0 | 0.0% | 0 | 0.0% | 0 | 0.0% | 0 | 0.0% | | |
| Total | 19 | 100.0% | 23 | 100.0% | 26 | 100.0% | 16 | 100.0% | 4 | 100.0% | 18 | 100.0% | 7 | 100.0% | 5 | 100.0% | 9 | 100.0% | 43 | 100.0% | | |
| Q46. How is the transfer or college success skills course credit applied? (Select all that apply.) | | | | | | | | | | | | | | | | | | | | | | |
| As an elective | 8 | 42.1% | 11 | 47.8% | 13 | 50.0% | 6 | 37.5% | 1 | 25.0% | 4 | 22.2% | 5 | 71.4% | 3 | 60.0% | 6 | 66.7% | 19 | 44.2% | | |
| Toward general education requirements | 9 | 47.4% | 10 | 43.5% | 10 | 38.5% | 9 | 56.3% | 3 | 75.0% | 11 | 61.1% | 2 | 28.6% | 2 | 40.0% | 2 | 22.2% | 20 | 46.5% | | |
| Toward major requirements | 2 | 10.5% | 0 | 0.0% | 2 | 7.7% | 0 | 0.0% | 0 | 0.0% | 1 | 5.6% | 1 | 14.3% | 0 | 0.0% | 0 | 0.0% | 2 | 4.7% | | |
| Other, please specify | 2 | 10.5% | 5 | 21.7% | 3 | 11.5% | 4 | 25.0% | 0 | 0.0% | 5 | 27.8% | 1 | 14.3% | 0 | 0.0% | 1 | 11.1% | 7 | 16.3% | | |
| I don't know | 0 | 0.0% | 0 | 0.0% | 0 | 0.0% | 0 | 0.0% | 0 | 0.0% | 0 | 0.0% | 0 | 0.0% | 0 | 0.0% | 0 | 0.0% | 0 | 0.0% | | |
| Total | 19 | 100.0% | 23 | 100.0% | 26 | 100.0% | 16 | 100.0% | 4 | 100.0% | 18 | 100.0% | 7 | 100.0% | 5 | 100.0% | 9 | 100.0% | 43 | 100.0% | | |
| Q129. Can students apply financial aid toward the tuition and fees associated with the transfer or college success skills course? | | | | | | | | | | | | | | | | | | | | | | |
| Yes | 19 | 100.0% | 20 | 90.9% | 24 | 96.0% | 15 | 93.8% | 4 | 100.0% | 17 | 94.4% | 7 | 100.0% | 5 | 100.0% | 7 | 87.5% | 40 | 95.2% | | |
| No | 0 | 0.0% | 1 | 4.5% | 0 | 0.0% | 1 | 6.3% | 0 | 0.0% | 1 | 5.6% | 0 | 0.0% | 0 | 0.0% | 0 | 0.0% | 1 | 2.4% | | |
| I don't know | 0 | 0.0% | 1 | 4.5% | 1 | 4.0% | 0 | 0.0% | 0 | 0.0% | 0 | 0.0% | 0 | 0.0% | 0 | 0.0% | 1 | 11.1% | 1 | 2.4% | | |
| Total | 19 | 100.0% | 22 | 100.0% | 25 | 100.0% | 16 | 100.0% | 4 | 100.0% | 18 | 100.0% | 7 | 100.0% | 5 | 100.0% | 8 | 100.0% | 42 | 100.0% | | |
| Q47. Select the five most important course objectives for the transfer or college success skills course: | | | | | | | | | | | | | | | | | | | | | | |
| Academic planning | 13 | 68.4% | 10 | 43.5% | 15 | 57.7% | 8 | 50.0% | 1 | 25.0% | 13 | 72.2% | 5 | 71.4% | 2 | 40.0% | 3 | 33.3% | 24 | 55.8% | | |

*Table continues on page 112*

*Table continued from page 111*

| Survey question/responses | Institutional type | | | | Institution control | | | | Number of undergraduates enrolled | | | | | | | | | | Total | |
|---|---|---|---|---|---|---|---|---|---|---|---|---|---|---|---|---|---|---|---|---|
| | Two-year | | Four-year | | Public | | Private | | Under 1,000 | | 1,000-4,999 | | 5,999-9,999 | | 10,000-19,999 | | 20,000 and above | | | |
| | Freq. | % | Freq | % | Freq. | % | Freq. | % | Freq. | % | Freq. | % | Freq. | % | Freq. | % | Freq. | % | Freq. | % |
| Academic success strategies | 16 | 84.2% | 15 | 65.2% | 22 | 84.6% | 9 | 56.3% | 3 | 75.0% | 11 | 61.1% | 5 | 71.4% | 0 | 0.0% | 8 | 88.9% | 32 | 74.4% |
| Analytical, critical-thinking, or problem-solving skills | 2 | 10.5% | 5 | 21.7% | 3 | 11.5% | 4 | 25.0% | 1 | 25.0% | 5 | 27.8% | 0 | 0.0% | 0 | 0.0% | 1 | 11.1% | 7 | 16.3% |
| Career exploration and/or preparation | 13 | 68.4% | 7 | 30.4% | 17 | 65.4% | 3 | 18.8% | 0 | 0.0% | 10 | 55.6% | 3 | 42.9% | 2 | 40.0% | 5 | 55.6% | 20 | 46.5% |
| Civic engagement | 0 | 0.0% | 1 | 4.3% | 0 | 0.0% | 1 | 6.3% | 0 | 0.0% | 0 | 0.0% | 1 | 14.3% | 0 | 0.0% | 0 | 0.0% | 1 | 2.3% |
| Common transfer-year experience | 1 | 5.3% | 4 | 17.4% | 2 | 7.7% | 3 | 18.8% | 2 | 50.0% | 2 | 11.1% | 1 | 14.3% | 0 | 0.0% | 1 | 11.1% | 6 | 14.0% |
| Connection with the institution or campus | 4 | 21.1% | 8 | 34.8% | 5 | 19.2% | 7 | 43.8% | 0 | 0.0% | 7 | 38.9% | 3 | 42.9% | 0 | 0.0% | 2 | 22.2% | 12 | 27.9% |
| Developmental education, remediation, and/or review | 0 | 0.0% | 0 | 0.0% | 0 | 0.0% | 0 | 0.0% | 0 | 0.0% | 0 | 0.0% | 0 | 0.0% | 0 | 0.0% | 0 | 0.0% | 0 | 0.0% |
| Digital literacy | 0 | 0.0% | 0 | 0.0% | 0 | 0.0% | 0 | 0.0% | 0 | 0.0% | 0 | 0.0% | 0 | 0.0% | 0 | 0.0% | 0 | 0.0% | 0 | 0.0% |
| Discipline-specific knowledge | 0 | 0.0% | 0 | 0.0% | 0 | 0.0% | 0 | 0.0% | 0 | 0.0% | 0 | 0.0% | 0 | 0.0% | 0 | 0.0% | 0 | 0.0% | 0 | 0.0% |
| Financial literacy | 4 | 21.1% | 1 | 4.3% | 5 | 19.2% | 0 | 0.0% | 0 | 0.0% | 3 | 16.7% | 0 | 0.0% | 1 | 20.0% | 1 | 11.1% | 5 | 11.6% |
| Gateway course completion | 0 | 0.0% | 0 | 0.0% | 0 | 0.0% | 0 | 0.0% | 0 | 0.0% | 0 | 0.0% | 0 | 0.0% | 0 | 0.0% | 0 | 0.0% | 0 | 0.0% |
| Graduate or professional school preparation (e.g., pre-med, pre-law) | 0 | 0.0% | 0 | 0.0% | 0 | 0.0% | 0 | 0.0% | 0 | 0.0% | 0 | 0.0% | 0 | 0.0% | 0 | 0.0% | 0 | 0.0% | 0 | 0.0% |
| Health and wellness | 1 | 5.3% | 0 | 0.0% | 1 | 3.8% | 0 | 0.0% | 0 | 0.0% | 0 | 0.0% | 0 | 0.0% | 1 | 20.0% | 0 | 0.0% | 1 | 2.3% |
| Information literacy | 1 | 5.3% | 0 | 0.0% | 1 | 3.8% | 0 | 0.0% | 0 | 0.0% | 0 | 0.0% | 0 | 0.0% | 0 | 0.0% | 1 | 11.1% | 1 | 2.3% |
| Integrative and applied learning | 0 | 0.0% | 1 | 4.3% | 0 | 0.0% | 1 | 6.3% | 1 | 25.0% | 0 | 0.0% | 0 | 0.0% | 0 | 0.0% | 0 | 0.0% | 1 | 2.3% |
| Intercultural competence, diversity skills, or engaging with different perspectives | 3 | 15.8% | 5 | 21.7% | 4 | 15.4% | 4 | 25.0% | 1 | 25.0% | 4 | 22.2% | 2 | 28.6% | 1 | 20.0% | 0 | 0.0% | 8 | 18.6% |

*Table continues on page 113*

*Table continued from page 112*

| Survey question/responses | Institutional type | | | | Institution control | | | | Number of undergraduates enrolled | | | | | | | | | | | | Total | |
|---|---|---|---|---|---|---|---|---|---|---|---|---|---|---|---|---|---|---|---|---|---|---|
| | Two-year | | Four-year | | Public | | Private | | Under 1,000 | | 1,000-4,999 | | 5,999-9,999 | | 10,000-19,999 | | 20,000 and above | | | | | |
| | Freq. | % | Freq | % | Freq. | % | Freq. | % | Freq. | % | Freq. | % | Freq. | % | Freq. | % | Freq. | % | Freq. | % | | |
| Introduction to a major, discipline, or career path | 7 | 36.8% | 5 | 21.7% | 8 | 30.8% | 4 | 25.0% | 0 | 0.0% | 4 | 22.2% | 5 | 71.4% | 2 | 40.0% | 1 | 11.1% | 12 | 27.9% | | |
| Introduction to institutional-specific academic expectations | 1 | 5.3% | 5 | 21.7% | 2 | 7.7% | 4 | 25.0% | 2 | 50.0% | 2 | 11.1% | 1 | 14.3% | 0 | 0.0% | 1 | 11.1% | 6 | 14.0% | | |
| Introduction to the liberal arts | 0 | 0.0% | 1 | 4.3% | 0 | 0.0% | 1 | 6.3% | 1 | 25.0% | 0 | 0.0% | 1 | 14.3% | 0 | 0.0% | 0 | 0.0% | 2 | 4.7% | | |
| Knowledge of institution or campus resources and services | 11 | 57.9% | 12 | 52.2% | 16 | 61.5% | 7 | 43.8% | 2 | 50.0% | 9 | 50.0% | 4 | 57.1% | 2 | 40.0% | 7 | 77.8% | 24 | 55.8% | | |
| Major exploration | 5 | 26.3% | 1 | 4.3% | 6 | 23.1% | 0 | 0.0% | 0 | 0.0% | 2 | 11.1% | 0 | 0.0% | 2 | 40.0% | 2 | 22.2% | 6 | 14.0% | | |
| On-time graduation rates (i.e., 4-year or 6-year graduation rate for transfers) | 0 | 0.0% | 3 | 13.0% | 1 | 3.8% | 2 | 12.5% | 1 | 25.0% | 1 | 5.6% | 0 | 0.0% | 0 | 0.0% | 1 | 11.1% | 3 | 7.0% | | |
| Oral communication skills | 1 | 5.3% | 2 | 8.7% | 1 | 3.8% | 2 | 12.5% | 1 | 25.0% | 0 | 0.0% | 0 | 0.0% | 1 | 20.0% | 1 | 11.1% | 3 | 7.0% | | |
| Persistence of transfer students | 2 | 10.5% | 5 | 21.7% | 2 | 7.7% | 5 | 31.3% | 1 | 25.0% | 4 | 22.2% | 0 | 0.0% | 1 | 20.0% | 0 | 0.0% | 7 | 16.3% | | |
| Personal exploration or development | 2 | 10.5% | 3 | 13.0% | 2 | 7.7% | 3 | 18.8% | 1 | 25.0% | 3 | 16.7% | 0 | 0.0% | 1 | 20.0% | 0 | 0.0% | 5 | 11.6% | | |
| Project planning, teamwork, or management skills | 2 | 10.5% | 1 | 4.3% | 2 | 7.7% | 1 | 6.3% | 0 | 0.0% | 0 | 0.0% | 0 | 0.0% | 2 | 40.0% | 1 | 11.1% | 3 | 7.0% | | |
| Retention of transfer students | 0 | 0.0% | 9 | 39.1% | 2 | 7.7% | 16 | 100.0% | 2 | 50.0% | 4 | 22.2% | 1 | 14.3% | 0 | 0.0% | 2 | 22.2% | 9 | 20.9% | | |
| Social support networks (e.g., peer connections and friendships) | 1 | 5.3% | 6 | 26.1% | 5 | 19.2% | 7 | 43.8% | 0 | 0.0% | 2 | 11.1% | 1 | 14.3% | 0 | 0.0% | 4 | 44.4% | 7 | 16.3% | | |
| Student-faculty interaction | 3 | 15.8% | 1 | 4.3% | 3 | 11.5% | 2 | 12.5% | 0 | 0.0% | 3 | 16.7% | 1 | 14.3% | 0 | 0.0% | 0 | 0.0% | 4 | 9.3% | | |
| Writing skills | 1 | 5.3% | 1 | 4.3% | 1 | 3.8% | 1 | 6.3% | 0 | 0.0% | 1 | 5.6% | 0 | 0.0% | 1 | 20.0% | 0 | 0.0% | 2 | 4.7% | | |
| Other, please specify | 1 | 5.3% | 3 | 13.0% | 4 | 15.4% | 1 | 6.3% | 0 | 0.0% | 0 | 0.0% | 0 | 0.0% | 1 | 20.0% | 3 | 33.3% | 4 | 9.3% | | |
| Total | 19 | 100.0% | 23 | 100.0% | 26 | 100.0% | 16 | 100.0% | 4 | 100.0% | 18 | 100.0% | 21 | 100.0% | 5 | 100.0% | 9 | 100.0% | 43 | 100.0% | | |

*Table continues on page 114*

*Table continued from page 113*

|  | Institutional type | | | | Institution control | | | | Number of undergraduates enrolled | | | | | | | | | | | | Total | |
|---|---|---|---|---|---|---|---|---|---|---|---|---|---|---|---|---|---|---|---|---|---|---|
|  | Two-year | | Four-year | | Public | | Private | | Under 1,000 | | 1,000-4,999 | | 5,999-9,999 | | 10,000-19,999 | | 20,000 and above | | | |
| Survey question/responses | Freq. | % | Freq | % | Freq. | % | Freq. | % | Freq. | % | Freq. | % | Freq. | % | Freq. | % | Freq. | % | Freq. | % |
| Q48. Select the five most important topics that comprise the content of the transfer or college success skills course: | | | | | | | | | | | | | | | | | | | | |
| Academic integrity | 1 | 5.3% | 3 | 13.0% | 1 | 3.8% | 3 | 18.8% | 1 | 25.0% | 3 | 16.7% | 1 | 14.3% | 0 | 0.0% | 0 | 0.0% | 5 | 11.6% |
| Academic planning or advising | 15 | 78.9% | 15 | 65.2% | 18 | 69.2% | 12 | 75.0% | 2 | 50.0% | 14 | 77.8% | 6 | 85.7% | 3 | 60.0% | 5 | 55.6% | 30 | 69.8% |
| Academic success resources | 10 | 52.6% | 12 | 52.2% | 11 | 42.3% | 11 | 68.8% | 3 | 75.0% | 12 | 66.7% | 4 | 57.1% | 3 | 60.0% | 1 | 11.1% | 23 | 53.5% |
| Academic success strategies (e.g., study skills, time management) | 14 | 73.7% | 16 | 69.6% | 19 | 73.1% | 11 | 68.8% | 0 | 0.0% | 11 | 61.1% | 4 | 57.1% | 0 | 0.0% | 7 | 77.8% | 31 | 72.1% |
| Alcohol awareness and safety | 0 | 0.0% | 0 | 0.0% | 0 | 0.0% | 0 | 0.0% | 0 | 0.0% | 0 | 0.0% | 0 | 0.0% | 0 | 0.0% | 0 | 0.0% | 0 | 0.0% |
| Basic needs (including housing, food, transportation, and childcare, among other topics) | 2 | 10.5% | 2 | 8.7% | 3 | 11.5% | 1 | 6.3% | 0 | 0.0% | 0 | 0.0% | 2 | 28.6% | 1 | 20.0% | 1 | 11.1% | 4 | 9.3% |
| Campus activities and involvement | 5 | 26.3% | 9 | 39.1% | 8 | 30.8% | 6 | 37.5% | 1 | 25.0% | 9 | 50.0% | 1 | 14.3% | 0 | 0.0% | 3 | 33.3% | 14 | 32.6% |
| Campus history and traditions | 0 | 0.0% | 1 | 4.3% | 0 | 0.0% | 1 | 6.3% | 0 | 0.0% | 1 | 5.6% | 0 | 0.0% | 0 | 0.0% | 0 | 0.0% | 1 | 2.3% |
| Campus policies and community standards | 0 | 0.0% | 2 | 8.7% | 1 | 3.8% | 1 | 6.3% | 0 | 0.0% | 1 | 5.6% | 0 | 0.0% | 0 | 0.0% | 1 | 11.1% | 2 | 4.7% |
| Campus resources | 5 | 26.3% | 8 | 34.8% | 7 | 26.9% | 6 | 37.5% | 0 | 0.0% | 7 | 38.9% | 3 | 42.9% | 0 | 0.0% | 3 | 33.3% | 13 | 30.2% |
| Campus safety | 0 | 0.0% | 0 | 0.0% | 0 | 0.0% | 0 | 0.0% | 0 | 0.0% | 0 | 0.0% | 0 | 0.0% | 0 | 0.0% | 0 | 0.0% | 0 | 0.0% |
| Campus tour | 0 | 0.0% | 0 | 0.0% | 0 | 0.0% | 0 | 0.0% | 0 | 0.0% | 0 | 0.0% | 0 | 0.0% | 0 | 0.0% | 0 | 0.0% | 0 | 0.0% |
| Career exploration or preparation | 8 | 42.1% | 7 | 30.4% | 11 | 42.3% | 4 | 25.0% | 1 | 25.0% | 5 | 27.8% | 2 | 28.6% | 3 | 60.0% | 5 | 55.6% | 16 | 37.2% |
| Commuter issues | 0 | 0.0% | 0 | 0.0% | 0 | 0.0% | 0 | 0.0% | 0 | 0.0% | 0 | 0.0% | 0 | 0.0% | 0 | 0.0% | 0 | 0.0% | 0 | 0.0% |
| Course registration procedures | 2 | 10.5% | 5 | 21.7% | 3 | 11.5% | 4 | 25.0% | 1 | 25.0% | 3 | 16.7% | 2 | 28.6% | 1 | 20.0% | 1 | 11.1% | 8 | 18.6% |
| Critical thinking | 0 | 0.0% | 4 | 17.4% | 1 | 3.8% | 3 | 18.8% | 1 | 25.0% | 1 | 5.6% | 1 | 14.3% | 1 | 20.0% | 0 | 0.0% | 4 | 9.3% |

*Table continues on page 115*

*Table continued from page 114*

| Survey question/responses | Institutional type | | | | Institution control | | | | Number of undergraduates enrolled | | | | | | | | | | | | Total | |
|---|---|---|---|---|---|---|---|---|---|---|---|---|---|---|---|---|---|---|---|---|---|---|
| | Two-year | | Four-year | | Public | | Private | | Under 1,000 | | 1,000-4,999 | | 5,999-9,999 | | 10,000-19,999 | | 20,000 and above | | | |
| | Freq. | % | Freq | % | Freq. | % | Freq. | % | Freq. | % | Freq. | % | Freq. | % | Freq. | % | Freq. | % | Freq. | % |
| Discipline-specific content | 0 | 0.0% | 0 | 0.0% | 0 | 0.0% | 0 | 0.0% | 0 | 0.0% | 0 | 0.0% | 0 | 0.0% | 0 | 0.0% | 0 | 0.0% | 0 | 0.0% |
| Diversity/equity/inclusion issues | 4 | 21.1% | 6 | 26.1% | 7 | 26.9% | 3 | 18.8% | 1 | 25.0% | 5 | 27.8% | 1 | 14.3% | 1 | 20.0% | 2 | 22.2% | 10 | 23.3% |
| Financial information, including financial aid and scholarships | 8 | 42.1% | 3 | 13.0% | 10 | 38.5% | 1 | 6.3% | 0 | 0.0% | 5 | 27.8% | 2 | 28.6% | 1 | 20.0% | 3 | 33.3% | 11 | 25.6% |
| Financial literacy | 6 | 31.6% | 1 | 4.3% | 7 | 26.9% | 0 | 0.0% | 0 | 0.0% | 3 | 16.7% | 1 | 14.3% | 1 | 20.0% | 2 | 22.2% | 7 | 16.3% |
| Global learning | 0 | 0.0% | 0 | 0.0% | 0 | 0.0% | 0 | 0.0% | 0 | 0.0% | 0 | 0.0% | 0 | 0.0% | 0 | 0.0% | 0 | 0.0% | 0 | 0.0% |
| Health and wellness | 1 | 5.3% | 1 | 4.3% | 2 | 7.7% | 0 | 0.0% | 0 | 0.0% | 0 | 0.0% | 0 | 0.0% | 1 | 20.0% | 1 | 11.1% | 2 | 4.7% |
| Information literacy | 2 | 10.5% | 0 | 0.0% | 2 | 7.7% | 0 | 0.0% | 0 | 0.0% | 0 | 0.0% | 1 | 14.3% | 0 | 0.0% | 1 | 11.1% | 2 | 4.7% |
| Library literacy | 1 | 5.3% | 1 | 4.3% | 1 | 3.8% | 1 | 6.3% | 1 | 25.0% | 1 | 2.6% | 0 | 0.0% | 0 | 0.0% | 0 | 0.0% | 2 | 4.7% |
| Navigating transfer-related policies | 7 | 36.8% | 4 | 17.4% | 8 | 30.8% | 3 | 18.8% | 0 | 0.0% | 5 | 27.8% | 2 | 28.6% | 2 | 40.0% | 2 | 22.2% | 11 | 25.6% |
| Professional trends and issues | 0 | 0.0% | 2 | 8.7% | 1 | 3.8% | 1 | 6.3% | 0 | 0.0% | 1 | 5.6% | 0 | 0.0% | 0 | 0.0% | 1 | 11.1% | 2 | 4.7% |
| Relationship issues (e.g., interpersonal skills, conflict resolution) | 1 | 5.3% | 1 | 4.3% | 1 | 3.8% | 1 | 6.3% | 1 | 25.0% | 0 | 0.0% | 1 | 14.3% | 0 | 0.0% | 0 | 0.0% | 2 | 4.7% |
| Sexual assault and dating violence | 0 | 0.0% | 0 | 0.0% | 0 | 0.0% | 0 | 0.0% | 0 | 0.0% | 0 | 0.0% | 0 | 0.0% | 0 | 0.0% | 0 | 0.0% | 0 | 0.0% |
| School-life balance | 2 | 10.5% | 1 | 4.3% | 2 | 7.7% | 1 | 6.3% | 0 | 0.0% | 1 | 5.6% | 0 | 0.0% | 2 | 40.0% | 0 | 0.0% | 3 | 7.0% |
| Social connections | 0 | 0.0% | 5 | 21.7% | 2 | 7.7% | 3 | 18.8% | 1 | 25.0% | 2 | 11.1% | 0 | 0.0% | 0 | 0.0% | 2 | 22.2% | 5 | 11.6% |
| Undergraduate research | 1 | 5.3% | 0 | 0.0% | 1 | 3.8% | 0 | 0.0% | 0 | 0.0% | 0 | 0.0% | 0 | 0.0% | 0 | 0.0% | 1 | 11.1% | 1 | 2.3% |
| Writing skills | 0 | 0.0% | 3 | 13.0% | 0 | 0.0% | 3 | 18.8% | 2 | 50.0% | 0 | 0.0% | 1 | 14.3% | 0 | 0.0% | 0 | 0.0% | 3 | 7.0% |
| Other, please specify | 0 | 0.0% | 3 | 13.0% | 3 | 11.5% | 0 | 0.0% | 0 | 0.0% | 0 | 0.0% | 0 | 0.0% | 0 | 0.0% | 3 | 33.3% | 3 | 7.0% |
| Total | 19 | 100.0% | 23 | 100.0% | 26 | 100.0% | 16 | 100.0% | 4 | 100.0% | 18 | 100.0% | 21 | 100.0% | 5 | 100.0% | 9 | 100.0% | 43 | 100.0% |

*Table continues on page 116*

*Table continued from page 115*

| | Institutional type | | | | Institution control | | | | Number of undergraduates enrolled | | | | | | | | | | | Total | |
| | Two-year | | Four-year | | Public | | Private | | Under 1,000 | | 1,000-4,999 | | 5,999-9,999 | | 10,000-19,999 | | 20,000 and above | | | |
| Survey question/responses | Freq. | % | Freq | % | Freq. | % | Freq. | % | Freq. | % | Freq. | % | Freq. | % | Freq. | % | Freq. | % | Freq. | % |
|---|---|---|---|---|---|---|---|---|---|---|---|---|---|---|---|---|---|---|---|---|
| Q49. As of fall 2021, in what format(s) is your institution's transfer or college success skills course taught? (Select all that apply.) | | | | | | | | | | | | | | | | | | | | |
| Face-to-face | 12 | 63.2% | 19 | 82.6% | 18 | 69.2% | 13 | 81.3% | 4 | 100.0% | 11 | 61.1% | 6 | 85.7% | 3 | 60.0% | 8 | 88.9% | 32 | 74.4% |
| Virtual | 12 | 63.2% | 4 | 17.4% | 14 | 53.8% | 2 | 12.5% | 2 | 50.0% | 4 | 22.2% | 3 | 42.9% | 3 | 60.0% | 5 | 55.6% | 17 | 39.5% |
| Hybrid (including face-to-face and virtual components) | 15 | 78.9% | 8 | 34.8% | 19 | 73.1% | 4 | 25.0% | 2 | 50.0% | 8 | 44.4% | 4 | 57.1% | 3 | 60.0% | 7 | 77.8% | 24 | 55.8% |
| Total | 19 | 100.0% | 23 | 100.0% | 26 | 100.0% | 16 | 100.0% | 4 | 100.0% | 18 | 100.0% | 21 | 100.0% | 5 | 100.0% | 9 | 100.0% | 43 | 100.0% |
| Q51. Who teaches the transfer or college success skills course? (Select all that apply). | | | | | | | | | | | | | | | | | | | | |
| Academic advisors | 9 | 47.4% | 13 | 56.5% | 13 | 50.0% | 9 | 56.3% | 2 | 50.0% | 11 | 61.1% | 4 | 57.1% | 3 | 60.0% | 3 | 33.3% | 23 | 53.5% |
| Adjunct faculty | 11 | 57.9% | 3 | 13.0% | 12 | 46.2% | 2 | 12.5% | 3 | 75.0% | 4 | 22.2% | 3 | 42.9% | 3 | 60.0% | 2 | 22.2% | 15 | 34.9% |
| Full-time, non-tenure-track faculty | 15 | 78.9% | 7 | 30.4% | 16 | 61.5% | 6 | 37.5% | 2 | 50.0% | 10 | 55.6% | 4 | 57.1% | 4 | 80.0% | 3 | 33.3% | 23 | 53.5% |
| Tenure-track faculty | 7 | 36.8% | 6 | 26.1% | 9 | 34.6% | 4 | 25.0% | 1 | 25.0% | 3 | 16.7% | 4 | 57.1% | 2 | 40.0% | 3 | 33.3% | 13 | 30.2% |
| Student affairs professionals | 5 | 26.3% | 9 | 39.1% | 7 | 26.9% | 7 | 43.8% | 1 | 25.0% | 8 | 44.4% | 2 | 28.6% | 2 | 40.0% | 1 | 11.1% | 14 | 32.6% |
| Graduate students | 0 | 0.0% | 0 | 0.0% | 0 | 0.0% | 0 | 0.0% | 1 | 25.0% | 0 | 0.0% | 0 | 0.0% | 0 | 0.0% | 0 | 0.0% | 1 | 2.3% |
| Undergraduate students | 0 | 0.0% | 1 | 4.3% | 1 | 3.8% | 0 | 0.0% | 0 | 0.0% | 0 | 0.0% | 0 | 0.0% | 0 | 0.0% | 1 | 11.1% | 1 | 2.3% |
| Other, please specify | 3 | 15.8% | 6 | 26.1% | 5 | 19.2% | 4 | 25.0% | 1 | 25.0% | 5 | 27.8% | 0 | 0.0% | 1 | 20.0% | 2 | 22.2% | 9 | 20.9% |
| I don't know | 0 | 0.0% | 0 | 0.0% | 0 | 0.0% | 0 | 0.0% | 0 | 0.0% | 0 | 0.0% | 0 | 0.0% | 0 | 0.0% | 0 | 0.0% | 0 | 0.0% |
| Total | 19 | 100.0% | 23 | 100.0% | 26 | 100.0% | 16 | 100.0% | 4 | 100.0% | 18 | 100.0% | 21 | 100.0% | 5 | 100.0% | 9 | 100.0% | 43 | 100.0% |
| Q52. Has your transfer or college success skills course been formally assessed or evaluated within the last four years? | | | | | | | | | | | | | | | | | | | | |
| Yes | 13 | 68.4% | 10 | 43.5% | 17 | 65.4% | 6 | 37.5% | 4 | 100.0% | 9 | 50.0% | 2 | 28.6% | 3 | 60.0% | 6 | 66.7% | 24 | 55.8% |
| No | 4 | 21.1% | 6 | 26.1% | 5 | 19.2% | 5 | 31.3% | 0 | 0.0% | 6 | 33.3% | 2 | 28.6% | 1 | 20.0% | 1 | 11.1% | 10 | 23.3% |
| I don't know | 2 | 10.5% | 7 | 30.4% | 4 | 15.4% | 5 | 31.1% | 0 | 0.0% | 3 | 16.7% | 3 | 42.9% | 1 | 20.0% | 2 | 22.2% | 9 | 20.9% |
| Total | 19 | 100.0% | 23 | 100.0% | 26 | 100.0% | 16 | 100.0% | 4 | 100.0% | 18 | 100.0% | 7 | 100.0% | 5 | 100.0% | 9 | 100.0% | 43 | 100.0% |

*Table continues on page 117*

*Table continued from page 116*

| Survey question/responses | Institutional type | | | | Institution control | | | | Number of undergraduates enrolled | | | | | | | | | | | | Total | |
| --- | --- | --- | --- | --- | --- | --- | --- | --- | --- | --- | --- | --- | --- | --- | --- | --- | --- | --- | --- | --- | --- | --- |
| | Two-year | | Four-year | | Public | | Private | | Under 1,000 | | 1,000-4,999 | | 5,999-9,999 | | 10,000-19,999 | | 20,000 and above | | | | | |
| | Freq. | % | Freq | % | Freq. | % | Freq. | % | Freq. | % | Freq. | % | Freq. | % | Freq. | % | Freq. | % | Freq. | % | Freq. | % |
| Q53. What type of assessment was conducted? (Select all that apply). | | | | | | | | | | | | | | | | | | | | | | |
| Analysis of institutional data (e.g., GPA, retention rates, graduation) | 10 | 76.9% | 5 | 55.6% | 12 | 75.0% | 3 | 50.0% | 3 | 75.0% | 6 | 66.7% | 1 | 50.0% | 2 | 66.7% | 4 | 80.0% | 16 | 69.6% |
| Direct assessment of student learning outcomes | 9 | 69.2% | 6 | 66.7% | 10 | 62.5% | 5 | 83.3% | 0 | 0.0% | 6 | 66.7% | 1 | 50.0% | 2 | 66.7% | 3 | 60.0% | 16 | 69.6% |
| Focus groups with faculty | 3 | 23.1% | 4 | 44.4% | 4 | 25.0% | 3 | 50.0% | 2 | 50.0% | 2 | 22.2% | 1 | 50.0% | 0 | 0.0% | 2 | 40.0% | 7 | 30.4% |
| Focus groups with professional staff | 1 | 7.7% | 1 | 11.1% | 2 | 12.5% | 0 | 0.0% | 0 | 0.0% | 0 | 0.0% | 1 | 50.0% | 0 | 0.0% | 1 | 20.0% | 2 | 8.7% |
| Focus groups with students | 3 | 23.1% | 2 | 22.2% | 4 | 25.0% | 1 | 16.7% | 1 | 25.0% | 2 | 22.2% | 0 | 0.0% | 1 | 33.3% | 1 | 20.0% | 5 | 21.7% |
| Individual interviews with faculty | 1 | 7.7% | 1 | 11.1% | 1 | 6.3% | 1 | 16.7% | 1 | 25.0% | 1 | 11.1% | 1 | 50.0% | 0 | 0.0% | 0 | 0.0% | 3 | 13.0% |
| Individual interviews with orientation staff | 0 | 0.0% | 0 | 0.0% | 0 | 0.0% | 0 | 0.0% | 0 | 0.0% | 0 | 0.0% | 0 | 0.0% | 0 | 0.0% | 0 | 0.0% | 0 | 0.0% |
| Individual interviews with students | 1 | 7.7% | 1 | 11.1% | 1 | 6.3% | 1 | 16.7% | 1 | 25.0% | 0 | 0.0% | 0 | 0.0% | 0 | 0.0% | 1 | 20.0% | 2 | 8.7% |
| Program review | 9 | 69.2% | 2 | 22.2% | 10 | 62.5% | 1 | 16.7% | 2 | 50.0% | 5 | 55.6% | 1 | 50.0% | 2 | 66.7% | 2 | 40.0% | 12 | 52.2% |
| Student course evaluation | 9 | 69.2% | 6 | 66.7% | 11 | 68.8% | 4 | 66.7% | 3 | 75.0% | 6 | 66.7% | 0 | 0.0% | 2 | 66.7% | 3 | 60.0% | 16 | 69.6% |
| Survey instrument | 0 | 0.0% | 3 | 33.3% | 2 | 12.5% | 1 | 16.7% | 1 | 25.0% | 0 | 0.0% | 0 | 0.0% | 0 | 0.0% | 2 | 40.0% | 3 | 13.0% |
| Other, please specify | 0 | 0.0% | 0 | 0.0% | 0 | 0.0% | 0 | 0.0% | 0 | 0.0% | 0 | 0.0% | 0 | 0.0% | 0 | 0.0% | 0 | 0.0% | 0 | 0.0% |
| Total | 13 | 100.0% | 9 | 100.0% | 16 | 100.0% | 6 | 100.0% | 4 | 100.0% | 9 | 100.0% | 2 | 100.0% | 3 | 100.0% | 5 | 100.0% | 23 | 100.0% |
| Q54. In your opinion, considering costs (including staff time and resources) and educational gains, how valuable is your institution's transfer or college student success skills in supporting transfer student success? | | | | | | | | | | | | | | | | | | | | | | |
| Low benefit | 0 | 0.0% | 1 | 4.5% | 0 | 0.0% | 1 | 6.3% | 1 | 25.0% | 0 | 0.0% | 0 | 0.0% | 0 | 0.0% | 0 | 0.0% | 1 | 2.4% |
| Low-medium benefit | 2 | 10.5% | 1 | 4.5% | 2 | 8.0% | 1 | 6.3% | 0 | 0.0% | 2 | 11.1% | 0 | 0.0% | 0 | 0.0% | 1 | 12.5% | 3 | 7.1% |
| Medium benefit | 2 | 10.5% | 6 | 27.3% | 5 | 20.0% | 3 | 18.8% | 0 | 0.0% | 2 | 11.1% | 3 | 42.9% | 1 | 20.0% | 2 | 25.0% | 8 | 19.0% |

*Table continues on page 118*

*Table continued from page 117*

| Survey question/responses | Institutional type | | | | Institution control | | | | Number of undergraduates enrolled | | | | | | | | | | | | Total | |
|---|---|---|---|---|---|---|---|---|---|---|---|---|---|---|---|---|---|---|---|---|---|---|
| | Two-year | | Four-year | | Public | | Private | | Under 1,000 | | 1,000-4,999 | | 5,999-9,999 | | 10,000-19,999 | | 20,000 and above | | | |
| | Freq. | % | Freq | % | Freq. | % | Freq. | % | Freq. | % | Freq. | % | Freq. | % | Freq. | % | Freq. | % | Freq. | % |
| Medium-high benefit | 4 | 21.1% | 5 | 22.7% | 5 | 20.0% | 4 | 25.0% | 1 | 25.0% | 6 | 33.3% | 0 | 0.0% | 1 | 20.0% | 2 | 25.0% | 10 | 23.8% |
| High benefit | 11 | 57.9% | 8 | 36.4% | 13 | 52.0% | 6 | 37.5% | 2 | 50.0% | 7 | 38.9% | 4 | 57.1% | 3 | 60.0% | 3 | 37.5% | 19 | 45.2% |
| Unable to judge | 0 | 0.0% | 1 | 4.5% | 0 | 0.0% | 1 | 6.3% | 0 | 0.0% | 1 | 5.6% | 0 | 0.0% | 0 | 0.0% | 0 | 0.0% | 1 | 2.4% |
| Total | 19 | 100.0% | 22 | 100.0% | 25 | 100.0% | 16 | 100.0% | 4 | 100.0% | 18 | 100.0% | 7 | 100.0% | 5 | 100.0% | 8 | 100.0% | 42 | 100.0% |
| Q57. Does your institution offer orientation programming for incoming transfer/transfer-intending students? | | | | | | | | | | | | | | | | | | | | |
| Yes | 24 | 50.0% | 72 | 80.0% | 44 | 62.9% | 51 | 76.1% | 11 | 68.8% | 46 | 73.0% | 13 | 61.9% | 11 | 57.9% | 15 | 78.9% | 96 | 69.6% |
| No | 23 | 47.9% | 14 | 15.6% | 24 | 34.3% | 13 | 19.4% | 5 | 31.3% | 15 | 23.8% | 8 | 38.1% | 6 | 31.6% | 3 | 15.8% | 37 | 26.8% |
| I don't know | 1 | 2.1% | 4 | 4.4% | 2 | 2.9% | 3 | 4.5% | 0 | 0.0% | 2 | 3.2% | 0 | 0.0% | 2 | 10.5% | 1 | 5.3% | 5 | 3.6% |
| Total | 48 | 100.0% | 90 | 100.0% | 70 | 100.0% | 67 | 100.0% | 16 | 100.0% | 63 | 100.0% | 21 | 100.0% | 19 | 100.0% | 19 | 100.0% | 138 | 100.0% |
| Q130. Which best describes the orientation programming your institution offers for incoming transfer/transfer-intending students? | | | | | | | | | | | | | | | | | | | | |
| My institution offers an orientation specifically for transfer/transfer-intending students | 2 | 8.3% | 37 | 52.1% | 18 | 40.9% | 21 | 42.0% | 4 | 36.4% | 16 | 35.6% | 5 | 38.5% | 6 | 54.5% | 8 | 53.3% | 39 | 41.1% |
| My institution offers an orientation, but transfer/transfer-intending students attend the same sessions as first-year students | 15 | 62.5% | 16 | 22.5% | 16 | 36.4% | 14 | 28.0% | 4 | 36.4% | 15 | 33.3% | 5 | 38.5% | 2 | 18.2% | 5 | 33.3% | 31 | 32.6% |
| My institution offers an orientation that all incoming students attend, but there are specific programs and sessions for transfers/transfer-intending students | 5 | 20.8% | 17 | 23.9% | 7 | 15.9% | 15 | 30.0% | 3 | 27.3% | 13 | 28.9% | 3 | 23.1% | 2 | 18.2% | 1 | 6.7% | 22 | 23.2% |
| Other, please specify | 2 | 8.3% | 1 | 1.4% | 3 | 6.8% | 0 | 0.0% | 0 | 0.0% | 1 | 2.2% | 0 | 0.0% | 1 | 9.1% | 1 | 6.7% | 3 | 3.2% |
| Total | 24 | 100.0% | 71 | 100.0% | 44 | 100.0% | 50 | 100.0% | 11 | 100.0% | 45 | 100.0% | 13 | 100.0% | 11 | 100.0% | 15 | 100.0% | 95 | 100.0% |

*Table continues on page 119*

*Table continued from page 118*

| | Institutional type | | | | Institution control | | | | Number of undergraduates enrolled | | | | | | | | | | | Total | |
| | Two-year | | Four-year | | Public | | Private | | Under 1,000 | | 1,000-4,999 | | 5,999-9,999 | | 10,000-19,999 | | 20,000 and above | | | |
| Survey question/responses | Freq. | % | Freq | % | Freq. | % | Freq. | % | Freq. | % | Freq. | % | Freq. | % | Freq. | % | Freq. | % | Freq. | % |
|---|---|---|---|---|---|---|---|---|---|---|---|---|---|---|---|---|---|---|---|---|
| Q58. Does your institution offer orientation programming for incoming students who transfer outside of the fall semester or quarter (i.e., students who transfer in the winter, spring, or summer semesters or quarters)? | | | | | | | | | | | | | | | | | | | | |
| Yes | 19 | 79.2% | 63 | 88.7% | 38 | 86.4% | 43 | 86.0% | 7 | 63.6% | 38 | 84.4% | 13 | 100.0% | 10 | 90.9% | 14 | 93.3% | 82 | 86.3% |
| No | 4 | 16.7% | 7 | 9.9% | 5 | 11.4% | 6 | 12.0% | 4 | 36.4% | 6 | 13.3% | 0 | 0.0% | 0 | 0.0% | 1 | 6.7% | 11 | 11.6% |
| I don't know | 1 | 4.2% | 1 | 1.4% | 1 | 2.3% | 1 | 2.0% | 0 | 0.0% | 1 | 2.2% | 0 | 0.0% | 1 | 9.1% | 0 | 0.0% | 2 | 2.1% |
| Total | 24 | 100.0% | 71 | 100.0% | 44 | 100.0% | 50 | 100.0% | 11 | 100.0% | 45 | 100.0% | 13 | 100.0% | 11 | 100.0% | 15 | 100.0% | 95 | 100.0% |
| Q131. Are incoming transfer/transfer-intending students required to participate in orientation programming at your institution? | | | | | | | | | | | | | | | | | | | | |
| Yes | 16 | 66.7% | 49 | 69.0% | 27 | 61.4% | 37 | 74.0% | 9 | 81.8% | 33 | 73.3% | 8 | 61.5% | 5 | 45.5% | 10 | 66.7% | 65 | 68.4% |
| No | 7 | 29.2% | 21 | 29.6% | 16 | 36.4% | 12 | 24.0% | 2 | 18.2% | 12 | 26.7% | 4 | 30.8% | 5 | 45.5% | 5 | 33.3% | 28 | 29.5% |
| I don't know | 1 | 4.2% | 1 | 1.4% | 1 | 2.3% | 1 | 2.0% | 0 | 0.0% | 0 | 0.0% | 1 | 7.7% | 1 | 9.1% | 0 | 0.0% | 2 | 2.1% |
| Total | 24 | 100.0% | 71 | 100.0% | 44 | 100.0% | 50 | 100.0% | 11 | 100.0% | 45 | 100.0% | 13 | 100.0% | 11 | 100.0% | 15 | 100.0% | 95 | 100.0% |
| Q59. What is the approximate percentage of incoming transfer/transfer-intending students who participate in orientation programming at your institution? | | | | | | | | | | | | | | | | | | | | |
| Less than 10% | 0 | 0.0% | 2 | 2.8% | 2 | 4.5% | 0 | 0.0% | 0 | 0.0% | 1 | 2.2% | 1 | 7.7% | 0 | 0.0% | 0 | 0.0% | 2 | 2.1% |
| 10-19% | 0 | 0.0% | 3 | 4.2% | 2 | 4.5% | 1 | 2.0% | 0 | 0.0% | 1 | 2.2% | 1 | 7.7% | 1 | 9.1% | 0 | 0.0% | 3 | 3.2% |
| 20-29% | 2 | 8.3% | 2 | 2.8% | 4 | 9.1% | 0 | 0.0% | 0 | 0.0% | 1 | 2.2% | 1 | 7.7% | 2 | 18.2% | 0 | 0.0% | 4 | 4.2% |
| 30-39% | 2 | 8.3% | 1 | 1.4% | 2 | 4.5% | 1 | 2.0% | 0 | 0.0% | 3 | 6.7% | 0 | 0.0% | 0 | 0.0% | 0 | 0.0% | 3 | 3.2% |
| 40-49% | 1 | 4.2% | 2 | 2.8% | 1 | 2.3% | 2 | 4.0% | 0 | 0.0% | 3 | 6.7% | 0 | 0.0% | 0 | 0.0% | 0 | 0.0% | 3 | 3.2% |
| 50-59% | 1 | 4.2% | 2 | 2.8% | 1 | 2.3% | 2 | 4.0% | 0 | 0.0% | 3 | 6.7% | 0 | 0.0% | 0 | 0.0% | 0 | 0.0% | 3 | 3.2% |
| 60-69% | 0 | 0.0% | 2 | 2.8% | 1 | 2.3% | 1 | 2.0% | 1 | 9.1% | 1 | 2.2% | 0 | 0.0% | 0 | 0.0% | 0 | 0.0% | 2 | 2.1% |
| 70-79% | 0 | 0.0% | 9 | 12.7% | 2 | 4.5% | 7 | 14.0% | 1 | 9.1% | 4 | 8.9% | 1 | 7.7% | 0 | 0.0% | 3 | 20.0% | 9 | 9.5% |
| 80-89% | 1 | 4.2% | 8 | 11.3% | 5 | 11.4% | 4 | 8.0% | 2 | 18.2% | 4 | 8.9% | 0 | 0.0% | 2 | 18.2% | 2 | 13.3% | 10 | 10.5% |

*Table continues on page 120*

*Table continued from page 119*

| Survey question/responses | Institutional type | | | | Institution control | | | | Number of undergraduates enrolled | | | | | | | | | | Total | |
|---|---|---|---|---|---|---|---|---|---|---|---|---|---|---|---|---|---|---|---|---|
| | Two-year | | Four-year | | Public | | Private | | Under 1,000 | | 1,000-4,999 | | 5,999-9,999 | | 10,000-19,999 | | 20,000 and above | | | |
| | Freq. | % | Freq | % | Freq. | % | Freq. | % | Freq. | % | Freq. | % | Freq. | % | Freq. | % | Freq. | % | Freq. | % |
| 90-100% | 8 | 33.3% | 32 | 45.1% | 13 | 29.5% | 26 | 52.0% | 7 | 63.6% | 15 | 33.3% | 6 | 46.2% | 3 | 27.3% | 8 | 53.3% | 39 | 41.1% |
| I don't know | 9 | 37.5% | 8 | 11.3% | 11 | 25.0% | 6 | 12.0% | 0 | 0.0% | 9 | 20.0% | 3 | 23.1% | 3 | 27.3% | 2 | 13.3% | 17 | 17.9% |
| Total | 24 | 100.0% | 71 | 100.0% | 44 | 100.0% | 50 | 100.0% | 11 | 100.0% | 45 | 100.0% | 13 | 100.0% | 11 | 100.0% | 15 | 100.0% | 95 | 100.0% |

Q60. Generally, which of the following types of orientation activities does your institution offer for incoming transfer/transfer-intending students? (Select all that apply.)

| Survey question/responses | Two-year Freq. | % | Four-year Freq | % | Public Freq. | % | Private Freq. | % | Under 1,000 Freq. | % | 1,000-4,999 Freq. | % | 5,999-9,999 Freq. | % | 10,000-19,999 Freq. | % | 20,000 and above Freq. | % | Total Freq. | % |
|---|---|---|---|---|---|---|---|---|---|---|---|---|---|---|---|---|---|---|---|---|
| Bridge programs | 3 | 12.5% | 2 | 2.8% | 3 | 6.8% | 2 | 4.0% | 0 | 0.0% | 1 | 2.2% | 3 | 23.1% | 0 | 0.0% | 1 | 6.7% | 5 | 5.3% |
| On-campus pre-term activities | 12 | 50.0% | 30 | 42.3% | 20 | 45.5% | 21 | 42.0% | 6 | 54.5% | 19 | 42.2% | 6 | 46.2% | 8 | 72.7% | 3 | 20.0% | 42 | 44.2% |
| Online orientation | 20 | 83.3% | 40 | 56.3% | 38 | 86.4% | 22 | 44.0% | 3 | 27.3% | 26 | 57.8% | 9 | 69.2% | 9 | 81.8% | 14 | 93.3% | 61 | 64.2% |
| Outdoor adventure/ wilderness experience | 0 | 0.0% | 8 | 11.3% | 1 | 2.3% | 7 | 14.0% | 1 | 9.1% | 3 | 6.7% | 3 | 23.1% | 1 | 9.1% | 0 | 0.0% | 8 | 8.4% |
| Pre-term advising or registration | 16 | 66.7% | 58 | 81.7% | 34 | 77.3% | 40 | 80.0% | 9 | 81.8% | 37 | 82.2% | 10 | 76.9% | 9 | 81.8% | 10 | 66.7% | 75 | 78.9% |
| Programs for specific student populations (e.g., first-generation students, racially/ethnically minoritized students, etc.) | 8 | 33.3% | 15 | 21.1% | 15 | 34.1% | 8 | 16.0% | 0 | 0.0% | 12 | 26.7% | 2 | 15.4% | 4 | 36.4% | 5 | 33.3% | 23 | 24.2% |
| Spirit camps | 0 | 0.0% | 0 | 0.0% | 0 | 0.0% | 0 | 0.0% | 0 | 0.0% | 0 | 0.0% | 0 | 0.0% | 0 | 0.0% | 0 | 0.0% | 0 | 0.0% |
| Welcome week | 12 | 50.0% | 39 | 54.9% | 28 | 63.6% | 23 | 46.0% | 6 | 54.5% | 23 | 51.1% | 5 | 38.5% | 7 | 63.6% | 11 | 73.3% | 52 | 54.7% |
| Other, please specify | 5 | 20.8% | 1 | 1.4% | 5 | 11.4% | 1 | 2.0% | 1 | 9.1% | 3 | 6.7% | 1 | 7.7% | 0 | 0.0% | 1 | 6.7% | 6 | 6.3% |
| Total | 24 | 100.0% | 71 | 100.0% | 44 | 100.0% | 50 | 100.0% | 11 | 100.0% | 45 | 100.0% | 13 | 100.0% | 11 | 100.0% | 15 | 100.0% | 95 | 100.0% |

Q61. Are incoming transfer/transfer-intending students able to select the orientation programming in which they want to participate?

| Survey question/responses | Two-year Freq. | % | Four-year Freq | % | Public Freq. | % | Private Freq. | % | Under 1,000 Freq. | % | 1,000-4,999 Freq. | % | 5,999-9,999 Freq. | % | 10,000-19,999 Freq. | % | 20,000 and above Freq. | % | Total Freq. | % |
|---|---|---|---|---|---|---|---|---|---|---|---|---|---|---|---|---|---|---|---|---|
| Yes, but some forms are mandatory | 3 | 12.5% | 23 | 32.4% | 12 | 27.3% | 14 | 28.0% | 3 | 27.3% | 13 | 28.9% | 2 | 15.4% | 4 | 36.4% | 5 | 33.3% | 27 | 28.4% |
| Yes, they can select any and all forms in which they want to participate | 9 | 37.5% | 18 | 25.4% | 16 | 36.4% | 11 | 22.0% | 0 | 0.0% | 10 | 22.2% | 7 | 53.8% | 5 | 45.5% | 5 | 33.3% | 27 | 28.4% |

*Table continues on page 121*

*Table continued from page 120*

| Survey question/responses | Institutional type | | | | Institution control | | | | Number of undergraduates enrolled | | | | | | | | | | | | Total | |
| --- | --- | --- | --- | --- | --- | --- | --- | --- | --- | --- | --- | --- | --- | --- | --- | --- | --- | --- | --- | --- | --- | --- |
| | Two-year | | Four-year | | Public | | Private | | Under 1,000 | | 1,000-4,999 | | 5,999-9,999 | | 10,000-19,999 | | 20,000 and above | | | | | |
| | Freq. | % | Freq | % | Freq. | % | Freq. | % | Freq. | % | Freq. | % | Freq. | % | Freq. | % | Freq. | % | Freq. | % | Freq. | % |
| No, they do not have a choice | 10 | 41.7% | 26 | 36.6% | 14 | 31.8% | 21 | 42.0% | 8 | 72.7% | 19 | 42.2% | 3 | 23.1% | 1 | 9.1% | 4 | 26.7% | 35 | 36.8% | | |
| I don't know | 2 | 8.3% | 4 | 5.6% | 2 | 4.5% | 4 | 8.0% | 0 | 0.0% | 3 | 6.7% | 1 | 7.7% | 1 | 9.1% | 1 | 6.7% | 6 | 6.3% | | |
| Total | 24 | 100.0% | 71 | 100.0% | 44 | 100.0% | 50 | 100.0% | 11 | 100.0% | 45 | 100.0% | 13 | 100.0% | 11 | 100.0% | 15 | 100.0% | 95 | 100.0% | | |
| Q63. Which of the following activities does your campus' orientation programming include? (Select all that apply.) | | | | | | | | | | | | | | | | | | | | | | |
| Academic advising | 20 | 83.3% | 60 | 84.5% | 39 | 88.6% | 41 | 82.0% | 9 | 81.8% | 39 | 86.7% | 11 | 84.6% | 0 | 0.0% | 11 | 73.3% | 81 | 85.3% | | |
| College- or university-specific policies | 21 | 87.5% | 63 | 88.7% | 40 | 90.9% | 43 | 86.0% | 10 | 90.9% | 38 | 84.4% | 12 | 92.3% | 0 | 0.0% | 13 | 86.7% | 84 | 88.4% | | |
| Common reading (i.e., a book or article read before and discussed during orientation) | 2 | 8.3% | 13 | 18.3% | 3 | 6.8% | 11 | 22.0% | 2 | 18.2% | 5 | 11.1% | 5 | 38.5% | 1 | 9.1% | 1 | 6.7% | 14 | 14.7% | | |
| Community building | 7 | 29.2% | 42 | 59.2% | 17 | 38.6% | 32 | 64.0% | 8 | 72.7% | 21 | 46.7% | 10 | 76.9% | 6 | 54.5% | 5 | 33.3% | 50 | 52.6% | | |
| Convocations or other celebratory activities or traditions | 1 | 4.2% | 33 | 46.5% | 10 | 22.7% | 24 | 48.0% | 4 | 36.4% | 14 | 31.1% | 7 | 53.8% | 6 | 54.5% | 4 | 26.7% | 35 | 36.8% | | |
| Discussion about finances | 10 | 41.7% | 35 | 49.3% | 25 | 56.8% | 20 | 40.0% | 4 | 36.4% | 20 | 44.4% | 5 | 38.5% | 8 | 72.7% | 9 | 60.0% | 46 | 48.4% | | |
| Discussion of personal issues and challenges | 11 | 45.8% | 29 | 40.8% | 20 | 45.5% | 20 | 40.0% | 5 | 45.5% | 18 | 40.0% | 5 | 38.5% | 7 | 63.6% | 5 | 33.3% | 40 | 42.1% | | |
| Discussions about health and wellness on campus | 15 | 62.5% | 43 | 60.6% | 30 | 68.2% | 28 | 56.0% | 6 | 54.5% | 25 | 55.6% | 10 | 76.9% | 8 | 72.7% | 9 | 60.0% | 58 | 61.1% | | |
| Discussions about identity, diversity, equity, and/or social justice | 7 | 29.2% | 38 | 53.5% | 19 | 43.2% | 26 | 52.0% | 5 | 45.5% | 18 | 40.0% | 7 | 53.8% | 5 | 45.5% | 10 | 66.7% | 45 | 47.4% | | |
| Employment opportunities | 6 | 25.0% | 19 | 26.8% | 10 | 22.7% | 15 | 30.0% | 3 | 27.3% | 12 | 26.7% | 6 | 46.2% | 5 | 45.5% | 0 | 0.0% | 26 | 27.4% | | |
| Introduction to campus facilities | 15 | 62.5% | 51 | 71.8% | 34 | 77.3% | 32 | 64.0% | 8 | 72.7% | 30 | 66.7% | 6 | 46.2% | 10 | 90.9% | 9 | 60.0% | 67 | 70.5% | | |
| Introduction to campus resources and services | 20 | 83.3% | 68 | 95.8% | 40 | 90.9% | 47 | 94.0% | 9 | 81.8% | 43 | 95.6% | 12 | 92.3% | 10 | 90.9% | 14 | 93.3% | 88 | 92.6% | | |

*Table continues on page 122*

*Table continued from page 121*

| Survey question/responses | Institutional type | | | | Institution control | | | | Number of undergraduates enrolled | | | | | | | | | | | | Total | |
| --- | --- | --- | --- | --- | --- | --- | --- | --- | --- | --- | --- | --- | --- | --- | --- | --- | --- | --- | --- | --- | --- | --- |
| | Two-year | | Four-year | | Public | | Private | | Under 1,000 | | 1,000-4,999 | | 5,999-9,999 | | 10,000-19,999 | | 20,000 and above | | | | | |
| | Freq. | % | Freq | % | Freq. | % | Freq. | % | Freq. | % | Freq. | % | Freq. | % | Freq. | % | Freq. | % | Freq. | % |
| Social engagement opportunities | 10 | 41.7% | 49 | 69.0% | 25 | 56.8% | 34 | 68.0% | 7 | 63.6% | 27 | 60.0% | 9 | 69.2% | 9 | 81.8% | 8 | 53.3% | 60 | 63.2% |
| Placement testing | 15 | 62.5% | 19 | 26.8% | 21 | 47.7% | 13 | 26.0% | 4 | 36.4% | 15 | 33.3% | 7 | 53.8% | 5 | 45.5% | 4 | 26.7% | 35 | 36.8% |
| Registration or course enrollment | 16 | 66.7% | 45 | 63.4% | 32 | 72.7% | 29 | 58.0% | 6 | 54.5% | 31 | 68.9% | 9 | 69.2% | 8 | 72.7% | 8 | 53.3% | 62 | 65.3% |
| Sessions for family members | 8 | 33.3% | 34 | 47.9% | 19 | 43.2% | 22 | 44.0% | 5 | 45.5% | 17 | 37.8% | 8 | 61.5% | 6 | 54.5% | 5 | 33.3% | 41 | 43.2% |
| Structured interaction with faculty | 6 | 25.0% | 24 | 33.8% | 11 | 25.0% | 19 | 38.0% | 6 | 54.5% | 15 | 33.3% | 7 | 53.9% | 3 | 27.3% | 0 | 0.0% | 31 | 32.6% |
| Other, please specify | 1 | 4.2% | 1 | 1.4% | 1 | 2.3% | 1 | 2.0% | 0 | 0.0% | 1 | 2.2% | 0 | 0.0% | 0 | 0.0% | 1 | 6.7% | 2 | 2.1% |
| Total | 24 | 100.0% | 71 | 100.0% | 44 | 100.0% | 50 | 100.0% | 11 | 100.0% | 45 | 100.0% | 13 | 100.0% | 11 | 100.0% | 15 | 100.0% | 95 | 100.0% |
| Q62. Which incoming transfer/transfer-intending students, by category, are not required to participate in orientation programming? (Select all that apply.) | | | | | | | | | | | | | | | | | | | | |
| All transfer/transfer-intending students are required to participate | 12 | 50.0% | 28 | 39.4% | 16 | 36.4% | 23 | 46.0% | 4 | 36.4% | 23 | 51.1% | 4 | 30.8% | 1 | 9.1% | 7 | 46.7% | 39 | 41.1% |
| Anyone not interested in participating | 3 | 12.5% | 19 | 26.8% | 12 | 27.3% | 10 | 20.0% | 1 | 9.1% | 7 | 15.6% | 5 | 38.5% | 4 | 36.4% | 5 | 33.3% | 22 | 23.2% |
| Adult learners | 3 | 12.5% | 10 | 14.1% | 7 | 15.9% | 6 | 12.0% | 0 | 0.0% | 6 | 13.3% | 2 | 15.4% | 1 | 9.1% | 4 | 26.7% | 13 | 13.7% |
| Formerly or currently incarcerated students | 2 | 8.3% | 4 | 5.6% | 5 | 11.4% | 1 | 2.0% | 0 | 0.0% | 1 | 2.2% | 2 | 15.4% | 1 | 9.1% | 2 | 13.3% | 6 | 6.3% |
| Full-time students | 2 | 8.3% | 4 | 5.6% | 5 | 11.4% | 1 | 2.0% | 0 | 0.0% | 1 | 2.2% | 2 | 15.4% | 1 | 9.1% | 2 | 13.3% | 6 | 6.3% |
| Honors students | 2 | 8.3% | 4 | 5.6% | 5 | 11.4% | 1 | 2.0% | 0 | 0.0% | 1 | 2.2% | 2 | 15.4% | 1 | 9.1% | 2 | 13.3% | 6 | 6.3% |
| Institutionally-deemed academically underprepared students (e.g., students enrolled in developmental or remedial courses) | 1 | 4.2% | 4 | 5.6% | 4 | 9.1% | 1 | 2.0% | 0 | 0.0% | 1 | 2.2% | 1 | 7.7% | 1 | 9.1% | 2 | 13.3% | 5 | 5.3% |
| International students | 1 | 4.2% | 3 | 4.2% | 3 | 6.8% | 1 | 2.0% | 0 | 0.0% | 1 | 2.2% | 0 | 0.0% | 1 | 9.1% | 2 | 13.3% | 4 | 4.2% |

*Table continues on page 123*

*Table continued from page 122*

| | Institutional type | | | | Institution control | | | | Number of undergraduates enrolled | | | | | | | | | | | Total | |
|---|---|---|---|---|---|---|---|---|---|---|---|---|---|---|---|---|---|---|---|---|---|---|
| | Two-year | | Four-year | | Public | | Private | | Under 1,000 | | 1,000-4,999 | | 5,999-9,999 | | 10,000-19,999 | | 20,000 and above | | | |
| Survey question/responses | Freq. | % | Freq | % | Freq. | % | Freq. | % | Freq. | % | Freq. | % | Freq. | % | Freq. | % | Freq. | % | Freq. | % |
| Learning community participants | 2 | 8.3% | 4 | 5.6% | 5 | 11.4% | 1 | 2.0% | 0 | 0.0% | 1 | 2.2% | 2 | 15.4% | 1 | 9.1% | 2 | 13.3% | 6 | 6.3% |
| Non-degree students | 6 | 25.0% | 24 | 33.8% | 16 | 36.4% | 14 | 28.0% | 3 | 27.3% | 11 | 24.4% | 4 | 30.8% | 6 | 54.5% | 7 | 46.7% | 31 | 32.6% |
| Online students | 2 | 8.3% | 10 | 14.1% | 7 | 15.9% | 5 | 10.0% | 0 | 0.0% | 3 | 6.7% | 2 | 15.4% | 3 | 27.3% | 4 | 26.7% | 12 | 12.6% |
| Part-time students | 4 | 16.7% | 7 | 9.9% | 7 | 15.9% | 4 | 8.0% | 0 | 0.0% | 4 | 8.9% | 2 | 15.4% | 2 | 18.2% | 3 | 20.0% | 11 | 11.6% |
| Preprofessional students (e.g., pre-law, pre-med) | 2 | 8.3% | 5 | 7.0% | 5 | 11.4% | 2 | 4.0% | 0 | 0.0% | 1 | 2.2% | 2 | 15.4% | 2 | 18.2% | 2 | 13.3% | 7 | 7.4% |
| Reentry students | 7 | 29.2% | 22 | 31.0% | 15 | 34.1% | 14 | 28.0% | 6 | 54.5% | 9 | 20.0% | 4 | 30.8% | 4 | 36.4% | 7 | 46.7% | 30 | 31.5% |
| Student athletes | 1 | 4.2% | 3 | 4.2% | 4 | 9.1% | 0 | 0.0% | 0 | 0.0% | 0 | 0.0% | 1 | 7.7% | 1 | 9.1% | 2 | 13.3% | 4 | 4.2% |
| Students caring for dependents | 2 | 8.3% | 4 | 5.6% | 5 | 11.4% | 1 | 2.0% | 0 | 0.0% | 1 | 2.2% | 2 | 15.4% | 1 | 9.1% | 2 | 13.3% | 6 | 6.3% |
| Students on probationary status | 2 | 8.3% | 4 | 5.6% | 5 | 11.4% | 1 | 2.0% | 0 | 0.0% | 1 | 2.2% | 2 | 15.4% | 1 | 9.1% | 2 | 13.3% | 6 | 6.3% |
| Students residing within a particular residence hall | 2 | 8.3% | 4 | 5.6% | 5 | 11.4% | 1 | 2.0% | 0 | 0.0% | 1 | 2.2% | 2 | 15.4% | 1 | 9.1% | 2 | 13.3% | 6 | 6.3% |
| Students within specific majors, please list: | 2 | 8.3% | 4 | 5.6% | 4 | 9.1% | 2 | 4.0% | 0 | 0.0% | 2 | 4.4% | 2 | 15.4% | 0 | 0.0% | 2 | 13.3% | 6 | 6.3% |
| TRIO participants | 2 | 8.3% | 4 | 5.6% | 5 | 11.4% | 1 | 2.0% | 0 | 0.0% | 1 | 2.2% | 2 | 15.4% | 1 | 9.1% | 2 | 13.3% | 6 | 6.3% |
| Undeclared students | 2 | 8.3% | 4 | 5.6% | 5 | 11.4% | 1 | 2.0% | 0 | 0.0% | 1 | 2.2% | 2 | 15.4% | 1 | 9.1% | 2 | 13.3% | 6 | 6.3% |
| Veterans | 2 | 8.3% | 4 | 5.6% | 5 | 11.4% | 1 | 2.0% | 0 | 0.0% | 1 | 2.2% | 2 | 15.4% | 1 | 9.1% | 2 | 13.3% | 6 | 6.3% |
| Visiting students | 5 | 20.8% | 10 | 14.1% | 13 | 29.5% | 2 | 4.0% | 2 | 18.2% | 3 | 6.7% | 2 | 15.4% | 4 | 36.4% | 5 | 33.3% | 16 | 16.8% |
| Other, please specify | 3 | 12.5% | 6 | 8.5% | 5 | 11.4% | 4 | 8.0% | 1 | 9.1% | 4 | 8.9% | 1 | 7.7% | 2 | 18.2% | 1 | 6.7% | 9 | 9.5% |
| I don't know | 1 | 4.2% | 3 | 4.2% | 2 | 4.5% | 2 | 4.0% | 0 | 0.0% | 1 | 2.2% | 1 | 7.7% | 1 | 9.1% | 1 | 6.7% | 4 | 4.2% |
| Total | 24 | 100.0% | 71 | 100.0% | 44 | 100.0% | 50 | 100.0% | 11 | 100.0% | 45 | 100.0% | 13 | 100.0% | 11 | 100.0% | 15 | 100.0% | 95 | 100.0% |

*Table continues on page 124*

*Table continued from page 123*

| Survey question/responses | Institutional type | | | | Institution control | | | | Number of undergraduates enrolled | | | | | | | | | | | | Total | |
| --- | --- | --- | --- | --- | --- | --- | --- | --- | --- | --- | --- | --- | --- | --- | --- | --- | --- | --- | --- | --- | --- | --- |
| | Two-year | | Four-year | | Public | | Private | | Under 1,000 | | 1,000-4,999 | | 5,999-9,999 | | 10,000-19,999 | | 20,000 and above | | | |
| | Freq. | % | Freq | % | Freq. | % | Freq. | % | Freq. | % | Freq. | % | Freq. | % | Freq. | % | Freq. | % | Freq. | % |
| Q110. Which campus unit directly administers orientation programming for incoming transfer/transfer-intending students? (Select all that apply.) | | | | | | | | | | | | | | | | | | | | |
| Academic affairs office | 1 | 4.3% | 15 | 21.7% | 5 | 11.9% | 11 | 22.4% | 3 | 27.3% | 7 | 15.9% | 3 | 25.0% | 2 | 18.2% | 1 | 7.1% | 16 | 17.4% |
| Academic department(s), please list | 0 | 0.0% | 9 | 13.0% | 2 | 4.8% | 7 | 14.3% | 0 | 0.0% | 5 | 11.4% | 1 | 8.3% | 2 | 18.2% | 1 | 7.1% | 9 | 9.8% |
| College or school (e.g., College of Liberal Arts) | 0 | 0.0% | 0 | 0.0% | 0 | 0.0% | 0 | 0.0% | 0 | 0.0% | 0 | 0.0% | 0 | 0.0% | 0 | 0.0% | 0 | 0.0% | 0 | 0.0% |
| Transfer program office | 1 | 4.3% | 2 | 2.9% | 1 | 2.4% | 2 | 4.1% | 0 | 0.0% | 3 | 6.8% | 0 | 0.0% | 0 | 0.0% | 0 | 0.0% | 3 | 3.3% |
| Student affairs/student services office | 21 | 91.3% | 41 | 59.4% | 32 | 76.1% | 29 | 59.2% | 8 | 72.7% | 29 | 65.9% | 8 | 66.6% | 7 | 63.6% | 10 | 71.4% | 62 | 67.4% |
| University college | 0 | 0.0% | 2 | 2.9% | 2 | 4.8% | 0 | 0.0% | 0 | 0.0% | 0 | 0.0% | 0 | 0.0% | 0 | 0.0% | 2 | 14.3% | 2 | 2.2% |
| Total | 23 | 100.0% | 69 | 100.0% | 42 | 100.0% | 49 | 100.0% | 11 | 100.0% | 44 | 100.0% | 12 | 100.0% | 11 | 100.0% | 14 | 100.0% | 92 | 100.0% |
| Q64. Has your orientation programming been formally assessed or evaluated within the last four years? | | | | | | | | | | | | | | | | | | | | |
| Yes | 8 | 33.3% | 24 | 33.8% | 14 | 31.8% | 17 | 34.0% | 6 | 54.5% | 13 | 28.9% | 5 | 38.5% | 4 | 36.4% | 4 | 26.7% | 32 | 33.7% |
| No | 12 | 50.0% | 21 | 29.6% | 16 | 36.4% | 17 | 34.0% | 2 | 18.2% | 24 | 53.3% | 3 | 23.1% | 1 | 9.1% | 3 | 20.0% | 33 | 34.7% |
| I don't know | 4 | 16.7% | 26 | 36.6% | 14 | 31.8% | 16 | 32.0% | 3 | 27.3% | 8 | 17.8% | 5 | 38.5% | 6 | 54.5% | 8 | 53.3% | 30 | 31.6% |
| Total | 24 | 100.0% | 71 | 100.0% | 44 | 100.0% | 50 | 100.0% | 11 | 100.0% | 45 | 100.0% | 13 | 100.0% | 11 | 100.0% | 15 | 100.0% | 95 | 100.0% |
| Q65. What type of assessment was conducted? (Select all that apply). | | | | | | | | | | | | | | | | | | | | |
| Analysis of institutional data (e.g., GPA, retention rates, graduation) | 3 | 37.5% | 18 | 75.0% | 9 | 64.3% | 12 | 70.6% | 4 | 66.7% | 8 | 61.5% | 3 | 60.0% | 3 | 75.0% | 0 | 0.0% | 22 | 68.8% |
| Direct assessment of student learning outcomes | 3 | 37.5% | 9 | 37.5% | 3 | 21.4% | 9 | 52.9% | 3 | 50.0% | 7 | 53.8% | 1 | 20.0% | 1 | 25.0% | 1 | 25.0% | 13 | 40.6% |
| Evaluation of student orientation leaders | 1 | 12.5% | 7 | 29.2% | 4 | 28.6% | 4 | 23.5% | 1 | 16.7% | 4 | 30.8% | 0 | 0.0% | 1 | 25.0% | 2 | 50.0% | 8 | 25.0% |
| Focus groups with faculty | 1 | 12.5% | 2 | 8.3% | 1 | 7.1% | 2 | 11.8% | 1 | 16.7% | 1 | 7.7% | 0 | 0.0% | 1 | 25.0% | 0 | 0.0% | 3 | 9.4% |

*Table continues on page 125*

*Table continued from page 124*

| Survey question/responses | Institutional type | | | | Institution control | | | | Number of undergraduates enrolled | | | | | | | | | | | | Total | |
| --- | --- | --- | --- | --- | --- | --- | --- | --- | --- | --- | --- | --- | --- | --- | --- | --- | --- | --- | --- | --- | --- | --- |
| | Two-year | | Four-year | | Public | | Private | | Under 1,000 | | 1,000-4,999 | | 5,999-9,999 | | 10,000-19,999 | | 20,000 and above | | | | | |
| | Freq. | % | Freq | % | Freq. | % | Freq. | % | Freq. | % | Freq. | % | Freq. | % | Freq. | % | Freq. | % | Freq. | % | | |
| Focus groups with professional staff | 3 | 37.5% | 4 | 16.7% | 5 | 35.7% | 2 | 11.8% | 1 | 16.7% | 2 | 15.4% | 2 | 40.0% | 1 | 25.0% | 1 | 25.0% | 7 | 21.9% | | |
| Focus groups with students | 2 | 25.0% | 8 | 33.3% | 4 | 28.6% | 6 | 35.3% | 1 | 16.7% | 6 | 46.2% | 1 | 20.0% | 1 | 25.0% | 1 | 25.0% | 10 | 31.3% | | |
| Individual interviews with faculty | 1 | 12.5% | 1 | 4.2% | 1 | 7.1% | 1 | 5.9% | 1 | 16.7% | 0 | 0.0% | 2 | 40.0% | 0 | 0.0% | 0 | 0.0% | 3 | 9.4% | | |
| Individual interviews with orientation staff | 2 | 25.0% | 6 | 25.0% | 2 | 14.3% | 6 | 35.3% | 1 | 16.7% | 4 | 30.8% | 2 | 40.0% | 1 | 25.0% | 0 | 0.0% | 8 | 25.0% | | |
| Individual interviews with students | 3 | 37.5% | 4 | 16.7% | 3 | 21.4% | 4 | 23.5% | 0 | 0.0% | 5 | 38.5% | 2 | 40.0% | 0 | 0.0% | 0 | 0.0% | 7 | 21.9% | | |
| Program review | 1 | 12.5% | 10 | 41.7% | 5 | 35.7% | 6 | 35.3% | 3 | 50.0% | 3 | 23.1% | 1 | 20.0% | 3 | 75.0% | 2 | 50.0% | 12 | 37.5% | | |
| Survey evaluation | 1 | 12.5% | 10 | 41.7% | 3 | 21.4% | 8 | 47.1% | 3 | 50.0% | 5 | 38.5% | 0 | 0.0% | 2 | 50.0% | 2 | 50.0% | 12 | 37.5% | | |
| Survey instrument | 7 | 87.5% | 16 | 66.7% | 13 | 92.9% | 9 | 52.9% | 4 | 66.7% | 9 | 69.2% | 2 | 40.0% | 0 | 0.0% | 3 | 75.0% | 22 | 68.8% | | |
| Other, please specify | 0 | 0.0% | 1 | 4.2% | 0 | 0.0% | 1 | 5.9% | 0 | 0.0% | 0 | 0.0% | 1 | 20.0% | 0 | 0.0% | 0 | 0.0% | 1 | 3.1% | | |
| Total | 8 | 100.0% | 24 | 100.0% | 14 | 100.0% | 50 | 100.0% | 6 | 100.0% | 13 | 100.0% | 5 | 100.0% | 4 | 100.0% | 4 | 100.0% | 32 | 100.0% | | |
| Q66. In your opinion, considering costs (including staff time and resources) and educational gains, how beneficial is your institution's orientation programming in supporting transfer student success? | | | | | | | | | | | | | | | | | | | | | | |
| Low benefit | 0 | 0.0% | 2 | 2.8% | 1 | 2.3% | 1 | 2.0% | 0 | 0.0% | 0 | 0.0% | 1 | 7.7% | 0 | 0.0% | 1 | 6.7% | 2 | 2.1% | | |
| Low-medium benefit | 2 | 8.3% | 8 | 11.3% | 5 | 11.4% | 5 | 10.0% | 0 | 0.0% | 8 | 17.8% | 0 | 0.0% | 1 | 9.1% | 1 | 6.7% | 10 | 10.5% | | |
| Medium benefit | 7 | 29.5% | 21 | 29.6% | 14 | 31.8% | 14 | 28.0% | 2 | 18.2% | 17 | 37.8% | 2 | 15.4% | 4 | 36.4% | 3 | 20.0% | 28 | 29.5% | | |
| Medium-high benefit | 6 | 25.0% | 25 | 35.2% | 13 | 29.5% | 18 | 36.0% | 7 | 63.6% | 12 | 26.7% | 7 | 53.8% | 2 | 18.2% | 4 | 26.7% | 32 | 33.7% | | |
| High benefit | 7 | 29.5% | 13 | 18.3% | 9 | 20.5% | 10 | 20.0% | 1 | 9.1% | 8 | 17.8% | 3 | 23.1% | 2 | 18.2% | 5 | 33.3% | 19 | 20.0% | | |
| Unable to judge | 2 | 8.3% | 2 | 2.8% | 9 | 20.5% | 2 | 4.0% | 1 | 9.1% | 0 | 0.0% | 0 | 0.0% | 2 | 18.2% | 1 | 6.7% | 4 | 4.2% | | |
| Total | 24 | 100.0% | 71 | 100.0% | 44 | 100.0% | 50 | 100.0% | 11 | 100.0% | 45 | 100.0% | 13 | 100.0% | 11 | 100.0% | 15 | 100.0% | 95 | 100.0% | | |

*Table continues on page 126*

*Table continued from page 125*

| Survey question/responses | Institutional type | | | | Institution control | | | | Number of undergraduates enrolled | | | | | | | | | | | | Total | |
|---|---|---|---|---|---|---|---|---|---|---|---|---|---|---|---|---|---|---|---|---|---|---|
| | Two-year | | Four-year | | Public | | Private | | Under 1,000 | | 1,000-4,999 | | 5,999-9,999 | | 10,000-19,999 | | 20,000 and above | | | |
| | Freq. | % | Freq | % | Freq. | % | Freq. | % | Freq. | % | Freq. | % | Freq. | % | Freq. | % | Freq. | % | Freq. | % |
| Q68. Does your institution offer academic advising to transfer/transfer-intending students? | | | | | | | | | | | | | | | | | | | | |
| Yes | 47 | 97.9% | 84 | 94.4% | 68 | 97.1% | 62 | 93.9% | 16 | 100.0% | 60 | 96.8% | 19 | 90.5% | 17 | 89.5% | 19 | 100.0% | 131 | 95.6% |
| No | 0 | 0.0% | 3 | 3.4% | 1 | 1.4% | 2 | 3.0% | 0 | 0.0% | 0 | 0.0% | 2 | 9.5% | 1 | 5.3% | 0 | 0.0% | 3 | 2.2% |
| I don't know | 1 | 2.1% | 2 | 2.2% | 1 | 1.4% | 2 | 3.0% | 0 | 0.0% | 2 | 3.2% | 0 | 0.0% | 1 | 5.3% | 0 | 0.0% | 3 | 2.2% |
| Total | 48 | 100.0% | 89 | 100.0% | 70 | 100.0% | 66 | 100.0% | 16 | 100.0% | 62 | 100.0% | 21 | 100.0% | 19 | 100.0% | 19 | 100.0% | 137 | 100.0% |
| Q132. When are incoming transfer/transfer-intending students at your institution first offered academic advising services? | | | | | | | | | | | | | | | | | | | | |
| Before they are admitted the institution | 13 | 28.8% | 27 | 32.1% | 21 | 31.8% | 18 | 29.0% | 7 | 43.8% | 13 | 22.0% | 8 | 44.4% | 6 | 35.3% | 6 | 31.6% | 40 | 31.0% |
| After students have confirmed their acceptance at the institution | 17 | 37.7% | 40 | 47.6% | 21 | 31.8% | 36 | 58.1% | 9 | 56.3% | 34 | 57.6% | 6 | 33.3% | 4 | 23.5% | 4 | 21.1% | 57 | 44.1% |
| During orientation | 6 | 13.3% | 11 | 13.1% | 12 | 18.8% | 5 | 8.1% | 0 | 0.0% | 7 | 11.8% | 2 | 11.1% | 3 | 17.6% | 5 | 26.3% | 17 | 13.2% |
| Other, please specify | 9 | 20.0% | 6 | 7.1% | 12 | 18.8% | 3 | 4.8% | 0 | 0.0% | 5 | 8.4% | 2 | 11.1% | 4 | 23.5% | 4 | 21.1% | 15 | 11.6% |
| Total | 45 | 100.0% | 84 | 100.0% | 66 | 100.0% | 62 | 100.0% | 16 | 100.0% | 59 | 100.0% | 18 | 100.0% | 17 | 100.0% | 19 | 100.0% | 129 | 100.0% |
| Q70. Are incoming transfer/transfer-intending students at your institution required to participate in academic advising? | | | | | | | | | | | | | | | | | | | | |
| Yes | 29 | 63.0% | 62 | 73.8% | 43 | 64.2% | 47 | 75.8% | 12 | 75.0% | 45 | 75.0% | 15 | 83.3% | 9 | 52.9% | 10 | 52.6% | 91 | 70.0% |
| No | 16 | 34.8% | 20 | 23.8% | 22 | 32.8% | 14 | 22.6% | 4 | 25.0% | 14 | 23.3% | 2 | 11.1% | 8 | 47.1% | 8 | 42.1% | 36 | 27.7% |
| I don't know | 1 | 2.2% | 2 | 2.4% | 2 | 3.0% | 1 | 1.6% | 0 | 0.0% | 1 | 1.7% | 1 | 5.6% | 0 | 0.0% | 1 | 5.3% | 3 | 2.3% |
| Total | 46 | 100.0% | 84 | 100.0% | 67 | 100.0% | 62 | 100.0% | 16 | 100.0% | 60 | 100.0% | 18 | 100.0% | 17 | 100.0% | 19 | 100.0% | 130 | 100.0% |
| Q69. What is the approximate percentage of incoming transfer/transfer-intending students who participate in academic advising at your institution? | | | | | | | | | | | | | | | | | | | | |
| 10% or less | 0 | 0.0% | 1 | 1.2% | 0 | 0.0% | 1 | 1.6% | 0 | 0.0% | 1 | 1.7% | 0 | 0.0% | 0 | 0.0% | 0 | 0.0% | 1 | 0.8% |
| 11-20% | 2 | 4.3% | 1 | 1.2% | 2 | 3.0% | 1 | 1.6% | 0 | 0.0% | 3 | 5.0% | 0 | 0.0% | 0 | 0.0% | 0 | 0.0% | 3 | 2.3% |
| 21-30% | 1 | 2.2% | 2 | 2.4% | 2 | 3.0% | 1 | 1.6% | 1 | 6.3% | 1 | 1.7% | 0 | 0.0% | 0 | 0.0% | 1 | 5.3% | 3 | 2.3% |

*Table continues on page 127*

*Table continued from page 126*

| Survey question/responses | Institutional type | | | | Institution control | | | | Number of undergraduates enrolled | | | | | | | | | | | | Total | |
| --- | --- | --- | --- | --- | --- | --- | --- | --- | --- | --- | --- | --- | --- | --- | --- | --- | --- | --- | --- | --- | --- | --- |
| | Two-year | | Four-year | | Public | | Private | | Under 1,000 | | 1,000-4,999 | | 5,999-9,999 | | 10,000-19,999 | | 20,000 and above | | | | | |
| | Freq. | % | Freq | % | Freq. | % | Freq. | % | Freq. | % | Freq. | % | Freq. | % | Freq. | % | Freq. | % | Freq. | % | | |
| 31-40% | 1 | 2.2% | 0 | 0.0% | 1 | 1.5% | 0 | 0.0% | 0 | 0.0% | 1 | 1.7% | 0 | 0.0% | 0 | 0.0% | 0 | 0.0% | 1 | 0.8% | | |
| 41-50% | 2 | 4.3% | 1 | 1.2% | 2 | 3.0% | 1 | 1.6% | 0 | 0.0% | 2 | 3.3% | 0 | 0.0% | 1 | 5.9% | 0 | 0.0% | 3 | 2.3% | | |
| 51-60% | 5 | 10.9% | 3 | 3.6% | 6 | 9.0% | 2 | 3.2% | 1 | 6.3% | 4 | 6.7% | 1 | 5.6% | 1 | 5.9% | 1 | 5.3% | 8 | 6.2% | | |
| 61-70% | 0 | 0.0% | 2 | 2.4% | 0 | 0.0% | 1 | 1.6% | 0 | 0.0% | 1 | 1.7% | 0 | 0.0% | 1 | 5.9% | 0 | 0.0% | 2 | 1.5% | | |
| 71-80% | 0 | 0.0% | 1 | 1.2% | 1 | 1.5% | 1 | 1.6% | 1 | 6.3% | 0 | 0.0% | 0 | 0.0% | 0 | 0.0% | 0 | 0.0% | 1 | 0.8% | | |
| 81-90% | 5 | 10.9% | 5 | 6.0% | 9 | 13.4% | 1 | 1.6% | 1 | 6.3% | 2 | 3.3% | 2 | 11.1% | 3 | 17.6% | 2 | 10.5% | 10 | 7.7% | | |
| 91-100% | 19 | 41.3% | 54 | 64.3% | 30 | 44.8% | 42 | 67.7% | 10 | 62.5% | 38 | 63.3% | 11 | 61.1% | 7 | 41.2% | 7 | 36.8% | 73 | 56.2% | | |
| I don't know | 11 | 23.9% | 14 | 16.7% | 14 | 20.9% | 11 | 17.7% | 2 | 12.5% | 7 | 11.7% | 4 | 22.2% | 4 | 23.5% | 8 | 42.1% | 25 | 19.2% | | |
| Total | 46 | 100.0% | 84 | 100.0% | 67 | 100.0% | 62 | 100.0% | 16 | 100.0% | 60 | 100.0% | 18 | 100.0% | 17 | 100.0% | 19 | 100.0% | 130 | 100.0% | | |
| Q71. Which of the following groups of incoming transfer/transfer-intending students are not required to participate in academic advising? (Select all that apply.) | | | | | | | | | | | | | | | | | | | | | | |
| All transfers/transfer-intending students are required to participate | 20 | 43.5% | 50 | 59.5% | 31 | 46.3% | 38 | 61.3% | 10 | 62.5% | 34 | 56.7% | 9 | 50.0% | 6 | 35.3% | 10 | 52.6% | 69 | 53.1% | | |
| Anyone not interested in participating | 10 | 21.7% | 16 | 19.0% | 16 | 23.9% | 10 | 16.1% | 3 | 18.8% | 10 | 16.7% | 2 | 11.1% | 5 | 29.4% | 6 | 31.6% | 26 | 20.0% | | |
| Adult learners | 1 | 2.2% | 5 | 6.0% | 5 | 7.5% | 1 | 1.6% | 1 | 6.3% | 0 | 0.0% | 0 | 0.0% | 3 | 17.6% | 2 | 10.5% | 6 | 4.6% | | |
| Formerly or currently incarcerated students | 2 | 4.3% | 5 | 6.0% | 6 | 9.0% | 1 | 1.6% | 1 | 6.3% | 1 | 1.7% | 0 | 0.0% | 3 | 17.6% | 2 | 10.5% | 7 | 5.4% | | |
| Full-time students | 1 | 2.2% | 4 | 4.8% | 4 | 6.0% | 1 | 1.6% | 1 | 6.3% | 0 | 0.0% | 0 | 0.0% | 2 | 11.8% | 2 | 10.5% | 5 | 3.8% | | |
| Honors students | 1 | 2.2% | 3 | 3.6% | 3 | 4.5% | 1 | 1.6% | 1 | 6.3% | 0 | 0.0% | 0 | 0.0% | 2 | 11.8% | 1 | 5.3% | 4 | 3.1% | | |
| Institutionally-deemed academically underprepared students (e.g., students enrolled in developmental or remedial courses) | 1 | 2.2% | 4 | 4.8% | 4 | 6.0% | 1 | 1.6% | 1 | 6.3% | 0 | 0.0% | 0 | 0.0% | 2 | 11.8% | 2 | 10.5% | 5 | 3.0% | | |

*Table continues on page 128*

*Table continued from page 127*

| Survey question/responses | Institutional type | | | | Institution control | | | | Number of undergraduates enrolled | | | | | | | | | | | | Total | |
|---|---|---|---|---|---|---|---|---|---|---|---|---|---|---|---|---|---|---|---|---|---|---|
| | Two-year | | Four-year | | Public | | Private | | Under 1,000 | | 1,000-4,999 | | 5,999-9,999 | | 10,000-19,999 | | 20,000 and above | | | | Total | |
| | Freq. | % | Freq | % | Freq. | % | Freq. | % | Freq. | % | Freq. | % | Freq. | % | Freq. | % | Freq. | % | Freq. | % | | |
| International students | 2 | 4.3% | 3 | 3.6% | 4 | 6.0% | 1 | 1.6% | 1 | 6.3% | 0 | 0.0% | 0 | 0.0% | 3 | 17.6% | 1 | 5.3% | 5 | 3.8% | | |
| Learning community participants | 1 | 2.2% | 3 | 3.6% | 3 | 4.5% | 1 | 1.6% | 1 | 6.3% | 0 | 0.0% | 0 | 0.0% | 2 | 11.8% | 1 | 5.3% | 4 | 3.1% | | |
| Non-degree students | 5 | 10.9% | 13 | 15.5% | 12 | 17.9% | 6 | 9.7% | 2 | 12.5% | 4 | 6.7% | 3 | 16.7% | 5 | 29.4% | 5 | 26.3% | 19 | 14.6% | | |
| Online students | 0 | 0.0% | 3 | 3.6% | 2 | 3.0% | 1 | 1.6% | 1 | 6.3% | 0 | 0.0% | 0 | 0.0% | 1 | 5.9% | 1 | 5.3% | 3 | 2.3% | | |
| Part-time students | 1 | 2.2% | 3 | 3.6% | 4 | 6.0% | 0 | 0.0% | 0 | 0.0% | 0 | 0.0% | 0 | 0.0% | 2 | 11.8% | 2 | 10.5% | 4 | 3.1% | | |
| Preprofessional students (e.g., pre-law, pre-med) | 1 | 2.2% | 2 | 2.4% | 3 | 4.5% | 0 | 0.0% | 0 | 0.0% | 0 | 0.0% | 0 | 0.0% | 2 | 11.8% | 1 | 5.3% | 3 | 2.3% | | |
| Reentry students | 6 | 13.0% | 8 | 9.5% | 10 | 14.9% | 4 | 6.5% | 4 | 25.0% | 0 | 0.0% | 4 | 22.2% | 3 | 17.6% | 4 | 21.1% | 15 | 11.5% | | |
| Student athletes | 1 | 2.2% | 3 | 3.6% | 3 | 4.5% | 1 | 1.6% | 1 | 6.3% | 0 | 0.0% | 0 | 0.0% | 2 | 11.8% | 1 | 5.3% | 4 | 3.1% | | |
| Students caring for dependents | 1 | 2.2% | 5 | 6.0% | 5 | 7.5% | 1 | 1.6% | 1 | 6.3% | 0 | 0.0% | 0 | 0.0% | 3 | 17.6% | 2 | 10.5% | 6 | 4.6% | | |
| Students on probationary status | 1 | 2.2% | 3 | 3.6% | 3 | 4.5% | 1 | 1.6% | 1 | 6.3% | 0 | 0.0% | 0 | 0.0% | 2 | 11.8% | 1 | 5.3% | 4 | 3.1% | | |
| Students residing within a particular residence hall | 1 | 2.2% | 4 | 4.8% | 4 | 6.0% | 1 | 1.6% | 1 | 6.3% | 0 | 0.0% | 0 | 0.0% | 2 | 11.8% | 2 | 10.5% | 5 | 3.8% | | |
| Students within specific majors, please list: | 2 | 4.3% | 5 | 6.0% | 5 | 7.5% | 2 | 3.2% | 1 | 6.3% | 1 | 1.7% | 1 | 5.6% | 2 | 11.8% | 2 | 10.5% | 7 | 5.4% | | |
| TRIO participants | 0 | 0.0% | 4 | 4.8% | 3 | 4.5% | 1 | 1.6% | 1 | 6.3% | 0 | 0.0% | 0 | 0.0% | 1 | 5.9% | 2 | 10.5% | 4 | 3.1% | | |
| Undeclared students | 2 | 4.3% | 4 | 4.8% | 5 | 7.5% | 1 | 1.6% | 1 | 6.3% | 0 | 0.0% | 0 | 0.0% | 3 | 17.6% | 2 | 10.5% | 6 | 4.6% | | |
| Veterans | 5 | 10.9% | 7 | 8.3% | 11 | 16.4% | 1 | 1.6% | 3 | 18.8% | 0 | 0.0% | 2 | 11.1% | 4 | 23.5% | 4 | 21.1% | 13 | 10.0% | | |
| Visiting Students | 7 | 15.2% | 6 | 7.1% | 9 | 13.4% | 4 | 6.5% | 0 | 0.0% | 6 | 10.0% | 1 | 5.6% | 2 | 11.8% | 4 | 21.1% | 13 | 10.0% | | |
| I don't know | 5 | 10.9% | 4 | 4.8% | 6 | 9.0% | 3 | 4.8% | 1 | 6.3% | 5 | 8.3% | 1 | 5.6% | 1 | 5.9% | 1 | 5.3% | 9 | 6.9% | | |
| Other, please specify | 1 | 2.2% | 1 | 0.9% | 1 | 1.1% | 1 | 1.6% | 0 | 0.0% | 1 | 1.7% | 1 | 5.6% | 0 | 0.0% | 0 | 0.0% | 2 | 1.2% | | |
| Total | 46 | 100.0% | 109 | 100.0% | 89 | 100.0% | 62 | 100.0% | 16 | 100.0% | 74 | 100.0% | 28 | 100.0% | 17 | 100.0% | 19 | 100.0% | 130 | 100.0% | | |

*Table continues on page 129*

*Table continued from page 128*

| | Institutional type | | | | Institution control | | | | Number of undergraduates enrolled | | | | | | | | | | | | Total | |
|---|---|---|---|---|---|---|---|---|---|---|---|---|---|---|---|---|---|---|---|---|---|---|---|
| | Two-year | | Four-year | | Public | | Private | | Under 1,000 | | 1,000-4,999 | | 5,999-9,999 | | 10,000-19,999 | | 20,000 and above | | | | | |
| Survey question/responses | Freq. | % | Freq | % | Freq. | % | Freq. | % | Freq. | % | Freq. | % | Freq. | % | Freq. | % | Freq. | % | Freq. | % |
| Q111. At your institution, are incoming transfer/transfer-intending students assigned an advisor? | | | | | | | | | | | | | | | | | | | | |
| Yes | 39 | 84.8% | 78 | 92.9% | 55 | 82.1% | 61 | 98.4% | 16 | 100.0% | 57 | 95.0% | 18 | 100.0% | 13 | 76.5% | 13 | 68.4% | 117 | 90.0% |
| No | 6 | 13.0% | 6 | 7.1% | 11 | 16.4% | 1 | 1.6% | 0 | 0.0% | 2 | 3.3% | 0 | 0.0% | 4 | 23.5% | 6 | 31.6% | 12 | 9.2% |
| I don't know | 1 | 2.2% | 0 | 0.0% | 1 | 1.5% | 0 | 0.0% | 0 | 0.0% | 1 | 1.7% | 0 | 0.0% | 0 | 0.0% | 0 | 0.0% | 1 | 0.8% |
| Total | 46 | 100.0% | 84 | 100.0% | 67 | 100.0% | 62 | 100.0% | 16 | 100.0% | 60 | 100.0% | 18 | 100.0% | 17 | 100.0% | 19 | 100.0% | 130 | 100.0% |
| Q72. At your institution, how frequently are transfer/transfer-intending students required to meet with their assigned advisor during their first year? | | | | | | | | | | | | | | | | | | | | |
| Only once, during the first term | 8 | 20.5% | 8 | 10.3% | 11 | 20.0% | 5 | 8.2% | 2 | 12.5% | 8 | 14.0% | 1 | 5.6% | 4 | 30.8% | 1 | 7.7% | 16 | 13.7% |
| Once during each term for the entire first year | 12 | 30.8% | 27 | 34.6% | 16 | 29.1% | 23 | 37.7% | 6 | 37.5% | 21 | 36.8% | 9 | 50.0% | 3 | 23.1% | 0 | 0.0% | 39 | 33.3% |
| Two or more times each term for the entire first year | 4 | 10.3% | 12 | 15.4% | 5 | 9.1% | 11 | 18.0% | 3 | 18.8% | 9 | 15.8% | 2 | 11.1% | 2 | 15.4% | 1 | 7.7% | 17 | 14.5% |
| Transfer/transfer-intending students are not required to meet with their assigned advisor | 9 | 23.1% | 11 | 14.1% | 12 | 21.8% | 7 | 11.5% | 3 | 18.8% | 6 | 10.5% | 3 | 16.7% | 1 | 7.7% | 6 | 46.2% | 19 | 16.2% |
| Other, please specify | 5 | 12.8% | 14 | 17.9% | 8 | 14.5% | 11 | 18.0% | 1 | 6.3% | 11 | 19.3% | 1 | 5.6% | 3 | 23.1% | 3 | 23.1% | 19 | 16.2% |
| I don't know | 1 | 2.6% | 6 | 7.7% | 3 | 5.5% | 4 | 6.6% | 1 | 6.3% | 2 | 3.5% | 2 | 11.1% | 0 | 0.0% | 2 | 15.4% | 7 | 6.0% |
| Total | 39 | 100.0% | 78 | 100.0% | 55 | 100.0% | 61 | 100.0% | 16 | 100.0% | 57 | 100.0% | 18 | 100.0% | 13 | 100.0% | 13 | 100.0% | 117 | 100.0% |
| Q73. At your institution, how frequently are transfer/transfer-intending students required to meet with their assigned advisor after their first year? | | | | | | | | | | | | | | | | | | | | |
| Once during each term | 9 | 23.1% | 34 | 43.6% | 14 | 25.5% | 29 | 47.5% | 7 | 43.8% | 25 | 43.9% | 7 | 38.9% | 4 | 30.8% | 0 | 0.0% | 43 | 36.8% |
| Once during the academic year | 6 | 15.4% | 5 | 6.4% | 6 | 10.9% | 5 | 8.2% | 2 | 12.5% | 7 | 12.3% | 2 | 11.1% | 0 | 0.0% | 0 | 0.0% | 11 | 9.4% |
| Two or more times each term for the entire first year | 1 | 2.6% | 6 | 7.7% | 2 | 3.6% | 5 | 0.2% | 1 | 6.3% | 5 | 8.8% | 0 | 0.0% | 1 | 7.7% | 1 | 7.7% | 8 | 6.8% |

*Table continues on page 130*

*Table continued from page 129*

| Survey question/responses | Institutional type | | | | Institution control | | | | Number of undergraduates enrolled | | | | | | | | | | | | Total | |
|---|---|---|---|---|---|---|---|---|---|---|---|---|---|---|---|---|---|---|---|---|---|---|
| | Two-year | | Four-year | | Public | | Private | | Under 1,000 | | 1,000-4,999 | | 5,999-9,999 | | 10,000-19,999 | | 20,000 and above | | | |
| | Freq. | % | Freq | % | Freq. | % | Freq. | % | Freq. | % | Freq. | % | Freq. | % | Freq. | % | Freq. | % | Freq. | % |
| Transfer/transfer-intending students are not required to meet with their assigned advisor after their first year | 15 | 38.5% | 15 | 19.2% | 21 | 38.2% | 8 | 13.1% | 3 | 18.8% | 10 | 17.5% | 4 | 22.2% | 3 | 23.1% | 9 | 69.2% | 29 | 24.8% |
| Transfer/transfer-intending students must meet with an advisor but this individual may not be their assigned advisor | 1 | 2.6% | 0 | 0.0% | 1 | 1.8% | 0 | 0.0% | 0 | 0.0% | 1 | 1.8% | 0 | 0.0% | 0 | 0.0% | 0 | 0.0% | 1 | 0.9% |
| Other, please specify | 5 | 12.8% | 12 | 15.4% | 7 | 12.7% | 10 | 16.4% | 1 | 6.3% | 8 | 14.0% | 2 | 11.1% | 5 | 38.5% | 1 | 7.7% | 17 | 14.5% |
| I don't know | 2 | 5.1% | 6 | 7.7% | 4 | 7.3% | 4 | 6.6% | 2 | 12.5% | 1 | 1.8% | 3 | 16.7% | 0 | 0.0% | 2 | 15.4% | 8 | 6.8% |
| Total | 39 | 100.0% | 78 | 100.0% | 55 | 100.0% | 61 | 100.0% | 16 | 100.0% | 57 | 100.0% | 18 | 100.0% | 13 | 100.0% | 13 | 100.0% | 117 | 100.0% |

Q137. At your institution, how frequently are transfer/transfer-intending students required to meet with an advisor during their first year?

| Survey question/responses | Two-year | | Four-year | | Public | | Private | | Under 1,000 | | 1,000-4,999 | | 5,999-9,999 | | 10,000-19,999 | | 20,000 and above | | Total | |
|---|---|---|---|---|---|---|---|---|---|---|---|---|---|---|---|---|---|---|---|---|
| Only once, during the first term | 0 | 0.0% | 1 | 16.7% | 1 | 8.3% | 0 | 0.0% | 0 | 0.0% | 0 | 0.0% | 0 | 0.0% | 0 | 0.0% | 1 | 16.7% | 1 | 7.7% |
| Once during each term for the entire first year | 0 | 0.0% | 1 | 16.7% | 1 | 8.3% | 0 | 0.0% | 0 | 0.0% | 1 | 33.3% | 0 | 0.0% | 0 | 0.0% | 0 | 0.0% | 1 | 7.7% |
| Two or more times each term for the entire first year | 1 | 14.3% | 0 | 0.0% | 1 | 8.3% | 0 | 0.0% | 0 | 0.0% | 0 | 0.0% | 0 | 0.0% | 0 | 0.0% | 1 | 16.7% | 1 | 7.7% |
| Transfer/transfer-intending students are not required to meet an advisor | 3 | 42.9% | 4 | 66.7% | 6 | 50.0% | 1 | 100.0% | 0 | 0.0% | 1 | 33.3% | 0 | 0.0% | 3 | 75.0% | 3 | 50.0% | 7 | 53.8% |
| Other, please specify | 3 | 42.9% | 0 | 0.0% | 3 | 25.0% | 0 | 0.0% | 0 | 0.0% | 1 | 33.3% | 0 | 0.0% | 1 | 25.0% | 1 | 16.7% | 3 | 23.1% |
| I don't know | 0 | 0.0% | 0 | 0.0% | 0 | 0.0% | 0 | 0.0% | 0 | 0.0% | 0 | 0.0% | 0 | 0.0% | 0 | 0.0% | 0 | 0.0% | 0 | 0.0% |
| Total | 7 | 100.0% | 6 | 100.0% | 12 | 100.0% | 1 | 100.0% | 0 | 0.0% | 3 | 100.0% | 0 | 0.0% | 4 | 100.0% | 6 | 100.0% | 13 | 100.0% |

Q138. At your institution, how frequently are transfer/transfer-intending students required to meet with an advisor after their first year?

| Survey question/responses | Two-year | | Four-year | | Public | | Private | | Under 1,000 | | 1,000-4,999 | | 5,999-9,999 | | 10,000-19,999 | | 20,000 and above | | Total | |
|---|---|---|---|---|---|---|---|---|---|---|---|---|---|---|---|---|---|---|---|---|
| Once during each term | 0 | 0.0% | 1 | 16.7% | 1 | 8.3% | 0 | 0.0% | 0 | 0.0% | 0 | 0.0% | 0 | 0.0% | 0 | 0.0% | 0 | 0.0% | 1 | 7.7% |
| Once during the academic year | 0 | 0.0% | 0 | 0.0% | 0 | 0.0% | 0 | 0.0% | 0 | 0.0% | 1 | 33.3% | 0 | 0.0% | 0 | 0.0% | 0 | 0.0% | 0 | 0.0% |

*Table continues on page 131*

*Table continued from page 130*

| Survey question/responses | Institutional type | | | | Institution control | | | | Number of undergraduates enrolled | | | | | | | | | | | | Total | |
|---|---|---|---|---|---|---|---|---|---|---|---|---|---|---|---|---|---|---|---|---|---|---|
| | Two-year | | Four-year | | Public | | Private | | Under 1,000 | | 1,000-4,999 | | 5,999-9,999 | | 10,000-19,999 | | 20,000 and above | | | | | |
| | Freq. | % | Freq | % | Freq. | % | Freq. | % | Freq. | % | Freq. | % | Freq. | % | Freq. | % | Freq. | % | Freq. | % | | |
| Two or more times each term for the entire first year | 0 | 0.0% | 0 | 0.0% | 0 | 0.0% | 0 | 0.0% | 0 | 0.0% | 0 | 0.0% | 0 | 0.0% | 0 | 0.0% | 0 | 0.0% | 0 | 0.0% | | |
| Transfer/transfer-intending students are not required to meet an advisor after their first year | 4 | 57.1% | 5 | 83.3% | 8 | 66.7% | 1 | 100.0% | 0 | 0.0% | 1 | 33.3% | 0 | 0.0% | 3 | 75.0% | 5 | 83.3% | 9 | 69.2% | | |
| Other, please specify | 3 | 42.9% | 0 | 0.0% | 3 | 25.0% | 0 | 0.0% | 0 | 0.0% | 1 | 33.3% | 0 | 0.0% | 1 | 25.0% | 1 | 16.7% | 3 | 23.1% | | |
| I don't know | 0 | 0.0% | 0 | 0.0% | 0 | 0.0% | 0 | 0.0% | 0 | 0.0% | 0 | 0.0% | 0 | 0.0% | 0 | 0.0% | 0 | 0.0% | 0 | 0.0% | | |
| Total | 7 | 100.0% | 6 | 100.0% | 12 | 100.0% | 1 | 100.0% | 0 | 0.0% | 3 | 100.0% | 0 | 0.0% | 4 | 100.0% | 6 | 100.0% | 13 | 100.0% | | |
| U/4. How long has your institution provided targeted advising services and initiatives for transfer/transfer-intending students? | | | | | | | | | | | | | | | | | | | | | | |
| 2 years or less | 3 | 6.5% | 5 | 6.0% | 5 | 7.5% | 3 | 4.8% | 1 | 6.3% | 3 | 5.0% | 1 | 5.6% | 1 | 5.9% | 2 | 10.5% | 8 | 6.2% | | |
| 3-5 years | 7 | 15.2% | 17 | 20.2% | 10 | 14.9% | 13 | 21.0% | 7 | 43.8% | 10 | 16.7% | 2 | 11.1% | 4 | 23.5% | 1 | 5.3% | 24 | 18.5% | | |
| 6-10 years | 14 | 30.4% | 16 | 19.0% | 20 | 29.9% | 10 | 16.1% | 2 | 12.5% | 15 | 25.0% | 5 | 27.8% | 5 | 29.4% | 3 | 15.8% | 30 | 23.1% | | |
| 11-15 years | 0 | 0.0% | 6 | 7.1% | 3 | 4.5% | 3 | 4.8% | 0 | 0.0% | 2 | 3.3% | 2 | 11.1% | 1 | 5.9% | 1 | 5.3% | 6 | 4.6% | | |
| 16-20 years | 8 | 17.4% | 23 | 27.4% | 10 | 14.9% | 21 | 33.9% | 4 | 25.0% | 16 | 26.7% | 2 | 11.1% | 3 | 17.6% | 6 | 31.6% | 31 | 23.8% | | |
| More than 20 years | 0 | 0.0% | 0 | 0.0% | 0 | 0.0% | 0 | 0.0% | 0 | 0.0% | 0 | 0.0% | 0 | 0.0% | 0 | 0.0% | 0 | 0.0% | 0 | 0.0% | | |
| I don't know | 14 | 30.4% | 17 | 20.2% | 19 | 28.4% | 12 | 19.4% | 2 | 12.5% | 14 | 23.3% | 6 | 33.3% | 3 | 17.6% | 6 | 31.6% | 31 | 23.8% | | |
| Total | 46 | 100.0% | 84 | 100.0% | 67 | 100.0% | 62 | 100.0% | 16 | 100.0% | 60 | 100.0% | 18 | 100.0% | 17 | 100.0% | 19 | 100.0% | 130 | 100.0% | | |
| Q75. Which campus units directly administer academic advising for transfer/transfer-intending students? (Select all that apply.) | | | | | | | | | | | | | | | | | | | | | | |
| Academic affairs central office | 5 | 10.9% | 27 | 32.1% | 8 | 11.9% | 24 | 38.7% | 10 | 62.5% | 16 | 26.7% | 3 | 16.7% | 3 | 17.6% | 1 | 5.3% | 33 | 25.4% | | |
| Academic department(s), please specify | 14 | 30.4% | 19 | 22.6% | 17 | 25.4% | 16 | 25.8% | 1 | 6.3% | 22 | 36.7% | 6 | 33.3% | 1 | 5.9% | 3 | 15.8% | 33 | 25.4% | | |
| College or school (e.g., College of Liberal Arts) | 1 | 2.2% | 21 | 25.0% | 17 | 25.4% | 5 | 8.1% | 0 | 0.0% | 4 | 6.7% | 3 | 16.7% | 7 | 41.2% | 8 | 42.1% | 22 | 16.9% | | |

*Table continues on page 132*

*Table continued from page 131*

| Survey question/responses | Institutional type | | | | Institution control | | | | Number of undergraduates enrolled | | | | | | | | | | | | Total | |
|---|---|---|---|---|---|---|---|---|---|---|---|---|---|---|---|---|---|---|---|---|---|---|
| | Two-year | | Four-year | | Public | | Private | | Under 1,000 | | 1,000-4,999 | | 5,999-9,999 | | 10,000-19,999 | | 20,000 and above | | | |
| | Freq. | % | Freq | % | Freq. | % | Freq. | % | Freq. | % | Freq. | % | Freq. | % | Freq. | % | Freq. | % | Freq. | % |
| Transfer program office | 8 | 17.4% | 6 | 7.1% | 11 | 16.4% | 3 | 4.8% | 0 | 0.0% | 4 | 6.7% | 3 | 16.7% | 4 | 23.5% | 3 | 15.8% | 14 | 10.8% |
| Student affairs/student services office | 27 | 58.7% | 15 | 17.9% | 28 | 41.8% | 13 | 21.0% | 5 | 31.3% | 18 | 30.0% | 6 | 33.3% | 5 | 29.4% | 7 | 36.8% | 41 | 31.5% |
| University college | 0 | 0.0% | 3 | 3.6% | 3 | 4.5% | 0 | 0.0% | 0 | 0.0% | 0 | 0.0% | 0 | 0.0% | 0 | 0.0% | 3 | 15.8% | 3 | 2.3% |
| Other, please specify | 4 | 8.7% | 18 | 21.4% | 7 | 10.4% | 15 | 24.2% | 3 | 18.8% | 11 | 18.3% | 3 | 16.7% | 2 | 11.8% | 3 | 15.8% | 22 | 16.9% |
| Total | 46 | 100.0% | 84 | 100.0% | 67 | 100.0% | 62 | 100.0% | 16 | 100.0% | 60 | 100.0% | 18 | 100.0% | 17 | 100.0% | 19 | 100.0% | 130 | 100.0% |

Q76. Which of the following parties serve as academic advisors for transfer/transfer-intending students? (Select all that apply.)

| | Two-year | | Four-year | | Public | | Private | | Under 1,000 | | 1,000-4,999 | | 5,999-9,999 | | 10,000-19,999 | | 20,000 and above | | Total | |
|---|---|---|---|---|---|---|---|---|---|---|---|---|---|---|---|---|---|---|---|---|
| Professionally trained advisors | 37 | 80.4% | 59 | 70.2% | 59 | 88.1% | 37 | 59.7% | 8 | 50.0% | 38 | 63.3% | 17 | 94.4% | 15 | 88.2% | 18 | 94.7% | 96 | 73.8% |
| Faculty | 24 | 52.2% | 57 | 67.9% | 35 | 52.2% | 45 | 72.6% | 13 | 81.3% | 42 | 70.0% | 12 | 66.7% | 9 | 52.9% | 5 | 26.3% | 81 | 62.3% |
| College/university counselors | 13 | 28.3% | 9 | 10.7% | 15 | 22.4% | 7 | 11.3% | 1 | 6.3% | 10 | 16.7% | 3 | 16.7% | 3 | 17.6% | 5 | 26.3% | 22 | 16.9% |
| Staff at other institutions | 4 | 8.7% | 1 | 1.2% | 4 | 6.0% | 1 | 1.6% | 0 | 0.0% | 3 | 5.0% | 1 | 5.6% | 0 | 0.0% | 1 | 5.3% | 5 | 3.8% |
| Undergraduate peer mentors | 0 | 0.0% | 7 | 8.3% | 5 | 7.5% | 2 | 3.2% | 0 | 0.0% | 1 | 1.7% | 1 | 5.6% | 1 | 5.9% | 4 | 21.1% | 7 | 5.4% |
| Other, please specify | 2 | 4.3% | 9 | 10.7% | 3 | 4.5% | 8 | 12.9% | 2 | 12.5% | 8 | 13.3% | 0 | 0.0% | 1 | 5.9% | 1 | 5.3% | 12 | 9.2% |
| Total | 46 | 100.0% | 84 | 100.0% | 67 | 100.0% | 79 | 100.0% | 16 | 100.0% | 60 | 100.0% | 18 | 100.0% | 17 | 100.0% | 19 | 100.0% | 130 | 100.0% |

Q133. At your institution, do the parties that serve as academic advisors for transfer/transfer-intending students receive training about student transfer?

| | Two-year | | Four-year | | Public | | Private | | Under 1,000 | | 1,000-4,999 | | 5,999-9,999 | | 10,000-19,999 | | 20,000 and above | | Total | |
|---|---|---|---|---|---|---|---|---|---|---|---|---|---|---|---|---|---|---|---|---|
| Yes, all advisors for transfer/transfer-intending students are required to undergo training about student transfer | 32 | 69.6% | 38 | 45.2% | 40 | 59.7% | 30 | 48.4% | 10 | 62.5% | 29 | 48.3% | 11 | 61.1% | 9 | 56.2% | 12 | 63.2% | 71 | 55.4% |
| Yes, but only interested advisors receive training about student transfer | 9 | 19.6% | 19 | 22.6% | 16 | 23.9% | 12 | 19.4% | 2 | 12.5% | 14 | 23.3% | 3 | 16.7% | 5 | 31.2% | 4 | 21.1% | 28 | 21.9% |

*Table continues on page 133*

*Table continued from page 132*

| Survey question/responses | Institutional type | | | | Institution control | | | | Number of undergraduates enrolled | | | | | | | | | | | | Total | |
| --- | --- | --- | --- | --- | --- | --- | --- | --- | --- | --- | --- | --- | --- | --- | --- | --- | --- | --- | --- | --- | --- | --- |
| | Two-year | | Four-year | | Public | | Private | | Under 1,000 | | 1,000-4,999 | | 5,999-9,999 | | 10,000-19,999 | | 20,000 and above | | | | | |
| | Freq. | % | Freq | % | Freq. | % | Freq. | % | Freq. | % | Freq. | % | Freq. | % | Freq. | % | Freq. | % | Freq. | % | Freq. | % |
| No, advisors do not receive training about student transfer | 5 | 10.9% | 25 | 29.8% | 10 | 14.9% | 19 | 30.6% | 4 | 25.0% | 17 | 28.3% | 3 | 16.7% | 2 | 12.5% | 3 | 15.8% | 29 | 22.7% |
| Total | 46 | 100.0% | 84 | 100.0% | 67 | 100.0% | 62 | 100.0% | 16 | 100.0% | 60 | 100.0% | 18 | 100.0% | 16 | 100.0% | 19 | 100.0% | 128 | 100.0% |
| Q100. What forms of academic advising does your institution offer to transfer/transfer-intending students? (Select all that apply.) | | | | | | | | | | | | | | | | | | | | | | |
| One-on-one advising (i.e., students meet individually with advisors) | 46 | 100.0% | 81 | 96.4% | 65 | 97.0% | 61 | 98.4% | 0 | 0.0% | 59 | 98.3% | 18 | 100.0% | 17 | 100.0% | 17 | 89.5% | 127 | 97.7% |
| Group advising (i.e., multiple students meet with an advisor(s) concurrently) | 20 | 43.5% | 23 | 27.4% | 31 | 46.3% | 12 | 19.4% | 2 | 12.5% | 12 | 20.0% | 12 | 66.7% | 8 | 47.1% | 10 | 52.6% | 44 | 33.8% |
| Peer advising (i.e., select and trained peers meet with students and provide advising) | 2 | 4.3% | 13 | 15.5% | 10 | 14.9% | 5 | 8.1% | 0 | 0.0% | 2 | 3.3% | 3 | 16.7% | 3 | 17.6% | 7 | 36.8% | 15 | 11.5% |
| Online or distance advising | 32 | 69.6% | 52 | 61.9% | 50 | 74.6% | 34 | 54.8% | 7 | 43.8% | 33 | 55.0% | 14 | 77.8% | 14 | 82.4% | 17 | 89.5% | 85 | 65.4% |
| Other, please specify | 1 | 2.2% | 3 | 3.6% | 2 | 3.0% | 2 | 3.2% | 0 | 0.0% | 1 | 1.7% | 0 | 0.0% | 1 | 5.9% | 2 | 10.5% | 4 | 3.1% |
| Total | 46 | 100.0% | 84 | 100.0% | 67 | 100.0% | 62 | 100.0% | 16 | 100.0% | 60 | 100.0% | 18 | 100.0% | 17 | 100.0% | 19 | 100.0% | 130 | 100.0% |
| Q78. Does your institution use early warning/academic alert systems for transfer/transfer-intending students? | | | | | | | | | | | | | | | | | | | | | | |
| Yes | 40 | 87.0% | 64 | 76.2% | 55 | 82.1% | 48 | 77.4% | 12 | 75.0% | 51 | 85.0% | 15 | 83.3% | 14 | 82.4% | 12 | 63.2% | 104 | 80.0% |
| No | 6 | 13.0% | 14 | 16.7% | 10 | 14.9% | 10 | 16.1% | 3 | 18.8% | 7 | 11.7% | 3 | 16.7% | 3 | 17.6% | 4 | 21.1% | 20 | 15.4% |
| I don't know | 0 | 0.0% | 6 | 7.1% | 2 | 3.0% | 4 | 6.5% | 1 | 6.3% | 2 | 3.3% | 0 | 0.0% | 0 | 0.0% | 3 | 15.8% | 6 | 4.6% |
| Total | 46 | 100.0% | 84 | 100.0% | 67 | 100.0% | 62 | 100.0% | 16 | 100.0% | 60 | 100.0% | 18 | 100.0% | 17 | 100.0% | 19 | 100.0% | 130 | 100.0% |

*Table continues on page 134*

*Table continued from page 133*

| | Institutional type | | | | Institution control | | | | Number of undergraduates enrolled | | | | | | | | | | | Total | |
|---|---|---|---|---|---|---|---|---|---|---|---|---|---|---|---|---|---|---|---|---|---|---|
| | Two-year | | Four-year | | Public | | Private | | Under 1,000 | | 1,000-4,999 | | 5,999-9,999 | | 10,000-19,999 | | 20,000 and above | | | | | |
| Survey question/responses | Freq. | % | Freq | % | Freq. | % | Freq. | % | Freq. | % | Freq. | % | Freq. | % | Freq. | % | Freq. | % | Freq. | % |
| Q79. Please indicate the selection that best describes the early warning/academic alert system for transfer/transfer-intending students that is most prevalent at your institution. | | | | | | | | | | | | | | | | | | | | |
| An early warning tool that is entirely technology-based (such as a learner analytics platform that mines data to determine which students are at-risk and subsequently guides intervention) | 7 | 17.5% | 9 | 14.1% | 9 | 16.4% | 7 | 14.6% | 2 | 16.7% | 8 | 15.7% | 2 | 13.3% | 2 | 14.3% | 2 | 16.7% | 16 | 15.4% |
| An early warning system that is entirely human-based and relies on faculty, staff, and/or students observing behavior and then notifying someone so outreach can occur (such as a faculty referral system) | 14 | 35.0% | 21 | 32.8% | 16 | 29.1% | 18 | 37.5% | 3 | 25.0% | 18 | 35.3% | 7 | 46.7% | 2 | 14.3% | 4 | 33.3% | 34 | 32.7% |
| A hybrid approach that utilizes technology- and human-based approaches | 17 | 42.5% | 34 | 53.1% | 28 | 50.9% | 23 | 47.9% | 7 | 58.3% | 25 | 49.0% | 6 | 40.0% | 9 | 64.3% | 5 | 41.7% | 52 | 50.0% |
| Unable to judge | 2 | 5.0% | 0 | 0.0% | 2 | 3.6% | 0 | 0.0% | 0 | 0.0% | 0 | 0.0% | 0 | 0.0% | 1 | 7.1% | 1 | 8.3% | 2 | 1.9% |
| Total | 40 | 100.0% | 64 | 100.0% | 55 | 100.0% | 48 | 100.0% | 12 | 100.0% | 51 | 100.0% | 15 | 100.0% | 14 | 100.0% | 12 | 100.0% | 104 | 100.0% |
| Q80. Which employees at your institution participate in some aspect of early alert/academic warning systems for transfer/transfer-intending students? (Select all that apply.) | | | | | | | | | | | | | | | | | | | | |
| Academic advisors | 32 | 80.0% | 60 | 93.8% | 47 | 85.5% | 45 | 93.8% | 11 | 91.7% | 46 | 90.2% | 13 | 86.7% | 13 | 92.9% | 10 | 83.3% | 93 | 89.4% |
| Academic support personnel | 16 | 40.0% | 53 | 82.8% | 28 | 50.9% | 40 | 83.3% | 9 | 75.0% | 37 | 72.5% | 6 | 40.0% | 9 | 64.3% | 7 | 58.3% | 68 | 65.4% |
| Athletic department staff | 10 | 25.0% | 37 | 57.8% | 18 | 32.7% | 29 | 60.4% | 5 | 41.7% | 26 | 51.0% | 9 | 60.0% | 5 | 35.7% | 3 | 25.0% | 48 | 46.2% |
| Counseling/health services staff | 16 | 40.0% | 24 | 37.5% | 21 | 38.2% | 19 | 87.5% | 3 | 25.0% | 23 | 45.1% | 8 | 53.3% | 4 | 28.6% | 2 | 16.7% | 40 | 38.5% |
| Faculty/instructors | 37 | 92.5% | 57 | 89.1% | 51 | 92.7% | 42 | 87.5% | 11 | 91.7% | 45 | 88.2% | 0 | 0.0% | 13 | 92.9% | 10 | 83.3% | 94 | 90.4% |
| Information technology staff | 4 | 10.0% | 5 | 7.8% | 5 | 9.1% | 4 | 8.3% | 2 | 16.7% | 4 | 7.8% | 2 | 13.3% | 1 | 7.1% | 1 | 8.3% | 10 | 9.6% |
| Peer mentors | 2 | 5.0% | 10 | 15.6% | 5 | 9.1% | 7 | 14.6% | 0 | 0.0% | 6 | 11.8% | 3 | 20.0% | 0 | 0.0% | 3 | 25.0% | 12 | 11.5% |

*Table continues on page 135*

*Table continued from page 134*

| Survey question/responses | Institutional type | | | | Institution control | | | | Number of undergraduates enrolled | | | | | | | | | | | | Total | |
| --- | --- | --- | --- | --- | --- | --- | --- | --- | --- | --- | --- | --- | --- | --- | --- | --- | --- | --- | --- | --- | --- | --- |
| | Two-year | | Four-year | | Public | | Private | | Under 1,000 | | 1,000-4,999 | | 5,999-9,999 | | 10,000-19,999 | | 20,000 and above | | | | | |
| | Freq. | % | Freq | % | Freq. | % | Freq. | % | Freq. | % | Freq. | % | Freq. | % | Freq. | % | Freq. | % | Freq. | % | | |
| Residence life staff | 3 | 7.5% | 27 | 42.2% | 7 | 12.7% | 23 | 47.9% | 4 | 33.3% | 17 | 33.3% | 6 | 40.0% | 3 | 21.4% | 1 | 8.3% | 31 | 29.8% | | |
| Student affairs staff | 17 | 42.5% | 42 | 65.6% | 23 | 41.8% | 35 | 72.9% | 8 | 66.7% | 32 | 62.7% | 9 | 60.0% | 5 | 35.7% | 5 | 41.7% | 59 | 56.7% | | |
| Other, please specify | 2 | 5.0% | 3 | 4.7% | 3 | 5.5% | 2 | 4.2% | 0 | 0.0% | 2 | 3.9% | 0 | 0.0% | 2 | 14.3% | 1 | 8.3% | 5 | 4.8% | | |
| Total | 40 | 100.0% | 64 | 100.0% | 55 | 100.0% | 48 | 100.0% | 12 | 100.0% | 51 | 100.0% | 15 | 100.0% | 14 | 100.0% | 12 | 100.0% | 104 | 100.0% | | |

Q81. Which of the following describes the type of intervention that occurs? (Select all that apply.)

| Survey question/responses | Two-year | | Four-year | | Public | | Private | | Under 1,000 | | 1,000-4,999 | | 5,999-9,999 | | 10,000-19,999 | | 20,000 and above | | Total | |
| --- | --- | --- | --- | --- | --- | --- | --- | --- | --- | --- | --- | --- | --- | --- | --- | --- | --- | --- | --- | --- |
| | Freq. | % | Freq | % | Freq. | % | Freq. | % | Freq. | % | Freq. | % | Freq. | % | Freq. | % | Freq. | % | Freq. | % |
| Students are contacted by phone, letter, or electronic means (e.g., email and/or text "nudges") | 37 | 92.5% | 62 | 96.9% | 53 | 96.4% | 46 | 95.8% | 11 | 91.7% | 50 | 98.0% | 15 | 100.0% | 13 | 92.9% | 11 | 91.7% | 100 | 96.2% |
| Students are contacted in person | 19 | 47.5% | 34 | 53.1% | 25 | 45.5% | 27 | 56.3% | 6 | 50.0% | 27 | 52.9% | 8 | 53.3% | 6 | 42.9% | 5 | 41.7% | 52 | 50.0% |
| Students are informed about opportunities to seek assistance | 28 | 70.0% | 45 | 70.3% | 41 | 74.5% | 32 | 66.7% | 7 | 58.3% | 38 | 74.5% | 11 | 73.3% | 9 | 64.3% | 9 | 75.0% | 74 | 71.2% |
| Students are required by individual faculty members, another unit, or the institution to obtain assistance | 9 | 22.5% | 12 | 18.8% | 11 | 20.0% | 9 | 18.8% | 6 | 50.0% | 9 | 17.6% | 2 | 13.3% | 2 | 14.3% | 2 | 16.7% | 21 | 20.2% |
| Students' families are notified (with student waiver of privacy rights) | 4 | 10.0% | 6 | 9.4% | 5 | 9.1% | 5 | 10.4% | 2 | 16.7% | 5 | 9.8% | 2 | 13.3% | 0 | 0.0% | 1 | 8.3% | 10 | 9.6% |
| Other, please specify | 2 | 5.0% | 2 | 3.1% | 3 | 5.5% | 1 | 2.1% | 0 | 0.0% | 1 | 2.0% | 0 | 0.0% | 2 | 14.3% | 1 | 8.3% | 4 | 3.8% |
| Total | 40 | 100.0% | 64 | 100.0% | 55 | 100.0% | 48 | 100.0% | 12 | 100.0% | 51 | 100.0% | 15 | 100.0% | 14 | 100.0% | 12 | 100.0% | 104 | 100.0% |

Q82. Do transfer/transfer-intending students at your institution participate in guided pathways?

| Survey question/responses | Two-year | | Four-year | | Public | | Private | | Under 1,000 | | 1,000-4,999 | | 5,999-9,999 | | 10,000-19,999 | | 20,000 and above | | Total | |
| --- | --- | --- | --- | --- | --- | --- | --- | --- | --- | --- | --- | --- | --- | --- | --- | --- | --- | --- | --- | --- |
| | Freq. | % | Freq | % | Freq. | % | Freq. | % | Freq. | % | Freq. | % | Freq. | % | Freq. | % | Freq. | % | Freq. | % |
| Yes | 38 | 82.6% | 23 | 27.4% | 48 | 71.5% | 13 | 21.0% | 5 | 31.3% | 28 | 46.7% | 9 | 50.0% | 10 | 58.8% | 10 | 52.6% | 62 | 47.7% |
| No | 7 | 15.2% | 46 | 54.8% | 16 | 23.9% | 36 | 58.1% | 9 | 56.3% | 26 | 43.3% | 7 | 38.9% | 6 | 35.3% | 4 | 21.1% | 52 | 40.0% |
| I don't know | 1 | 2.2% | 15 | 17.9% | 3 | 4.5% | 13 | 21.0% | 2 | 12.5% | 6 | 10.0% | 2 | 11.1% | 1 | 5.9% | 5 | 26.3% | 16 | 12.3% |
| Total | 46 | 100.0% | 84 | 100.0% | 67 | 100.0% | 62 | 100.0% | 16 | 100.0% | 60 | 100.0% | 18 | 100.0% | 17 | 100.0% | 19 | 100.0% | 130 | 100.0% |

*Table continues on page 136*

*Table continued from page 135*

| Survey question/responses | Institutional type | | | | Institution control | | | | Number of undergraduates enrolled | | | | | | | | | | | | Total | |
|---|---|---|---|---|---|---|---|---|---|---|---|---|---|---|---|---|---|---|---|---|---|---|
| | Two-year | | Four-year | | Public | | Private | | Under 1,000 | | 1,000-4,999 | | 5,999-9,999 | | 10,000-19,999 | | 20,000 and above | | | |
| | Freq. | % | Freq | % | Freq. | % | Freq. | % | Freq. | % | Freq. | % | Freq. | % | Freq. | % | Freq. | % | Freq. | % |
| Q83. Do transfer/transfer-intending students at your institution participate in meta majors? | | | | | | | | | | | | | | | | | | | | |
| Yes | 23 | 50.0% | 4 | 4.8% | 25 | 37.3% | 2 | 3.2% | 1 | 6.3% | 7 | 11.7% | 7 | 38.9% | 7 | 41.2% | 5 | 26.3% | 27 | 20.8% |
| No | 15 | 32.6% | 67 | 79.8% | 31 | 46.3% | 50 | 80.6% | 13 | 81.3% | 43 | 71.7% | 8 | 44.4% | 7 | 41.2% | 11 | 57.9% | 82 | 63.1% |
| I don't know | 8 | 17.4% | 13 | 15.5% | 11 | 16.4% | 10 | 16.1% | 2 | 12.5% | 10 | 16.7% | 3 | 16.7% | 3 | 17.6% | 3 | 15.8% | 21 | 16.2% |
| Total | 46 | 100.0% | 84 | 100.0% | 67 | 100.0% | 62 | 100.0% | 16 | 100.0% | 60 | 100.0% | 18 | 100.0% | 17 | 100.0% | 19 | 100.0% | 130 | 100.0% |
| Q84. On your campus, how coordinated is academic advising for transfer/transfer-intending students? (Select the most appropriate answer.) | | | | | | | | | | | | | | | | | | | | |
| Totally decentralized, no coordination between any departments or units in transfer-year initiatives | 0 | 0.0% | 7 | 8.5% | 2 | 3.0% | 5 | 8.2% | 1 | 6.3% | 3 | 5.2% | 1 | 5.6% | 1 | 5.9% | 1 | 5.3% | 7 | 5.5% |
| Mostly decentralized, little coordination | 6 | 13.0% | 13 | 15.9% | 11 | 16.7% | 8 | 13.1% | 1 | 6.3% | 8 | 13.8% | 4 | 22.2% | 3 | 17.6% | 3 | 15.8% | 19 | 14.8% |
| Somewhere between decentralized/centralized, no to all coordinated | 17 | 37.0% | 22 | 26.8% | 28 | 42.4% | 11 | 18.0% | 4 | 25.0% | 16 | 27.6% | 6 | 33.3% | 6 | 35.3% | 7 | 36.8% | 39 | 30.5% |
| Almost all centralized, almost all coordinated | 11 | 23.9% | 24 | 29.3% | 13 | 19.7% | 21 | 34.4% | 6 | 37.5% | 16 | 27.6% | 2 | 11.1% | 4 | 23.5% | 7 | 36.8% | 35 | 27.3% |
| Totally centralized, all transfer-year initiatives are coordinated by a single director or office | 11 | 23.9% | 16 | 19.5% | 11 | 16.7% | 16 | 26.2% | 4 | 25.0% | 15 | 25.9% | 4 | 22.2% | 3 | 17.6% | 1 | 5.3% | 27 | 21.1% |
| Unable to judge | 1 | 2.2% | 0 | 0.0% | 1 | 1.5% | 0 | 0.0% | 0 | 0.0% | 0 | 0.0% | 1 | 5.6% | 0 | 0.0% | 0 | 0.0% | 1 | 0.8% |
| Total | 46 | 100.0% | 82 | 100.0% | 66 | 100.0% | 61 | 100.0% | 16 | 100.0% | 58 | 100.0% | 18 | 100.0% | 17 | 100.0% | 19 | 100.0% | 128 | 100.0% |
| Q85. Please identify the activities and processes related to academic advising in which your institution is currently engaged. (Select all that apply.) | | | | | | | | | | | | | | | | | | | | |
| Campuswide assessment and planning | 22 | 47.8% | 31 | 37.8% | 29 | 43.9% | 24 | 39.3% | 8 | 50.0% | 26 | 44.8% | 10 | 55.6% | 7 | 41.2% | 3 | 15.8% | 54 | 42.2% |
| Evaluation and continuous improvement of advising | 33 | 71.7% | 52 | 63.4% | 45 | 68.2% | 40 | 65.6% | 8 | 50.0% | 41 | 70.7% | 12 | 66.7% | 12 | 70.6% | 13 | 68.4% | 86 | 67.2% |

*Table continues on page 137*

*Table continued from page 136*

| Survey question/responses | Institutional type | | | | Institution control | | | | Number of undergraduates enrolled | | | | | | | | | | | | Total | |
| | Two-year | | Four-year | | Public | | Private | | Under 1,000 | | 1,000-4,999 | | 5,999-9,999 | | 10,000-19,999 | | 20,000 and above | | | |
| | Freq. | % | Freq | % | Freq. | % | Freq. | % | Freq. | % | Freq. | % | Freq. | % | Freq. | % | Freq. | % | Freq. | % |
| Leadership and change management | 6 | 13.0% | 22 | 26.8% | 14 | 21.2% | 14 | 23.0% | 3 | 18.8% | 9 | 15.5% | 4 | 22.2% | 4 | 23.5% | 8 | 42.1% | 28 | 21.9% |
| Ongoing professional development and training for advisors | 37 | 80.4% | 51 | 62.2% | 52 | 78.8% | 35 | 57.4% | 9 | 56.3% | 39 | 67.2% | 12 | 66.7% | 13 | 76.5% | 15 | 78.9% | 88 | 68.8% |
| Process mapping | 15 | 32.6% | 12 | 14.6% | 15 | 22.7% | 12 | 19.7% | 3 | 18.8% | 14 | 24.1% | 5 | 27.8% | 3 | 17.6% | 3 | 15.8% | 28 | 21.9% |
| Structure redesign | 15 | 32.6% | 13 | 15.9% | 19 | 28.8% | 9 | 14.8% | 3 | 18.8% | 10 | 17.2% | 7 | 38.9% | 2 | 11.8% | 7 | 36.8% | 29 | 22.7% |
| Technology and data governance and management | 11 | 23.9% | 20 | 24.4% | 17 | 25.8% | 14 | 23.0% | 4 | 25.0% | 12 | 20.7% | 6 | 33.3% | 4 | 23.5% | 6 | 31.6% | 32 | 25.0% |
| Technology selection (open response) | 3 | 6.5% | 2 | 2.4% | 4 | 6.1% | 1 | 1.6% | 1 | 6.3% | 2 | 3.4% | 1 | 5.6% | 0 | 0.0% | 1 | 5.3% | 5 | 3.9% |
| Other, please specify | 2 | 4.3% | 1 | 1.2% | 2 | 3.0% | 1 | 1.6% | 0 | 0.0% | 2 | 3.4% | 0 | 0.0% | 0 | 0.0% | 1 | 5.3% | 3 | 2.3% |
| My institution is not currently engaged in any activities or processes related to academic advising | 0 | 0.0% | 12 | 14.6% | 3 | 4.5% | 9 | 14.8% | 3 | 18.8% | 6 | 10.3% | 0 | 0.0% | 1 | 5.9% | 2 | 10.5% | 12 | 9.4% |
| Total | 46 | 100.0% | 82 | 100.0% | 66 | 100.0% | 61 | 100.0% | 16 | 100.0% | 58 | 100.0% | 18 | 100.0% | 17 | 100.0% | 19 | 100.0% | 128 | 100.0% |
| Q86. Has academic advising for transfer/transfer-intending students been formally assessed or evaluated in the last four years? | | | | | | | | | | | | | | | | | | | | |
| Yes | 22 | 47.8% | 20 | 24.4% | 28 | 42.4% | 14 | 23.0% | 3 | 18.8% | 21 | 36.2% | 9 | 50.0% | 5 | 29.4% | 4 | 21.1% | 42 | 32.8% |
| No | 15 | 32.6% | 37 | 45.1% | 22 | 33.3% | 29 | 47.5% | 7 | 43.8% | 25 | 43.1% | 6 | 33.3% | 6 | 35.3% | 7 | 36.8% | 51 | 39.8% |
| I don't know | 9 | 19.6% | 25 | 30.5% | 16 | 24.2% | 18 | 29.5% | 6 | 37.5% | 12 | 20.7% | 3 | 16.7% | 6 | 35.3% | 8 | 42.1% | 35 | 27.3% |
| Total | 46 | 100.0% | 82 | 100.0% | 66 | 100.0% | 61 | 100.0% | 16 | 100.0% | 58 | 100.0% | 18 | 100.0% | 17 | 100.0% | 19 | 100.0% | 128 | 100.0% |
| Q87. What type of assessment was conducted? (Select all that apply.) | | | | | | | | | | | | | | | | | | | | |
| Analysis of institutional data (e.g., GPA, retention rates, graduation) | 14 | 63.6% | 16 | 80.0% | 20 | 71.4% | 10 | 71.4% | 1 | 33.3% | 14 | 66.7% | 7 | 77.8% | 4 | 80.0% | 4 | 100.0% | 30 | 71.4% |

*Table continues on page 138*

*Table continued from page 137*

| Survey question/responses | Institutional type | | | | Institution control | | | | Number of undergraduates enrolled | | | | | | | | | | | | Total | |
| --- | --- | --- | --- | --- | --- | --- | --- | --- | --- | --- | --- | --- | --- | --- | --- | --- | --- | --- | --- | --- | --- | --- |
| | Two-year | | Four-year | | Public | | Private | | Under 1,000 | | 1,000-4,999 | | 5,999-9,999 | | 10,000-19,999 | | 20,000 and above | | | | | |
| | Freq. | % | Freq | % | Freq. | % | Freq. | % | Freq. | % | Freq. | % | Freq. | % | Freq. | % | Freq. | % | Freq. | % | | |
| Direct assessment of student learning outcomes | 6 | 27.3% | 7 | 35.0% | 7 | 25.0% | 6 | 42.9% | 0 | 0.0% | 9 | 42.9% | 3 | 33.3% | 1 | 20.0% | 0 | 0.0% | 13 | 31.0% | | |
| Focus groups with faculty | 6 | 27.3% | 8 | 40.0% | 9 | 32.1% | 5 | 35.7% | 1 | 33.3% | 8 | 38.1% | 1 | 11.1% | 1 | 20.0% | 3 | 75.0% | 14 | 33.3% | | |
| Focus groups with professional staff | 8 | 36.4% | 10 | 50.0% | 12 | 42.9% | 6 | 42.9% | 1 | 33.3% | 9 | 42.9% | 2 | 22.2% | 3 | 60.0% | 3 | 75.0% | 18 | 42.9% | | |
| Focus groups with students | 8 | 36.4% | 8 | 40.0% | 12 | 42.9% | 4 | 28.6% | 0 | 0.0% | 8 | 38.1% | 3 | 33.3% | 2 | 40.0% | 3 | 75.0% | 16 | 38.1% | | |
| Individual interviews with faculty | 1 | 4.5% | 4 | 20.0% | 3 | 10.7% | 2 | 14.3% | 0 | 0.0% | 2 | 9.5% | 1 | 11.1% | 1 | 20.0% | 1 | 25.0% | 5 | 11.9% | | |
| Individual interviews with orientation staff | 1 | 4.5% | 2 | 10.0% | 2 | 7.1% | 1 | 7.1% | 0 | 0.0% | 2 | 9.5% | 1 | 11.1% | 0 | 0.0% | 0 | 0.0% | 3 | 7.1% | | |
| Individual interviews with students | 3 | 13.6% | 4 | 20.0% | 5 | 17.9% | 2 | 14.3% | 0 | 0.0% | 5 | 23.8% | 1 | 11.1% | 1 | 20.0% | 0 | 0.0% | 7 | 16.7% | | |
| Program review | 9 | 40.9% | 5 | 25.0% | 11 | 39.3% | 3 | 21.4% | 0 | 0.0% | 9 | 42.9% | 2 | 22.2% | 2 | 40.0% | 1 | 25.0% | 14 | 33.3% | | |
| Student course evaluation | 0 | 0.0% | 8 | 40.0% | 3 | 10.7% | 5 | 35.7% | 0 | 0.0% | 2 | 9.5% | 1 | 11.1% | 1 | 20.0% | 1 | 25.0% | 8 | 19.0% | | |
| Survey instrument | 12 | 54.5% | 12 | 60.0% | 17 | 60.7% | 7 | 50.0% | 0 | 0.0% | 11 | 52.4% | 4 | 44.4% | 3 | 60.0% | 1 | 25.0% | 24 | 57.1% | | |
| I don't know | 0 | 0.0% | 0 | 0.0% | 0 | 0.0% | 0 | 0.0% | 0 | 0.0% | 0 | 0.0% | 0 | 0.0% | 0 | 0.0% | 0 | 0.0% | 0 | 0.0% | | |
| Other, please specify | 0 | 0.0% | 1 | 5.0% | 0 | 0.0% | 1 | 7.1% | 1 | 33.3% | 0 | 0.0% | 0 | 0.0% | 0 | 0.0% | 0 | 0.0% | 1 | 2.4% | | |
| Total | 22 | 100.0% | 20 | 100.0% | 28 | 100.0% | 65 | 100.0% | 3 | 100.0% | 53 | 100.0% | 9 | 100.0% | 5 | 100.0% | 4 | 100.0% | 42 | 100.0% | | |

Q88. Select the outcome(s) that were measured using the assessment methods indicated in the previous question. (Select all that apply.)

| Survey question/responses | Two-year | | Four-year | | Public | | Private | | Under 1,000 | | 1,000-4,999 | | 5,999-9,999 | | 10,000-19,999 | | 20,000 and above | | Total | |
| --- | --- | --- | --- | --- | --- | --- | --- | --- | --- | --- | --- | --- | --- | --- | --- | --- | --- | --- | --- | --- |
| Academic planning | 15 | 68.2% | 14 | 70.0% | 21 | 75.0% | 8 | 57.1% | 2 | 66.7% | 14 | 66.7% | 6 | 66.7% | 4 | 80.0% | 3 | 75.0% | 29 | 69.0% |
| Academic success strategies | 8 | 36.4% | 9 | 45.0% | 11 | 39.3% | 6 | 42.9% | 0 | 0.0% | 7 | 33.3% | 4 | 44.4% | 3 | 60.0% | 1 | 25.0% | 17 | 40.5% |
| Analytical, critical-thinking, or problem-solving skills | 2 | 9.1% | 4 | 20.0% | 4 | 14.3% | 2 | 14.3% | 0 | 0.0% | 4 | 19.0% | 2 | 22.2% | 0 | 0.0% | 0 | 0.0% | 6 | 14.3% |
| Career exploration and/or preparation | 8 | 36.4% | 7 | 35.0% | 11 | 39.3% | 4 | 28.6% | 0 | 0.0% | 9 | 42.9% | 5 | 55.6% | 0 | 0.0% | 1 | 25.0% | 15 | 35.7% |

*Table continues on page 139*

*Table continued from page 138*

| Survey question/responses | Institutional type | | | | Institution control | | | | Number of undergraduates enrolled | | | | | | | | | | | | Total | |
| --- | --- | --- | --- | --- | --- | --- | --- | --- | --- | --- | --- | --- | --- | --- | --- | --- | --- | --- | --- | --- | --- | --- |
| | Two-year | | Four-year | | Public | | Private | | Under 1,000 | | 1,000-4,999 | | 5,999-9,999 | | 10,000-19,999 | | 20,000 and above | | | | | |
| | Freq. | % | Freq | % | Freq. | % | Freq. | % | Freq. | % | Freq. | % | Freq. | % | Freq. | % | Freq. | % | Freq. | % | Freq. | % |
| Civic engagement | 1 | 4.5% | 2 | 10.0% | 1 | 3.6% | 2 | 14.3% | 0 | 0.0% | 1 | 4.8% | 2 | 22.2% | 0 | 0.0% | 0 | 0.0% | 3 | 7.1% |
| Common transfer-year experience | 4 | 18.2% | 3 | 15.0% | 5 | 17.9% | 2 | 14.3% | 0 | 0.0% | 3 | 14.3% | 3 | 33.3% | 0 | 0.0% | 1 | 25.0% | 7 | 16.7% |
| Connection with the institution or campus | 6 | 27.3% | 9 | 45.0% | 9 | 32.1% | 6 | 42.9% | 2 | 66.7% | 7 | 33.3% | 4 | 44.4% | 1 | 20.0% | 1 | 25.0% | 15 | 35.7% |
| Developmental education, remediation, and/or review | 4 | 18.2% | 1 | 5.0% | 5 | 17.9% | 0 | 0.0% | 0 | 0.0% | 3 | 14.3% | 1 | 11.1% | 1 | 20.0% | 0 | 0.0% | 5 | 11.9% |
| Digital literacy | 1 | 4.5% | 2 | 10.0% | 3 | 10.7% | 0 | 0.0% | 0 | 0.0% | 1 | 4.8% | 2 | 22.2% | 0 | 0.0% | 0 | 0.0% | 3 | 7.1% |
| Discipline-specific knowledge | 2 | 9.1% | 2 | 10.0% | 3 | 10.7% | 1 | 7.1% | 0 | 0.0% | 1 | 4.8% | 3 | 33.3% | 0 | 0.0% | 0 | 0.0% | 4 | 9.5% |
| Financial literacy | 0 | 0.0% | 2 | 10.0% | 0 | 0.0% | 2 | 14.3% | 0 | 0.0% | 1 | 4.8% | 1 | 11.0% | 0 | 0.0% | 0 | 0.0% | 2 | 4.8% |
| Gateway course completion | 5 | 22.7% | 3 | 15.0% | 6 | 21.4% | 2 | 14.3% | 1 | 33.3% | 4 | 19.0% | 3 | 33.3% | 0 | 0.0% | 0 | 0.0% | 8 | 19.0% |
| Graduate or professional school preparation (e.g., premed, prelaw) | 0 | 0.0% | 2 | 10.0% | 1 | 3.6% | 1 | 1.7% | 0 | 0.0% | 1 | 4.8% | 1 | 11.1% | 0 | 0.0% | 0 | 0.0% | 2 | 4.8% |
| Health and wellness | 4 | 18.2% | 4 | 20.0% | 4 | 14.3% | 4 | 28.6% | 0 | 0.0% | 4 | 19.0% | 3 | 33.3% | 1 | 20.0% | 0 | 0.0% | 8 | 19.0% |
| Information literacy | 2 | 9.1% | 3 | 15.0% | 3 | 10.7% | 2 | 14.3% | 0 | 0.0% | 2 | 9.5% | 3 | 33.3% | 0 | 0.0% | 0 | 0.0% | 5 | 11.9% |
| Integrative and applied learning | 1 | 4.5% | 1 | 5.0% | 2 | 7.1% | 0 | 0.0% | 0 | 0.0% | 1 | 4.8% | 1 | 11.1% | 0 | 0.0% | 0 | 0.0% | 2 | 4.8% |
| Intercultural competence, diversity skills, or engaging with different perspectives | 4 | 18.2% | 4 | 20.0% | 5 | 17.9% | 3 | 21.4% | 0 | 0.0% | 4 | 19.0% | 3 | 33.3% | 0 | 0.0% | 1 | 25.0% | 8 | 19.0% |
| Introduction to a major, discipline, or career path | 5 | 22.7% | 8 | 40.0% | 9 | 32.1% | 4 | 28.6% | 0 | 0.0% | 5 | 23.8% | 5 | 55.6% | 1 | 20.0% | 2 | 50.0% | 13 | 31.0% |
| Introduction to institutional specific academic expectations | 2 | 9.1% | 2 | 10.0% | 3 | 10.7% | 1 | 7.1% | 0 | 0.0% | 2 | 9.5% | 2 | 22.2% | 0 | 0.0% | 0 | 0.0% | 4 | 9.5% |
| Introduction to the liberal arts | 0 | 0.0% | 1 | 5.0% | 0 | 0.0% | 1 | 7.1% | 0 | 0.0% | 0 | 0.0% | 1 | 11.1% | 0 | 0.0% | 0 | 0.0% | 1 | 2.4% |

*Table continues on page 140*

*Table continued from page 139*

| | Institutional type | | | | Institution control | | | | Number of undergraduates enrolled | | | | | | | | | | Total | |
| | Two-year | | Four-year | | Public | | Private | | Under 1,000 | | 1,000-4,999 | | 5,999-9,999 | | 10,000-19,999 | | 20,000 and above | | | |
| Survey question/responses | Freq. | % | Freq | % | Freq. | % | Freq. | % | Freq. | % | Freq. | % | Freq. | % | Freq. | % | Freq. | % | Freq. | % |
|---|---|---|---|---|---|---|---|---|---|---|---|---|---|---|---|---|---|---|---|---|
| Knowledge of institution or campus resources and services | 8 | 36.4% | 9 | 45.0% | 11 | 39.3% | 6 | 42.9% | 2 | 66.7% | 9 | 42.9% | 4 | 44.4% | 2 | 40.0% | 2 | 50.0% | 17 | 40.5% |
| Major exploration | 7 | 31.8% | 5 | 25.0% | 11 | 39.3% | 1 | 7.1% | 0 | 0.0% | 5 | 23.8% | 4 | 44.4% | 2 | 40.0% | 1 | 25.0% | 12 | 28.6% |
| On-time graduation rates (i.e., 4-year or 6-year graduation rate for transfers) | 4 | 18.2% | 12 | 60.0% | 8 | 28.6% | 8 | 57.1% | 1 | 33.3% | 8 | 38.1% | 2 | 22.2% | 0 | 0.0% | 3 | 75.0% | 16 | 38.1% |
| Oral communication skills | 1 | 4.5% | 2 | 10.0% | 2 | 7.1% | 1 | 7.1% | 1 | 33.3% | 2 | 9.5% | 0 | 0.0% | 2 | 40.0% | 0 | 0.0% | 3 | 7.1% |
| Persistence of transfer students | 8 | 36.4% | 6 | 30.0% | 11 | 39.3% | 3 | 21.4% | 1 | 33.3% | 5 | 23.8% | 5 | 55.6% | 0 | 0.0% | 1 | 25.0% | 14 | 33.3% |
| Personal exploration or development | 4 | 18.2% | 0 | 0.0% | 4 | 14.3% | 0 | 0.0% | 0 | 0.0% | 3 | 14.3% | 1 | 11.1% | 0 | 0.0% | 0 | 0.0% | 4 | 9.5% |
| Project planning, teamwork, or management skills | 1 | 4.5% | 1 | 5.0% | 1 | 3.6% | 1 | 7.1% | 0 | 0.0% | 0 | 0.0% | 1 | 11.1% | 1 | 20.0% | 1 | 25.0% | 2 | 4.8% |
| Retention of transfer students | 8 | 36.4% | 7 | 35.0% | 12 | 42.9% | 3 | 21.4% | 0 | 0.0% | 5 | 23.8% | 5 | 55.6% | 0 | 0.0% | 0 | 0.0% | 15 | 35.7% |
| Social support networks (e.g., friendships) | 0 | 0.0% | 1 | 5.0% | 0 | 0.0% | 1 | 7.1% | 0 | 0.0% | 0 | 0.0% | 1 | 11.1% | 0 | 0.0% | 0 | 0.0% | 1 | 2.4% |
| Student-faculty interaction | 5 | 22.7% | 6 | 30.0% | 6 | 21.4% | 5 | 35.7% | 2 | 66.7% | 5 | 23.8% | 2 | 22.2% | 0 | 0.0% | 2 | 50.0% | 11 | 26.2% |
| Writing skills | 3 | 13.6% | 4 | 20.0% | 5 | 17.9% | 2 | 14.3% | 0 | 0.0% | 4 | 19.0% | 3 | 33.3% | 0 | 0.0% | 0 | 0.0% | 7 | 16.7% |
| Other, please specify | 1 | 4.5% | 1 | 5.0% | 1 | 3.6% | 1 | 7.1% | 0 | 0.0% | 1 | 4.8% | 0 | 0.0% | 1 | 20.0% | 0 | 0.0% | 2 | 4.8% |
| Total | 22 | 100.0% | 20 | 100.0% | 28 | 100.0% | 14 | 100.0% | 20 | 100.0% | 21 | 100.0% | 9 | 100.0% | 5 | 100.0% | 20 | 100.0% | 127 | 100.0% |

Q89. In your opinion, considering costs (including staff time and resources) and educational gains, how beneficial are your institution's advising practices in supporting transfer student success?

| Survey question/responses | Freq. | % | Freq | % | Freq. | % | Freq. | % | Freq. | % | Freq. | % | Freq. | % | Freq. | % | Freq. | % | Freq. | % |
|---|---|---|---|---|---|---|---|---|---|---|---|---|---|---|---|---|---|---|---|---|
| Low benefit | 0 | 0.0% | 2 | 2.4% | 1 | 1.5% | 1 | 1.6% | 0 | 0.0% | 0 | 0.0% | 1 | 5.6% | 0 | 0.0% | 1 | 5.3% | 2 | 1.6% |
| Between low-medium benefit | 0 | 0.0% | 5 | 6.1% | 1 | 1.5% | 4 | 6.6% | 1 | 6.3% | 3 | 5.2% | 0 | 0.0% | 0 | 0.0% | 1 | 5.3% | 5 | 3.9% |
| Medium benefit | 14 | 30.4% | 24 | 29.3% | 22 | 33.3% | 15 | 24.6% | 4 | 25.0% | 17 | 29.3% | 6 | 33.3% | 6 | 35.3% | 4 | 21.1% | 37 | 28.9% |
| Between medium-high benefit | 12 | 26.1% | 22 | 26.8% | 17 | 25.8% | 17 | 27.9% | 8 | 50.0% | 12 | 20.7% | 4 | 22.2% | 4 | 23.5% | 6 | 31.6% | 34 | 26.6% |

*Table continues on page 141*

*Table continued from page 140*

| Survey question/responses | Institutional type | | | | Institution control | | | | Number of undergraduates enrolled | | | | | | | | | | | | Total | |
|---|---|---|---|---|---|---|---|---|---|---|---|---|---|---|---|---|---|---|---|---|---|---|
| | Two-year | | Four-year | | Public | | Private | | Under 1,000 | | 1,000-4,999 | | 5,999-9,999 | | 10,000-19,999 | | 20,000 and above | | | |
| | Freq. | % | Freq | % | Freq. | % | Freq. | % | Freq. | % | Freq. | % | Freq. | % | Freq. | % | Freq. | % | Freq. | % |
| High benefit | 19 | 41.3% | 28 | 34.1% | 24 | 36.4% | 23 | 37.7% | 3 | 18.8% | 24 | 41.4% | 7 | 38.9% | 7 | 41.2% | 7 | 36.8% | 48 | 37.5% |
| Unable to judge | 1 | 2.2% | 1 | 1.2% | 1 | 1.5% | 1 | 1.6% | 0 | 0.0% | 2 | 3.4% | 0 | 0.0% | 0 | 0.0% | 0 | 0.0% | 2 | 1.6% |
| Total | 46 | 100.0% | 82 | 100.0% | 66 | 100.0% | 61 | 100.0% | 20 | 100.0% | 58 | 100.0% | 18 | 100.0% | 17 | 100.0% | 19 | 100.0% | 128 | 100.0% |

# References

American Association of Colleges and Universities. (2023). *High-impact practices.* https://www.aacu.org/trending-topics/high-impact

Bailey, T. R., Jaggars, S. S., & Jenkins, D. (2015). *Redesigning America's community colleges: A clearer path to student success.* Harvard University Press.

Castro, E. L., & Cortez, E. (2016). Exploring the lived experiences and intersectionalities of Mexican community college transfer students: Qualitative insights toward expanding a transfer receptive culture. *Community College Journal of Research and Practice, 41*(2), 1–16.

Causey, J., Gardner, A., Kim, H., Lee, S., Pevitz, A., Ryu, M., Scheetz, A., & Shapiro, D. (2022). *COVID-19: Transfer, mobility, and progress, the 9th in the series.* National Student Clearinghouse Research Center. https://nscresearchcenter.org/wp-content/uploads/COVIDTransfer2YrofPandemic.pdf

Center for Community College Student Engagement. (2013). *A matter of degrees: High-impact practices for community college student engagement.* Community College Leadership Program, The University of Texas at Austin. https://cccse.org/sites/default/files/Matter_of_Degrees_2.pdf

Center for Community College Student Engagement. (2018). *Show me the way: The power of advising in community colleges.* Department of Educational Leadership and Policy, Program in Higher Education Leadership, College of Education, The University of Texas at Austin. https://cccse.org/sites/default/files/Show_Me_The_Way.pdf

Center for Community College Student Engagement. (2020). *The intersection of work and learning: Findings from entering students in community colleges.* Department of Educational Leadership and Policy, College of Education, The University of Texas at Austin. https://cccse.org/sites/default/files/WorkingLearner.pdf

Chase, M. M., Dowd, A. C., Pazich, L. B., & Bensimon, E. M. (2012). Transfer equity for "minoritized" students: A critical policy analysis of seven states. *Educational Policy, 28*(5), 669–717.

Cohen, A. M., Brawer, F. B., & Kisker, C. B. (2013). *The American community college* (6th ed.). Jossey-Bass.

Community College Research Center. (2023). *Community college FAQs.* https://ccrc.tc.columbia.edu/Community-College-FAQs.html

Cooper, D. M., Nguyen, A., Karandjeff, K., Brohawn, K., Purnell, R., Kretz, A., Rodriguez-Kiino, D., Chaplot, P., Nguyen, K. (2020, May). *Students speak their truth about transfer: What they need to get through the gate.* The RP Group. https://rpgroup.org/Portals/0/Documents/Projects/ThroughtheGate/RPGroup_TheTruthAboutTransfer_TTGPhase3_R3%5b79%5d.pdf?ver=2020-05-18-171449-773

Crisp, G., Doran, E., Carales, V., & Potts, C. (2020). Disrupting the dominant discourse: Exploring the mentoring experiences of Latinx community college students. *Journal for the Study of Postsecondary and Tertiary Education, 5,* 57–78.

Crisp, G., Kolby, E., & Potter, C. (2022). Centering equity in transfer partnerships. *Journal of College Orientation, Transition, and Retention, 29*(2), 1–21.

Crisp, G., & Núñez, A.-M. (2014). Understanding the racial transfer gap: Modeling underrepresented minority and nonminority students' pathways from two- to four-year institutions. *The Review of Higher Education, 37*(3), 291–320.

Del Real Viramontes, J. R. (2020). Latina/o transfer students and community cultural wealth: Expanding the transfer receptive culture framework. *Community College Journal of Research and Practice. 45*(12), 855–870.

Fay, M. P., Jaggars, S. S., & Farakish, N. (2022). "Lost in the shuffle": How relationships and personalized advisement shape transfer aspirations and outcomes for community college students. *Community College Review, 50*(4), 366–390.

Fematt, V. L., Grimm, R. P., Nylund-Gibson, K., Gerber, M. M., Brenner, M. B., & Solórzano, D. (2021). Identifying transfer student subgroups by academic and social adjustment: A latent class analysis. *Community College Journal of Research and Practice, 45*(3), 167–183.

Fink, J., Garcia Tulloch, A., Steiger, J., & Reddy, V. (2023). *Advancing equity with effective community college transfer pathways.* The Campaign for College Opportunity. https://collegecampaign.org/wp-content/uploads/2023/11/2023_AEEIEA_Briefs_TransferBrief_AdvancingEquity.small_.pdf

Fishman, R., & Nguyen, S. (2021, January 14). *Where did all the students go? Understanding the enrollment decline at community colleges during the pandemic.* New America. https://www.newamerica.org/education-policy/edcentral/community-college-enrollment-survey/

Flaga, C. T. (2006). The process of transition for community college transfer students. *Community College Journal of Research and Practice, 30*(1), 3–19.

Hernández, I., Hernández, S., & de la Teja M. H. (2017, May). *Five things student affairs professionals can do to support Latinx/a/o students in community colleges* (Five Things Issue Brief Series). NASPA Research and Policy Institute. https://www.naspa.org/files/dmfile/5Things_LATINX_DOWNLOAD.pdf

HigherEd Direct. (n.d.). *The higher education search engine—updated continuously.* https://hepinc.com

Hoover, S. C. (2010). Designing orientation and transition programs for transfer students. In J. Ward-Roof (Ed.), *Designing successful transitions: A guide for orienting students to college* (Monograph No. 13, 3rd ed., pp. 181–192). National Resource Center for The First-Year Experience and Students in Transition.

Hunter, M. S., & White, E. R. (2004). Could fixing academic advising fix higher education? *About Campus, 9*(1), 20–25.

Jain, D., Herrera, A., Bernal, S., & Solorzano, D. (2011). Critical race theory and the transfer function: Introducing a transfer receptive culture. *Community College Journal of Research and Practice, 35*(3), 252–256.

Keup, J. R., & Young, D. G. (2022). Being HIP: Advising as an emerging high-impact practice. *New Directions for Higher Education, 2021*(195–196), 91–99.

Kuh, G. D. (2008). *High-impact educational practices: What they are, who has access to them, and why they matter.* Association of American Colleges & Universities. https://www.aacu.org/publication/high-impact-educational-practices-what-they-are-who-has-access-to-them-and-why-they-matter

Laanan, F. S. (2007). Studying transfer students: Part II: Dimensions of transfer students' adjustment. *Community College Journal of Research and Practice, 31*, 37–59.

Melguizo, T., Kienzl, G. S., & Alfonso, M. (2011). Comparing the educational attainment of community college transfer students and four-year college rising juniors using propensity score matching methods. *The Journal of Higher Education, 82*(3), 265–291.

National Student Clearinghouse Research Center. (2022). *COVID-19: Transfer, mobility, and progress: First two years of the pandemic report.* https://nscresearchcenter.org/wp-content/uploads/COVIDTransfer2YrofPandemic.pdf

National Student Clearinghouse Research Center. (2024, February 28). *Transfer and progress: Fall 2023 report.* http://nscresearchcenter.org/transfer-and-progress

Núñez, A.-M., & Yoshimi, J. (2016). A phenomenology of transfer: Students' experiences at a receiving institution. *Innovative Higher Education, 42*(2), 173–187.

Peska, S. F. (2011). One size does not fit all: Tailoring orientation services to mid-year transfer students. *The Journal of College Orientation and Transition, 18*(2), 33–44.

Provencher, A., & Kassel, R. (2019). High-impact practices and sophomore retention: Examining the effects of selection bias. *Journal of College Student Retention: Research, Theory & Practice, 21*(2), 221–241.

Roberts, L. M., Welsh, M. E., & Dudek, B. (2019). Instruction and outreach for transfer students: A Colorado case study. *College & Research Libraries, 80*(1), 94–122.

Santiago, D. A., & Stettner, A. (2013). *Supporting Latino community college students: An investment in our economic future.* Excelencia in Education.

Schudde, L., Bradley, D., & Absher, C. (2020). Navigating vertical transfer online: Access to and usefulness of transfer information on community college websites. *Community College Review, 48*(1), 3–30.

Schudde, L., Jabbar, H., & Hartman, C. (2021). How political and ecological contexts shape community college transfer. *Sociology of Education, 94*(1), 65–83.

Shapiro, D., Dundar, A., Huie, F., Wakhungu, P.K., Bhimdiwali, A., Nathan, A., & Youngsik, H. (2018, July). *Transfer and mobility: A national view of student movement in postsecondary institutions, Fall 2011 cohort* (Signature Report No. 15). National Student Clearinghouse Research Center.

Taylor, J. L., & Jain, D. (2017). The multiple dimensions of transfer: Examining the transfer function in American higher education. *Community College Review, 45*(4), 273–293.

Tobolowsky, B. F., & Cox, B. E. (2012). Rationalizing neglect: An institutional response to transfer students. *The Journal of Higher Education, 83*(3), 389–410.

Townsend, B. K., Wilson, K. (2006). "A hand hold for a little bit": Factors facilitating the success of community college transfer students to a large research university. *Journal of College Student Development, 47*, 439–456.

Wyner, J., Deane, K. C., Jenkins, D., & Fink, J. (2016). *The transfer playbook: Essential practices for two- and four-year colleges.* Community College Research Center, Teachers College, Columbia University. https://ccrc.tc.columbia.edu/media/k2/attachments/transfer-playbook-essential-practices.pdf

Zhang, Y. (2016). An overlooked population in community college: International students' (in) validation experiences with academic advising. *Community College Review, 44*(2), 153–170. https://doi.org/10.1177/0091552116633293

# About the Authors

***Dr. Catherine Hartman*** is an Assistant Professor of Community College Leadership at North Carolina State University and a Faculty Scholar at the Belk Center for Community College Leadership and Research. Catherine also serves as an affiliate scholar at the National Resource Center for The First-Year Experience and Students in Transition. Her research focuses on community college student engagement, transfer student success, and community college leadership.

***Dr. Jeffrey Mayo*** is the Director of the First-Year Experience Office at The University of Texas at Austin. His work focuses on creating learning communities, student engagement opportunities, and mentorship for students to set a strong trajectory toward their academic and personal goals. His research interests have centered on transfer student socio-academic belonging, Latinx community college student success, and online education.